Historic Virginia Homes and Churches

Robert Alexander Lancaster

HISTORIC VIRGINIA
HOMES AND CHURCHES

HISTORIC VIRGINIA HOMES AND CHURCHES

BY ROBERT A. LANCASTER, JR.

WITH 316 ILLUSTRATIONS

PHILADELPHIA AND LONDON
J. B. LIPPINCOTT COMPANY
MCMXV

PUBLISHED OCTOBER, 1915

PRINTED BY J. B. LIPPINCOTT COMPANY
AT THE WASHINGTON SQUARE PRESS
PHILADELPHIA, U.S.A.

GORDONSDALE, FAUQUIER COUNTY
See page 384

PREFACE

THIS work includes practically all of the principal Colonial homes of historic interest in the State of Virginia now standing and many which have been destroyed, together with the churches most likely to engage attention.

In 1888 the writer began to gather photographs of historic buildings in Virginia for his private collection, and later, upon the request of friends, decided to publish them. The making of the collection as complete as possible and the gathering of the historical data have involved years of labor and much travelling in conveyances of many sorts and by foot. It may be said that the work was done at the psychological time, for much information gathered in past years would now be impossible to secure and much of that recently added will soon be as inaccessible. The information has been made as full as the great number of houses treated would allow.

As alterations in buildings have been frequent, the writer's aim in such cases has been to secure pictures of as early a period as possible while they were in their original condition, so as to show the character of houses and churches our ancestors built. For instance, the picture shown of St. John's Church, Hampton, was taken from one published some fifty years ago rather than from one showing it as it is to-day after the original has been altered. The photographs of Montpelier, Eagle Point, Belleville, and many other places, also show these edifices before the existing alterations were made.

The author wishes to acknowledge with thanks the great assistance rendered by Mrs. Mary Newton Stanard, and Mr. William Clayton Torrence, Secretary of the Valentine Museum, and Mr. William G. Stanard, Secretary of the Virginia Historical Society, without whose help he could not have secured much valuable information. He also appreciates the assistance rendered by Mrs. Sally Nelson Robins, Mr. G. C. Callahan of Philadelphia, Mrs. I. H. Carrington, Miss Kate Mason Roland, Mrs. James Lyons, Mrs. John Dunn, Mrs. Philip A. Bruce, the late General William B. Taliaferro and his family, Mr. Carter Wellford, Mr. Morgan P. Robinson, the late Thomas Bolling, Mr. Preston Cocke, Mr. Thomas N. Carter, the officers of the R. F. and P. R. R., C. and O. Ry., and Tidewater and Western R. R. and Hon. F. B. Hutton and Miss Ellen W. Preston of Abingdon, Va.; and to Mr. H. P. Cook for a few pictures from his collection; also the hospitality extended at the various homes visited in making the collection.

R. A. L., Jr.

Richmond, July, 1915

BROOK HILL, HENRICO COUNTY
See page 113

CONTENTS

All houses and names of families mentioned in this book are contained in the index, pages 503–527.

SABINE HALL, GARDEN FRONT
See page 333

ILLUSTRATIONS

PART II—HAMPTON ROADS AND THE LOWER JAMES

PART III—RICHMOND, MANCHESTER AND THE UPPER JAMES

PART IV—GLOUCESTER AND THE YORK RIVER COUNTRY

PART V—THE RAPPAHANNOCK AND POTOMAC

PART VI—PIEDMONT AND THE SOUTH SI

PART VII—BEYOND THE MOUNTAINS

PART VIII—THE EASTERN SHORE

HISTORIC VIRGINIA HOMES AND CHURCHES

PART I

JAMESTOWN WILLIAMSBURG YORKTOWN

JAMESTOWN

THE story of Virginia, as of America, begins at Jamestown.

On December 20, 1606, three ships, the *Susan Constant,* the *Godspeed* and the *Discovery,* dropped down the Thames from London. Through the months of January, February, March and nearly all of April, they bore steadily across the Atlantic. They were mere toys—white dots on the bosom of the vasty deep—yet they were bringing a new order of things to a New World—they were bringing England to the Red Man's Land.

Aboard them were Captain Christopher Newport, Admiral of the fleet, and one hundred and three stout-hearted, adventurous spirits, fifty-four of whom were "gentlemen," four "carpenters" and twenty-four "laborers." Seven of these were to form the Council of State to govern the Colony they were coming to plant. These were Edward Maria Wingfield, Bartholomew Gosnold, Christopher Newport, John Smith, John Ratcliffe, John Martin, George Kendall, but the document appointing them was brought in a sealed box which was not to be opened, "nor the governors known until they reached land." There was also a godly Church of England minister, Reverend Robert Hunt, for the instructions of the King's Council for Virginia had warned them that "every plantation which our Heavenly Father has not planted shall be rooted out."

Upon April 26, they arrived at the Cape, which they

named Henry for the Prince of Wales. There they set up a cross, then sailed into Chesapeake Bay and up James River.

Upon May 18, when the beauty of the spring season made them think that they had found in Virginia " earth's only paradise," they chose the site for Jamestown and with their ships floating in six fathoms of water made fast to the trees upon the bank.

On the fourteenth, they put themselves and their goods ashore, and gentlemen and laborers alike fell to work cutting down trees to make a clearing for their fort, within which rude cabins were soon built. " For a church," says Captain John Smith, " wee did hang . . . an old saile to three or foure trees to shadow us from the Sunne, our walles were railes of wood, our seats unhewed trees, till we cut plankes, our Pulpit a bar of wood nailed to two neighbouring trees . . . this was our Church till we built a homely thing like a barne, set upon crachets covered with rafters, sedge and earth; so was also the walls. The best of our houses (were) of the like curiosity, but the most part, farre much worse workmanship, that neither could well defend wind or rain; yet we had daily common Prayer morning and evening every Sunday, two sermons, and every three months the holy communion till our minister died: but our prayers daily, with our homily on Sunday, we continued two or three years after, till more Preachers came."

Spring in Virginia was full of fair promises, but with summer came the deadly " ague and fever " and other diseases caused by the swampy situation and bad drinking water. Danger from the Indians was ever present; food became scarce; dissensions arose. Every one knows the story of the trying years that followed, with Captain Smith's strenuous efforts to keep the colony alive, his capture by the Indians and rescue by Pocahontas, the colonists' devoted friend. Its climax was reached in the " starving time "—the winter of 1609–1610—when only the arrival of Lord Delaware with provisions and new settlers saved Jamestown from being abandoned.

AMBLER HOUSE, JAMESTOWN

JAMESTOWN CHURCH AND OLD TOWER

After this, though there were still great suffering and many deaths, Virginia grew in strength. In 1614 the baptism of Pocahontas and her marriage with John Rolfe made a bond of friendship between the red man and the white. In 1619 Virginians were given the right to share in their own government. A popular legislature was authorized and the House of Burgesses, the first representative Assembly, not only of America, but of all the King's Colonies, met on July 30, in the church. In this year also twenty picked maidens, " pure and undefiled," were sent over to make homes for such of the bachelor settlers as were willing to pay for their transportation—provided said bachelors took the fancy of the maids—and when the pairing off was accomplished Parson Bucke united the twenty happy pairs in holy wedlock.

These auspicious events were followed by a frightful disaster—the Indian Massacre of 1622, when nearly four hundred Colonists were murdered, but from which Jamestown escaped, thanks to timely warning.

The year 1635 saw at Jamestown the first American revolutionary movement. The people, tired of Governor Harvey's misrule, " thrust him out " of office and shipped him to England.

Years of quick growth, but full of interest, followed —then, in the spring of 1652, the loyal Virginians assembled at Jamestown to defend the rights of King Charles, but were forced to surrender, on easy terms, to the Parliament fleet.

It was at Jamestown, too, that the most dramatic scenes of the famous Bacon's Rebellion were enacted in 1676, when the town was burned, leaving only the ruined church tower standing. A final burning of the State House, in 1698, caused the removal of the Colonial government to Williamsburg.

After " James City " ceased to be even a village, and most of its site became the property of one family, Travis, it still retained its right to send a member to the House of

Burgesses, a privilege not taken away until the formation of the State in 1776. The Mr. Travis of the day was the returning officer, and the only voter and he, or his nominee, the member. A member of Congress who once heard of this on a visit to Jamestown said he now understood why the place had once been called " Earth's only paradise."

Still retaining its privileges as a town—though only a town in name—Jamestown was long without a history. Cornwallis camped there June 4–9, 1781, and on June 6, gave Lafayette a beating. In September, 1781, the first French troops, arriving in Virginia for the Yorktown campaign, landed at Jamestown.

In 1861, the Confederate fort which adds much of picturesqueness to this historic spot was built, by order of General Robert E. Lee.

About a quarter of a mile below the church tower, upon a level grass plot, stand the ruins of a Colonial mansion known as the Ambler House. This house was built some time in the latter part of the eighteenth century by the Huguenot, Edward Jacqueline, a member of the House of Burgesses and a large land holder at Jamestown. From him the house passed to his descendants of the well-known Ambler family, and continued in their possession until the first part of the nineteenth century, when it was sold. It has since frequently changed hands and has been three times burned, though the massive old walls still stand firm.

Upon May 3, 1893, Mr. and Mrs. Edward E. Barney, then owners of Jamestown Island, moved by a broad and generous spirit of patriotism, presented the twenty-two and a half acres of land upon which are the tower, churchyard and Confederate fort to the Association for the Preservation of Virginia Antiquities.[1]

---

[1] See also Yonge, *The Site of Old " James Towne," 1607–1698. A Brief Historical and Topographical Sketch of the First American Metropolis.* Richmond: 1907. This monograph was published serially in *The Virginia Magazine of History and Biography*, xi, 257–276, 393–414; xii, 33–54, 113–133.

FOUNDATIONS OF OLD JAMESTOWN CHURCH

Through the efforts of this organization, the United States Government has placed a splendid sea-wall along the shore of the island exposed to the encroachment of the river, which had already made serious inroads. In 1901 excavations at the rear of the tower brought to light the foundations, brick aisles and chancel of the church, and some exceedingly interesting tombs. A most interesting feature of the " excavations " is a small wall which may be seen, in the illustration of the foundations of the church, immediately inside the outer right-hand larger wall. This smaller wall is in all probability a part of the foundation of the earliest church on this site and hence of the building in which sat the first " Assembly of the representatives of the People " called together in the New World. In order to protect these relics from the weather, and as a memorial to the first settlers, the National Society of the Colonial Dames of America has restored the outer walls of the church building, in part, over the original foundations. Other excavations, in 1903, unearthed the foundation of a block of five or six connected buildings, including those of the State House burned by Bacon, in 1676.

Many interesting memorials have been placed at Jamestown in honor of the year 1907. Among these is a granite shaft, erected by the United States Government; stately entrance gates by the Colonial Dames of America,—a different organization from the one which restored the church, —a bronze statue of Captain John Smith by Mr. and Mrs. Joseph Bryan; a rest house—patterned after the Malvern Hill Mansion—by the Daughters of the American Revolution; ornamental fountain by the Massachusetts Society of Colonial Wars; a monument to the first House of Burgesses, by the Norfolk branch of the Association for the Preservation of Virginia Antiquities.

An improvement which might have saved many lives in the early days of storm and stress, if it only could have been made three hundred years ago, is a fine artesian well which supplies the island with a generous amount of pure, sparkling and delicious water.

WILLIAMSBURG

A straggling, mile-long " city," with eighteenth century houses and shady streets and here and there open spaces of greensward where trees have plenty of room to grow and young children to play; a city dominated by a venerable church with ivied walls and white spire, within a high-walled, mossy graveyard; and by a venerable college within a wide green campus; a village out of an old story book! On a June day the gardens are overflowing with bloom and sweet odors, and the music of singing birds, and cows browse, blissful and unafraid, upon the grass and buttercups that the inhabitants with rare sense of the fitness of things allow to spring unrebuked in the streets.

Such is Williamsburg.

After the destruction of Jamestown it was decided to remove the seat of government of Virginia to a situation less popular with malaria and mosquitoes. The site chosen was the Middle Plantation, a little village upon high ground some seven miles back from Jamestown and the river. Its name was changed forthwith to Williamsburg after the reigning king of England and Virginia. The first plan was to lay out the streets to form a monogram of the letters W and M, the initials of their majesties William and Mary, but this was abandoned. Instead, Duke of Gloucester Street and its parallel thoroughfares were intersected at right angles by other highways bearing names suggestive of royalty and state. Along these streets many of the houses, where the lights of other days lived and moved and had their being, may still be found.

The Capitol and Governor's Palace have disappeared, but the site of the former is preserved; the Palace Green is the Palace Green still, and the college and the church still carry on the good works for which they were originally designed.

WILLIAM AND MARY COLLEGE

In the midst of its shady campus stands William and Mary, looking straight up the Duke of Gloucester Street, which was originally closed at the opposite end by the

WILLIAM AND MARY COLLEGE, WILLIAMSBURG

Capitol building and grounds. It is built after the favorite Colonial manner, of red brick with glazed " headers," and with a triple-arched brick porch and a white cupola. Some distance in the foreground, upon the main walk, is a white marble statue of Norborne Berkeley, Baron de Botetourt 1718–1770), Governor-in-chief of Virginia 1768 to 1770, with a high-flown inscription.

William and Mary was the first American college save one, the first to have chairs of Law, Political Economy, Modern Languages and History, the first to establish elective and honor systems and class lectures and to award medals, and its Phi Beta Kappa was the first Greek letter fraternity in the United States.

It was through the untiring efforts of the Reverend James Blair, D.D. (1655–1743), Rector of Bruton Parish, that the College Charter was granted, in 1693, by their gracious majesties whose names it bears: " that the Church in Virginia may be furnished with a seminary of Ministers of the Gospel, and that the youth may be piously educated in good letters and manners and that the Christian religion may be propagated among the Western Indians, to the glory of Almighty God." Sir Christopher Wren is believed to have been the architect, and good Parson Blair was fittingly made its first president.[2]

Of this old college it has been said that " more illustrious men, in proportion to the numbers educated there, have gone out to make it and themselves famous than from any other literary institution on this Continent."

Presidents of the United States, judges, chancellors, statesmen and divines, warriors and gentlemen fill the rolls of its venerable record. General Washington was its first chancellor after the Revolution, and to name only a few of the distinguished sons of this Alma Mater, three presidents of the United States—Thomas Jefferson, James Monroe, John Tyler—were educated there, as were

[2] Motley, *Life of Commissary James Blair* (Johns Hopkins University Studies, Series xix, No. 10).

Chief Justice John Marshall; Peyton Randolph, first President of the Continental Congress; Chancellor George Wythe, and Governor Edmund Randolph.

He spake truly who declared, " Its name must ever be associated with the deeds of the great and good."

The college library contains some treasures in the way of rare books and interesting portraits. Many of the books were presents from the royal governors of Virginia and contain book plates bearing coats-of-arms of their donors.

Among the rules of the college was one that no student should keep a race-horse, and another that drinking should be confined to the moderation that becomes a prudent and industrious student. A practical, if somewhat unique, officer for the college was named on June 26, 1761, when it was " Resolved that Mrs. Foster be appointed stocking-mender in the college and that she be paid annually the sum of twelve pounds provided she furnish herself with lodging, diet, fire and candles."

The college continued in successful operation until the Revolution, when a company of volunteers was raised among the students and commanded by some of the professors. When the James River peninsula became the seat of war the exercises were temporarily suspended and the buildings were occupied in succession by the troops of the British and allied armies. The college has been thrice destroyed by fire,—first in 1705, again not long before the War between the States and again during that conflict by Federal soldiers,—but the Colonial builders laid their massive brick-work to stand, and it has, each time, been restored within the same walls.

THE BRAFFERTON BUILDING

WILLIAM AND MARY COLLEGE

Upon the college green to the right of the main building stands the commodious and substantial building known as the Brafferton, the first Indian School of any consequence in America. The Honorable Robert Boyle, of

England, who died in 1691, directed in his will that his executors should apply his personal estate to such charitable and pious uses as they, in their discretion, should see fit. The fund was invested in an English estate called Brafferton, and the rents, subject to ninety pounds given to Harvard University, were paid the President and professors of William and Mary for the purpose of establishing and maintaining a department for Indians. The result was the Brafferton, where Indian youths were supported and taught until the Revolution.

The Brafferton is now used as one of the college dormitories.

THE PRESIDENT'S HOUSE

WILLIAM AND MARY COLLEGE

To the left of the college and immediately across the campus from the Brafferton is a dignified mansion built, like the college and the Brafferton, of dark red brick with glazed " headers " and, like the Brafferton, too, in plan, with the addition of the square, pillared porch. It was built in 1732 and as the home of a long succession of honored presidents of William and Mary has enjoyed a rich social history. It has its place in war history as well, for Lord Cornwallis made it his headquarters not long before the Yorktown campaign. It was also occupied by the French troops at the time of the siege of Yorktown and by them was accidentally burned, but was rebuilt at the cost —tradition says—of the private purse of King Louis XVI.

THE BLAIR HOUSE

Passing from the college grounds into Duke of Gloucester Street, a few steps bring you to a long, low, white frame cottage, with one story and a dormer and with two street entrances, a short distance apart, each of which is reached by worn white marble steps.

Modest as this homestead looks, it was the residence of two very distinguished men—John Blair (1686–1771),

President of the Council of State and Acting Governor of Virginia, and his son, John Blair (died, 1800), Justice of the United States Supreme Court.[3]

BLAIR HOUSE, WILLIAMSBURG

BRUTON CHURCH

Foot-worn stone steps lead to a heavy iron gate set in a wall of checkered brick-work. The gate gives entrance to the old town's Holy of Holies—Bruton Parish Church and Churchyard. The green " God's acre " is filled with tombstones, many of them bearing arms and interesting epitaphs in English or Latin. The old sanctuary is built in the shape of a Roman cross, with a square entrance tower, of the familiar dull red and glazed brick. The tower is surmounted by a white wooden steeple from one side of which the town clock, which tradition says was formerly in the Capitol, keeps a watchful eye upon the town. The

[3] Blair family: *William and Mary College Quarterly Historical Magazine*, v, p. 279; Horner, *The History of the Blair, Banister and Braxton Families* (Philadelphia, 1898).

bell, which both cries the hours with silvery sound and calls the people to church, bears the inscription, " The gift of James Tarpley in Bruton Parish, 1761."

Bruton has been longer in continuous use than any other Episcopal church in America. The parish was established when Williamsburg was still Middle Plantation and antedates College, Capitol and Palace. The first

BRUTON CHURCH, WILLIAMSBURG

church was doubtless of wood, but in 1676 a brick one was built upon " land sufficient for the Church and Churchyard " given by Colonel John Page—first of the Page family in Virginia—who also subscribed " twenty pounds sterling " to the building fund.

Upon October 1, 1706, " The vestry, considering ye great charge ye parish hath been at for ye repairing of ye Church, and how bad a condition it still is in," ordered that " twenty thousand pounds of tobacco be levied this year for and towards building a new church." This (the present) building was finished in 1715 and stands upon the original site. It was said to have been "adorned as the best Churches in London." There were the high-back pews and tall pulpit of the time. The Governor's pew was slightly elevated from the main floor and over it stretched a silken canopy around which the Governor's name was wrought in letters of gold. In this pew splendidly worshipped the royal governors, Nicholson, Jennings, Spotswood, Drysdale, Gooch, Dinwiddie, Fauquier, Lord Botetourt and Lord Dunmore, while in other pews have sat burgesses and councillors, patriots, scholars and statesmen without number. To name only the greatest in this remarkable galaxy—George Washington, Thomas Jefferson, Patrick Henry, George Mason, and John Marshall all bowed the knee in this storied temple.

In 1718 leave was given the students of William and Mary College to use the west gallery and to put a door with a lock and key to the stairs of said gallery, "the sexton to keep the key." In this gallery, while students at William and Mary, sat Peyton Randolph (1722–1775), President of the Continental Congress, and George Wythe (1726–1806), signer of the Declaration of Independence.

In 1721, it was ordered that a gallery be built in the south side of the church "for the boys of the parish."

In 1753, it was ordered that half of the south gallery be appropriated to the college students, and here, while students, sat Thomas Jefferson, James Monroe, Chief Justice Marshall, Governor Edmund Randolph, President John Tyler, and General Winfield Scott.

The north gallery was reserved for colored servants and was entered by a stairway from outside.

In 1755, it was ordered that a loft be built for the organ which had been brought from England, and upon which Mr. Peter Pelham was appointed to play.

Old Bruton is the fortunate possessor of three notable services of Communion silver, the most interesting of which was brought from Jamestown. It consists of a chalice, paten and alms-basin presented to Jamestown Church by Francis Moryson, Acting Governor of Virginia. The chalice and paten are inscribed: " Mixe not holy things with profane. Ex dono Francisci Morrison Armigeri anno Domi 1661," and the basin with arms, and " For the use of James City Parish Church." The " Queene Anne Service " is an exquisitely chased, two-handled cup and cover, and a paten, and bears arms. The " King George Service " consists of a flagon chalice and alms-basin. Each piece bears the royal arms and initials G III R, and the motto, " Honi soit qui mal y pense."

King Edward VII in 1907 gave a Bible and President Roosevelt a lectern for the Bible to rest upon, to this historic church, which has been beautifully and reverently restored to as nearly as possible its appearance in the days when it was the State Church of England's first colony in America.

THE PALACE GREEN

Beyond the church stretches the "Palace Green " where stood the Governor's palace, said to have been a " magnificent structure . . . finished and beautiful with gates, fine gardens, offices, walks, a fine canal, orchards, etc." And " likewise the ornamental addition of a good cupola or lantern, illuminating most of the town upon birth nights and other nights of occasional rejoicing."

The Palace was the very centre of social and ceremonious life in Colonial Virginia. It was there that the painted and powdered belles and beaux displayed to the best advantage their velvets and brocades, their jewelled buckles and falls of rich lace and also their accomplishments in the way of ornate manners and speech; there the minuet and the more lively country dances occupied the hours twixt candle-light and dawn when the birthday of his honor, the Governor of Virginia, or his Majesty, the King of England, was being celebrated, and upon other holidays.

WYTHE HOUSE

The square brick mansion over-run with ivy and Virginia creeper hard by the church was the home of the distinguished Revolutionary patriot and signer of the Declaration of Independence, George Wythe (1726–1806).[4] This house has figured in both history and fiction, for just before the Yorktown campaign General Washington took it for his headquarters and in recent times Miss Ellen

WYTHE HOUSE, WILLIAMSBURG

Glasgow made use of it as the home of Judge Bassett, one of the chief characters of her novel, *The Voice of the People.*

The Wythe House can boast of no less than three ghosts. Whoever sleeps in what was Judge Wythe's bedroom upon the night of the 8th of June is suddenly awakened by the touch of a cold hand upon his brow; the shadow of General Washington walks in the wide hall on moonlight nights, and, on occasion, a glimpse of the lovely Mrs.

[4] Wythe family: *William and Mary Quarterly,* ii, 69.

Skipwith, who was Miss Elizabeth Byrd, of "Westover," may be had, as she descends the broad, dark stairs.

SAUNDERS HOUSE

The picturesque mansion with the two-storied, pillared porch, just beyond the Wythe House, is the Saunders House—formerly the home of Mr. Robert Saunders[5] (a prominent gentleman of Williamsburg and a President of

SAUNDERS HOUSE, WILLIAMSBURG

William and Mary College) and his wife, who was Lucy Page, the youngest of the twenty children of Governor John Page.

About the year 1752 this house was occupied by Governor Robert Dinwiddie while the Palace was undergoing repairs.

PAGE HOUSE

Just across Palace Green from the Saunders House is the little old white frame, dormer-windowed cottage which was the town house of Governor John Page, of

[5] Saunders family: *William and Mary Quarterly*, xiv, p. 145 *et seq.*

" Rosewell." Hard by is the site of the old theatre which furnished Williamsburg folk with the diversion of the play. Both homestead and theatre figure conspicuously in Miss Mary Johnston's novel " Audrey," and since the publication of that book the cottage has been pointed out to visitors as " Audrey's house." Its panelled hall and parlor and unique stairway make it as quaint within as without, and one of the tiny window-panes in the parlor gives it a

PAGE HOUSE, WILLIAMSBURG

still further interest. Upon this pane a diamond from the finger of some fair one of over a century ago has scratched, so plainly that it may still be easily read, the initials " T. B." and the date " 1790 November 23," followed by the words, " O fatal day." The identity of " T. B." and the reason why November 23, 1790, was a " fatal day " are alike wrapped in mystery, which is fortunate, since it grants every reader of the haunting inscription liberty to give free rein to imagination and make his own story.

THE COURT HOUSE AND GREEN

Divided from the Palace Green by the street named for Lord Dunmore is Court Green, a broad grassy space, shaded by fine old trees.

Within it, upon the Duke of Gloucester Street side, stands the Court House, built in 1769, and upon it look a number of picturesque and charming old homesteads.

COURT HOUSE, WILLIAMSBURG

COURT GREEN HOUSES

TUCKER HOUSE

Facing the Court Green on its north side is a large, rambling, frame house which was the home of two members of a distinguished Virginia family, Judges St. George and Nathaniel Beverley Tucker.[6]

Beyond the Tucker House, on the north side of the

[6] Tucker family: *The Critic* (Richmond, Va.), Sept. 14, 1889.

street named for Governor Nicholson, which passes under a double row of large trees, several commodious frame

TUCKER HOUSE, WILLIAMSBURG

COLEMAN HOUSE, WILLIAMSBURG

homesteads of the Colonial period, with large gardens lying behind them, look upon the Court Green.

On the right-hand side of the cross street, as one turns to go to the station, is the house in which General Lafayette was entertained when he visited the Colonial capital in 1824.

COLEMAN HOUSE

A block further down Nicholson Street is to be noticed one of the most interesting of the old Williamsburg homes. The house is rich in heirlooms of the Tucker and Randolph families, and the terraced garden is beautiful and fragrant in summer with roses in endless variety, old-fashioned flowering shrubs, hyacinths and tulips, violets and lilies, great peonies—pink and white, each single blossom a bouquet.

THE POWDER HORN

Across Duke of Gloucester Street from the Court Green, but some distance back, stands one of the most

OLD POWDER HORN AT WILLIAMSBURG

interesting relics in America—the old Powder Horn. This curious looking little octagon-shaped house, with its high peaked roof, was built in 1714, during Governor Spotswood's administration, to hold the Colony's munitions of war, and was designed by the Governor himself. Its walls are strong and thick, and to add to its security it was formerly enclosed by a thick and high outer wall, running parallel to its eight sides.

It was from the Powder Horn that Lord Dunmore secretly removed the gunpowder for which Patrick Henry, at the head of his Hanover troops, made him pay. This incident, it will be remembered, resulted in Dunmore's flight from the capital and the patriotic Virginians putting themselves on record in a pledge to defend Virginia " or any sister colony "—fervently closing with, " God save the liberties of America."

Since the Revolution the Powder Horn has had a checkered history—serving in turn as a Baptist Church, a dancing school and a stable. During the War between the States the Confederates used it for its original purpose—a powder magazine and armory.

It is now the property of the Association for the Preservation of Virginia Antiquities, which has made it a museum of relics of Virginia's past.

RALEIGH TAVERN

From the Powder Horn on to the old Capitol grounds at the eastern end of the street may be seen numerous Colonial dwellings—though the open lots and new buildings show where many others have been destroyed by fire. The site of the most notable of these, Raleigh Tavern, has been recently marked by the Virginia Society of the Colonial Dames of America with a tablet.

This most famous of Colonial " guest houses " was a large, square, wooden building, two stories high, with eight dormer windows on each of its four sides. In a small portico over the Duke of Gloucester Street entrance stood, upon a pedestal which is now one of the relics of the Powder Horn Museum, a leaden bust of Sir Walter Raleigh. In 1742, the tavern was owned by John Blair, nephew of the

Commissary, and kept by one Henry Wetherburn. Mine host Wetherburn was evidently an expert mixer of the cup that cheers, if we may take a hint from the Goochland County records, from which we learn that William Randolph, of Tuckahoe, sold to his friend, Peter Jefferson —the father of Thomas Jefferson—200 acres of land for

RALEIGH TAVERN, WILLIAMSBURG, AND THE APOLLO ROOM

"Henry Wetherburn's biggest bowl of Arrack punch." The deed was duly recorded in Goochland and may be seen there to-day.

The chief glory of the Raleigh was a large banqueting hall with deep fireplaces at each end and carved wainscoting, named after an apartment in London Tavern, the "Apollo Room." The *Virginia Gazette* contains many allusions to entertainments and gatherings in this room, and it has been said that the Apollo "witnessed probably more scenes of brilliant festivity and political excitement than any other single apartment in North America." Thomas Jefferson was one of the gallants who danced at the balls held there. In a letter written in 1764 to his chum John Page,—afterward Governor of Virginia,—he wrote of having been "last night as merry as agreeable company and dancing with Belinda in the Apollo" could make him. But alas, he was not always so "merry" in the Apollo, for it was during a ball there that his "Belinda," as he elected to call the fair Rebecca Burwell, gave him the mitten.

The *Gazette* mentions a "genteele dinner" given by Peyton Randolph at the Raleigh, when "many loyal and patriotic toasts were drank, and the afternoon spent with cheerfulness and decorum." This was in 1768, and when, in the same year, Lord Botetourt came to be Governor of Virginia, he supped in state at the Raleigh, with the gentlemen of his Council.

During the days immediately preceding the Revolution the Raleigh became a favorite meeting place of the patriots. In 1773, Patrick Henry, Thomas Jefferson, the Lees, and a few others were accustomed to meet in a private room there, to consult on state affairs. In consequence of an agreement made there, Dabney Carr introduced in the House of Burgesses, on March 12 of that year, the resolutions for Inter-Colonial Committees of Correspondence.

When, in 1774, Lord Dunmore dissolved the Assembly that had protested against the shutting up of Boston Harbor and proclaimed June 1 a day of fast, it was to the Apollo Room that the indignant Burgesses adjourned and there drew up the famous resolution against the use of tea and other East Indian products.

Upon December 5, 1776, the Phi Beta Kappa—the first Greek letter society formed in America—was organized, by the students of William and Mary College, in the Apollo Room at the Raleigh.

This truly historic old tavern continued to be a popular place for banquets, assemblies, balls and political meetings until the year 1859, when, by unhappy accident, it was laid in ashes.

THE PARADISE HOUSE

On the left-hand side of Duke of Gloucester Street, not far below the Peninsula Hotel, may be seen a quaint brick dwelling known as the Paradise House.

When Philip Ludwell III (1716–1767) of Greenspring, Virginia, died in London—in which city he had taken up his abode—he left there two daughters, one of whom, Lucy, married, in 1769, John Paradise, Esq.,[7] . . . a gentleman well known in literary circles in London. He and his wife were identified with Doctor Johnson's famous set of literary lights and wits. Doctor Johnson sometimes dined with them and they are mentioned in "Boswell" and in Burney's *Memoirs*.

After her husband's death Madam Paradise returned to Virginia and was a personage in the society of Williamsburg, where she made her home, until her death in 1814. Among the articles of furniture which she brought over was the mahogany dining-table at which Johnson had been entertained, and which is still in Williamsburg.

It is probable that the house was formerly owned by Madam Paradise's father.

THE CARTER HOUSE

On the opposite side of the street from the Paradise House and somewhat farther down, is the many-dormered, white frame dwelling which was the town house of Robert Carter (1728–1804) of Nomini Hall, Westmoreland County, who was long a member of the Colonial Council and was familiarly known as "Councillor Carter."

Present-day readers have made the acquaintance of

---

[7] There is an interesting note on Paradise in *William and Mary Quarterly*, vi, 58.

Councillor Carter and his family and friends through the exceedingly quaint and delightful journal of Philip Vickers Fithian [8]—a tutor at Nomini just before the Revolution.

CARTER HOUSE, WILLIAMSBURG

THE OLD CAPITOL AND CLERK'S OFFICE

All that is left of that "noble, beautiful and commodious pile," the Capitol, within whose walls so much history, not only of Virginia but of America, was made, are the brick foundations lying across the foot of Duke of Gloucester Street and rising but little above the grass that fills the space between them with friendly green. They show the building to have been a large H-shaped structure, lying sideways to the street. The rear side was the House of Burgesses. The site is now the property of the Association for the Preservation of Virginia Antiquities, which

[8] Williams, *Philip Vickers Fithian, Journal and Letters, 1767–1774*, Princeton, 1900.

has placed upon it a granite boulder, bearing a bronze tablet appropriately inscribed, and capped the old brick-work with concrete, to prevent further decay.

Across Capitol Street on the left is a stout brick building, now part of a dwelling, but formerly the office of the Clerk of the House of Burgesses, or General Court.

GARRETT HOUSE

Following Capitol Street a short distance, still to the left, brings to view a long, rambling, white house in a shady, green lawn, which makes a charming picture of that interesting type of old-time Virginia homestead which grew with the needs of the family. The oldest part of this house was built by John Coke, a son of the distinguished family of Coke of Trusley and an ancestor of the late Senator Coke, of Texas. An extremely quaint stair-rail is one of the interesting interior details of this end of the house.

This, like many other of the Williamsburg homes, contains a fascinating collection of heirlooms—rare old mahogany, pictures, silver, and the like. Upon the parlor walls hangs, in a perfect state of preservation, the paper with the old-fashioned hunting-scene pattern which was the first wall-paper ever brought to Williamsburg.

BASSETT HALL

To the right of Capitol Street, on Francis Street—which is parallel with Duke of Gloucester—stands a large frame house, with square Colonial porches, in the midst of a lovely old flower garden. This is Bassett Hall, once the town home of the Bassett family of New Kent County.[9] Mrs. Bassett and Mrs. Washington (who were Dandridges) were sisters, and General Washington was often entertained at Bassett Hall.

---

[9] Bassett family: *Virginia Magazine of History and Biography*, iv, 162; vii, 399; and Keith, *The Ancestry of Benjamin Harrison . . . and Notes on Families Related*, Philadelphia, 1893, pp. 27–33.

It is said that the sweet Irish singer, Tom Moore, while a guest here composed his beautiful poem " To the Firefly "—suggested by the " firefly lamps " that sparkled among the flowers and shrubbery as he sat on the porch in the evening.

Bassett Hall was, in 1841, the home of President John Tyler.

RANDOLPH HOUSE

Just beyond Bassett Hall, on the same street, is the picturesque old homestead of Peyton Randolph, Attorney General of Virginia, Speaker of the House of Burgesses, and first President of the Continental Congress.

MASONIC TEMPLE

Still farther up Francis Street is a plain and now shabby frame house once used for Masonic meetings. Within this modest " Temple " was organized the first Grand Lodge of Masons in the Old Dominion.

CARY HOUSE

Turning into England Street, the tourist finds himself at the gate of a long, white, dormer-windowed cottage, in a green yard, with great shade-trees screening its square Colonial porch from the gaze of the over-curious.

This was the home of the lovely Cary sisters—Sarah and Mary [10]—where George Washington and George Fairfax did a-wooing go; Fairfax successfully, and Washington in vain.

TAZEWELL HALL

On England Street stands an old frame mansion of Colonial type. Its exterior is plain, but within it is very handsome, and the walls of its stately hall and rooms are made beautiful with carved mahogany panelling.

---

[10] Cary family: *The Critic* (Richmond, Va.), April 26, May 10 and 24, 1890.

This is Tazewell Hall, the home of Sir John Randolph (1693–1737)—one of the most distinguished lawyers of Colonial Virginia and Speaker of the House of Burgesses —and of his grandson Edmund Randolph (1753–1813), Governor of Virginia and Secretary of State of the United States.

The marriage, in 1776, of the Master of Tazewell Hall was announced in the *Virginia Gazette* in the following fashion:

TAZEWELL HALL, WILLIAMSBURG

" Edmund Randolph, Esq., Attorney General of Virginia, to Miss Betsy Nicholas,[11] a young lady whose amiable sweetness of disposition, joined with the finest intellectual accomplishments, cannot fail of rendering the worthy man of her choice completely happy."

[11] Nicholas family: *The Critic* (Richmond, Va.), August 30, 1890.

YORKTOWN

About nine miles distant from Williamsburg, upon a hill overlooking beautiful but now empty York River harbor, lies all that is left of Yorktown. This famous little town, built in 1691, was the successor of "York Plantation," which had already had an interesting history. It was never more than a village in size, but owing to its situation did a great shipping business for nearly a hundred years. An Englishman who had visited it published his impressions in the *London Magazine*, in 1764. He wrote:

"Yorktown . . . is situated on a rising ground, gently descending every way into a valley, and tho' but stragglingly built, yet makes no inconsiderable figure. You perceive a great air of opulence amongst the inhabitants who have (some of them) built themselves houses equal in magnificence to many of our superb ones at St. James, as those of Mr. Lightfoot, Nelson, etc., almost every considerable man keeps an equipage though they have no concern about the different colours of their coach horses, driving frequently black, white and chestnut in the same harness . . . the most considerable houses are brick, some handsome ones of wood—all built in the modern taste—and the lesser sort of plaster. There are some very pretty garden spots in the town; and the avenues leading to Williamsburg, Norfolk, etc., are prodigiously agreeable. The roads are . . . infinitely superior to most in England. The country surrounding is thickly overspread with plantations, and the planters live in a manner equal to men of the best fortune."

In achieving fame Yorktown bade farewell to fortune, for its prosperous career came to a sudden end with the Revolution; but perhaps it finds consolation in a secure place in history and the superb monument erected, in 1881, by the United States Government.

Traces of earthworks raised by the British still remain, though covered and altered in many places by the later Confederate fortifications.

NELSON HOUSE, YORKTOWN

CUSTOM HOUSE, YORKTOWN

THE CUSTOM HOUSE

The oldest brick building now standing in Yorktown is the Custom House, built in 1715. This interesting relic—the first Custom House in the United States—escaped serious damage during the famous siege.

THE NELSON HOUSE

Upon the brow of the hill, facing the river, a short distance away from the Custom House stands the picturesque old Nelson House. The massiveness of this commodious brick mansion, and its situation upon a terrace some distance above the street and within an old-fashioned walled garden whose entrance gates are guarded on each side by tall, thick box trees, give it an air of dignified seclusion and security. Indoors, the spacious rooms, with their deep window-seats and handsome wainscoting, produce a charming effect, while the interest that a touch of the mysterious gives is added by a hidden stairway leading to the garret, to which a secret panel in the dining-room woodwork gives entrance.

As the home of Thomas Nelson (1738–1789),[12] Governor of Virginia, Signer of the Declaration of Independence and Major General in the Revolutionary Army, and as the headquarters of Lord Cornwallis during the siege this house is the most historic as well as the most attractive now standing in Yorktown. It suffered a good deal of damage during the siege and a cannon ball embedded in the brick-work still bears witness to the bombardment, during which the patriotic General Nelson said to General Lafayette, " Spare no particle of my property so long as it affords comfort or shelter to the enemies of my country."

The site of the mansion of " Secretary " Nelson, uncle of General Nelson, which was destroyed during the siege

---

[12] Nelson family: See Page, *Genealogy of the Page Family*, p. 155 *et seq.* Interesting results from an investigation of the English ancestry of the Nelson family are given in *Virginia Magazine of History and Biography*, xiii, pp. 402–403; xvii, pp. 187–188.

is still pointed out. " Secretary " Nelson was brought out of Yorktown under a flag of truce and congratulated the American officers upon the havoc their bombardment was playing upon his own house.

THE CHURCH

In the churchyard a short distance away from the Nelson House may be seen the Nelson tombs. The church where this patriotic family worshipped and which was built in 1697 was burned in 1814, but was replaced by a small stone-marle building on the original site. The old bell of the earlier church bearing the inscription, " County of York, Virginia, 1725," was preserved and is still in use.

THE MOORE HOUSE

About three-quarters of a mile out of Yorktown, upon " Temple Farm," stands the " Moore House " where the

MOORE HOUSE, NEAR YORKTOWN

surrender of Cornwallis was drawn up and signed. The room made forever famous by this epoch-making agreement is still pointed out. The house is a very old one and is probably part of the residence of Colonel George Ludlow

(1596–1656), member of the Colonial Council, who was a kinsman of the English regicide, Edmund Ludlow, and is mentioned by him in his memoirs. Standing within a green lawn on a bold bluff of York River, the long, dormer-window farm-house makes a charming picture.

An interesting bit of history connected with "Temple Farm" is found in the fact that just about this site stood, more than a hundred years before the Revolution, the home of Captain Nicholas Martain (1591–1657), ancestor of General Washington and General Nelson and one of the leading spirits in the first rebellion against tyranny in Virginia, when, in 1634, the Colonists "thrust" the unpopular Governor, Sir John Harvey, out of office and shipped him to England.

Another historic spot near Yorktown is the field where Lord Cornwallis's men laid down their arms.

RINGFIELD HOUSE, YORK COUNTY

RINGFIELD

The most historic spot on York River—Yorktown—has been noticed. The only other place on that side of the river to be represented here is Ringfield, lying between the forks of King's Creek and Felgate's Creek. This plantation was first patented by Captain Robert Felgate, a prominent ship-captain of London, who made his will in 1640, leaving his estate to his brother, William Felgate, a skinner of London. At Felgate's death his widow, Mary, married (in 1660) Captain John Underhill, Jr., from the City of Worcester, England, from whom the Felgate plantation passed to Joseph Ring, a prominent planter, who probably built the house still standing. Since his time the place has been known as Ringfield. There were long to be seen there two old tombs of members of the Ring family, one having a mutilated coat-of-arms, but they have been lately removed to the old Bruton Churchyard, Williamsburg.

In about 1772, Ringfield belonged to Colonel Landon Carter (1710–1778) of Sabine Hall, Richmond County.

PORTO BELLO, NEAR WILLIAMSBURG

PORTO BELLO

Not far from Williamsburg on the north side of Queen's Creek, near its mouth, is Porto Bello, which was bought by Lord Dunsmore, in 1773. He built the present house. It has since had many owners, and is now owned by Mr. T. R. Daley.

PART II

HAMPTON ROADS AND THE LOWER JAMES

ST. PAUL'S CHURCH, NORFOLK

AS St. Paul's Church was the only building left standing after the fire which during the Revolution laid the town of Norfolk in ashes, it is, of course, the only Colonial building now to be found there. With its high-walled graveyard it makes the loveliest and most appealing spot in that city by the sea.

The church, which was built in 1739, is in the shape of a cross, and is completely mantled in ivy, save where the green is trimmed away to show the cannon-ball lodged in the wall by a gun on the frigate *Liverpool,* during the bombardment of Norfolk by Lord Dunmore, on New Year's Day, 1776.*

The Communion service was taken from the church by the British and carried to Scotland.

THE MYERS HOUSE, NORFOLK

The ivy-covered, brick dwelling now occupied by Mr. Barton Myers was built, in 1791, by Moses Myers, his great-grandfather. He was one of the most prominent ship owners and merchants of his day engaged in foreign trade, and was appointed by John Quincy Adams, Collector of Customs for the Port in 1828.

Five generations of the family have lived here. The house has always been noted for its hospitality and many of the most distinguished men who visited Norfolk were entertained within its hospitable walls, amongst them Henry Clay, who stayed here when he visited Norfolk during the Presidential campaign in 1844.

President Roosevelt, with members of his Cabinet, and James Bryce, British Ambassador, with their wives, were entertained here on the occasion of the opening of the Jamestown Exposition, April, 1907, as the guests of Mr. Harry St. George Tucker, President of the Exposition.

* See illustration, p. 43.

The American Architect and Building News, of Boston, in its portfolio of the Georgian Period, Part IV, published in Boston, in 1900, says, " The house we have chosen for illustration is by far the most interesting example of Georgian work to be found in Norfolk."

General Winfield Scott, on a visit to Norfolk, in 1850, was a guest here. His visit, and a description of the house was referred to in an article published by Mr. H. B. Bagnall in the *Ledger-Dispatch*.

ROLLESTON

In the Dutch-roofed portion of the house here presented we find all that is left of the habitation of one of Virginia's early settlers. In 1649—the year Charles I

ROLLESTON, PRINCESS ANNE COUNTY

was beheaded with other disappointed Cavaliers—William Moseley arrived on our shores from Rotterdam, Holland, bringing with him his wife Susannah and sons Arthur and William, grants of land in Lynnhaven Parish on Broad

ST. PAUL'S CHURCH, NORFOLK

MYERS HOUSE, NORFOLK

Creek, Lower Norfolk County, Virginia, a " Court Callender," a " Coat of Arms," old family portraits, one of them painted in the reign of Henry II and the rest by Van Dyck, and family jewels of rare value, showing how Englishmen cling to their old traditions and belongings even when colonizing in the wilderness. In 1650, alas! we find Susannah Moseley forced to sell her jewels for " Cattell," the gems, irony of Fate! being purchased by Francis Yardley, son of the Colonial Governor and leader of the Cromwellian party in Virginia.

Here in Lower Norfolk County, William Moseley built the house of our cut, calling it " Rolleston " after the Moseley seat, Rolleston Hall, in Staffordshire, England. These Virginia lands were escheated to the Commonwealth in the time of Cromwell, and, after the restoration of Charles II, were restored to the grandson of the emigrant, Colonel Edward Moseley, a man of great distinction in those parts, a member of the House of Burgesses, and one of Governor Spotswood's Knights of the Golden Horseshoe. The house still stands, and until the end of the War between the States (1865) was occupied by his lineal descendants.

THOROUGHGOOD HOUSE

In the early days of our country's history, as far back indeed as 1621, there came to Virginia from Lynn, in Norfolk, England, in the good ship *Charles*, a certain Adam Thoroughgood, who was destined to become, through his thrift and industry, a man of much distinction in the Colony. Perhaps, too, a strain of gentle blood, which flowed in him from a long line of English ancestors, enabled him to impress those early colonizers—an impression so lasting that to this day their descendants around Lynnhaven and Norfolk, in Virginia, still revere his memory.

He was the son of Thomas Thoroughgood, M.P., and brother of Sir John Thoroughgood, Knight of Kensington, England, whom he mentions in his will, and it is stated in the patent for 5350 acres of land granted him, that the grant is made "at the especial recommendation of him from their Lordships and others of his Majesties most humble privy Councell." He settled first at "Kicotan," now Hampton, Virginia, but in 1634, when this land was granted him in the same shire, he removed to Back River, naming it "Norfolk" County, and its beautiful Bay, "Lynnhaven." Here he built the quaint house, the gable

THOROUGHGOOD HOUSE, PRINCESS ANNE COUNTY
Built about 1635

end of which appears in our illustration, and so substantial was his work that now it still stands habitable and well preserved, with its walls of three feet thickness, its queer old wainscoting reaching the ceiling about the chimney pieces, and its secret closets running from gable to gable in which to hide from the Indians.

Here he amassed a large fortune, and rose to much

distinction in the Colony, being, in 1637, a member of the Council (our Colonial House of Lords) with Governor Harvey. But in 1640, he is dead, cut down before his prime, still, having accomplished enough in his thirty-seven years of life to make dwellers in those parts nearly 300 years later proud to claim descent from Captain Adam Thoroughgood.

ST. JOHN'S CHURCH, HAMPTON *

ST. JOHN'S CHURCH, HAMPTON

Across Hampton Roads from Norfolk is the still older town of Hampton, which, like Norfolk, has been destroyed by fire and rebuilt. During the War between the States, when the inhabitants set the torch to their own homes rather than let them give shelter to Northern soldiers, the massive walls of St. John's were the only relics left of Colonial Hampton.

There were churches in Hampton, which was first known by the name the Indians gave it, "Kicoughtan,"

* Picture from Lossing's *Field Book of the Revolution*, published 1850, vol. 2, p. 326.

from a very early date, but St. John's was not built until 1727. Like many of the Colonial churches it is cruciform and is surrounded by a graveyard filled with interesting old tombs. A number of these which were in existence in 1861 disappeared during the war.

St. John's possesses the oldest service of Communion silver in America. One of the pieces, a large cup, bears the inscription: "The Communion Cupp for St. Mary's Church in Smith Hundred, in Virginia," and the hall mark, 1617. Smith's Hundred was one of the large land grants along the Chickahominy, and the Hampton silver evidently belonged originally to a church there—long since disappeared.

An interesting window in St. John's is to the memory of Pocahontas, and was placed there by the Indian students of Hampton Normal School.

Notable among the beauties of the churchyard are the fine old weeping willows that shade it with their fringe-like foliage.

EASTERN SHORE CHAPEL, PRINCESS ANNE COUNTY

EASTERN SHORE CHAPEL

Soon after the opening of the earliest vestry books known to Bishop Meade is mention, in 1725, of an Eastern Shore Chapel. The present building was erected in 1754.

OLD BRICK CHURCH, ISLE OF WIGHT

Crossing again to the south side of James River, the traveller enters the county of Isle of Wight, whose chief interest is the Old Brick Church, some five miles from Smithfield.*

The Old Brick Church is as unique as it is picturesque. Tradition has long insisted that it was built in 1632, and this seemed to be confirmed during its restoration, when, in the débris scattered about, two old bricks with the traditional date baked into them were found. The zealous historian of the church has produced other strong arguments in favor of this date, in spite of which there are some who doubt. Whatever may be its exact age, it is certain that it was built early in the seventeenth century and it is the oldest brick Protestant church in the New World. A point of interest concerning it is that it was evidently of the same type as (and probably exactly like) the Jamestown Church, as the ruins of that historic sanctuary plainly show. These two were the only buttressed churches of the seventeenth century in America.

Fortunately, the Old Brick Church, while suffering much from neglect in the past, has remained unchanged in all of its essential features. The square entrance-tower, the frame-work of the round-headed windows with their lancet lights and the great east window (though their glasses were destroyed) have been preserved. Within the last few years the church has been completely restored and many handsome memorials placed in the beautiful old window frames.

---

* See illustration, p. 51.

BACON'S CASTLE

Not many miles above the Old Brick Church, in the adjoining county of Surry, is Bacon's Castle, perhaps the oldest of the homesteads in the James River region. Though a spacious addition, with commodious " built in " porches, tells a story of a later time, the steep roof, massive walls and huge chimneys of the original building stamp it at once as early Colonial. The deep window-seats, wainscoted walls and low ceilings, with their heavy oaken cross-beams, make the rooms exceedingly picturesque. In one instance the cross-beams are supported by a carved oak centre-post in the middle of the big room.

Bacon's Castle was built by Arthur Allen, who came to Virginia from England in 1649. He married Alice Tucker and died in 1670, leaving the plantation with the brick house, said to have been built in 1660, to his son and heir, Major Arthur Allen, sometime Speaker of the Virginia House of Burgesses. During Bacon's Rebellion the house of Major Allen, who was a friend of Governor Berkeley's, was seized, fortified and used as a stronghold by a party of Bacon's adherents, commanded by William Rookings, and was held for nearly four months.

In the journal of the Master of a Ship, who was aiding Governor Berkeley in this part of the country, is this entry: " The guard at Allen's brick house we hear is run away." On the next day the writer records the occupation of the " fort," as he calls it. The records of Surry County show that on July 3, 1677, Major Arthur Allen sued Mr. Robert Burgess " for that during the late most Horrid Rebellion he with others did seize and keep garrison in the plt's house neare fower months (bearing the title of Lieutenant Commander-in-Chief next to William Rookings)." From that time the house was known as Bacon's Castle.

Major Allen died in 1710 and the estate passed to his son, Arthur, who died in 1725, leaving an only son and heir, James, upon whose death it was inherited by his sister

ST. LUKE'S CHURCH, ISLE OF WIGHT COUNTY EARLY 17 C

Katherine, wife of Benjamin Cocke. In 1802 Allen Cocke left Bacon's Castle to his sister, Mrs. Bradley. After passing through the hands of several other owners it was bought by Mr. William A. Warren, of Surry, who gave it to the present owner, his son, Mr. Charles Walker Warren, as a wedding gift. This seems most fitting, for the bride was Miss Pegram, daughter of Mr. Blair Pegram, of Surry, and is related to the Allens, Cockes and other former owners of the old "Castle."

BACON'S CASTLE, SURRY COUNTY

About a quarter of a mile away from Bacon's Castle are the ivy-grown ruins of a Colonial church, with walls three feet thick. A brick found among these ruins bears the date 1736.

CARTER'S GROVE

Going up James River from Bacon's Castle and crossing to the north side, the next Colonial house of note is Carter's Grove, in the lower end of James City County. This fine old mansion was built by Carter Burwell in 1751. It stands on a bluff eighty feet high overlooking the river and, as may be imagined, the view from the windows is superb. The James is wide here and looking down stream the broad expanse of Burwell's Bay and still lower reaches may be seen. In front of the house, the hill has been cut down to form terraces below which a green field stretches away to the edge of the high river bank.

The house is commodious and handsome, but modern porches, while they add greatly to its comfort, mar the beauty of the exterior. Within, it is one of the most impressive examples of Colonial home-building left in Virginia. Walls of hall and rooms are panelled to the ceiling, where they are finished with beautiful cornices. The great central hall is spanned by a wide arch supported on either side by fluted pilasters, beneath which the fine old stairway, with its carved banisters, descends with majestic sweep. Along the hand-rail may still be seen the gashes made by the sabres of Tarleton's men, who paid their respects to Carter's Grove when raiding Virginia during the Revolution.

Some interesting details concerning the construction of the house are furnished by an old plantation account book of the Burwell family. This shows that the house was begun in June and finished in September. The labor was of course that of slaves, but a "master workman"—one David Minitree—was general director of construction and was brought from England, accompanied by his family, especially for this work. He was paid 115 pounds by Mr. Burwell for "building me a brick house according to agreement," and in addition received a present of 25 pounds. The timber used—25,000 feet of plank, at ten shillings a thousand, 40,000 shingles, at four shillings a thousand, and 15,000 lathes, at seven shillings a thousand—was evidently brought from a distance, as 32 pounds was paid for hauling it; but the bricks—460,000 at seventeen shillings a thousand—were made upon the place. Five hundred and forty squares of glass were used, at two and a half pence a square. The entire cost of building the house was five hundred pounds, which considering its substantial condition, after over a century and a half of wear and tear, seems most moderate.

THE HALL AT CARTER'S GROVE

CARTER'S GROVE, JAMES CITY COUNTY

Carter Burwell, builder and first master of Carter's Grove, was the son of Colonel Nathaniel Burwell, of Carter's Creek, and his wife, Elizabeth, daughter of Robert ("King") Carter. He was long a member of the House of Burgesses from James City County. He married Lucy, daughter of Honorable John Grymes (1693–1748) of Middlesex County, and had, among other children, (his eldest son) Colonel Nathaniel Burwell, who inherited Carter's Grove, but about the end of the eighteenth century moved to Clarke County, where he built Carter Hall. Since then Carter's Grove has had several owners, but has been best known as the hospitable home of Dr. Edwin Booth, who has, however, recently sold it.

THE WARREN HOUSE

Grays Creek, which flows into James River, opposite Jamestown, has at its mouth, on John Smith's map, "The New Fort." A short distance up the creek on a bluff on the "Smith Fort" farm are remains of earthworks, most probably a part of the "New Fort" built in 1608 or 1609.

On "Smith's Fort" is an old brick residence exactly fifty feet long, which is the oldest house in Virginia whose exact date can be ascertained.* The records show that Thomas Rolfe, the son of Pocahontas, owned 1200 acres here which he sold to Thomas Warren (ancestor of the well-known Surry family). Depositions on record at Surry Court House state that the Warrens' "fifty foot brick house" at Smith's Fort was built in 1654. After passing through many different hands, the house and a hundred or so acres of land adjoining are the property of a prosperous negro family.

FOUR MILE TREE

Going on up the south side of the river, the traveller soon has a view of Four Mile Tree—a name evidently given the plantation on account of some conspicuous tree

* See illustration at head of Index.

which distinguished it in early times. The mansion stands upon a steep, round-top hill overlooking the river and from the remnants of terraces and high box-hedges that may be still seen was, evidently, in its day, a place of beauty as well as consequence.

As early as 1637, Henry Browne * patented 2250 acres "at the Four Mile Tree" and a little later 900 acres adjoining. The estate remained in the Browne family, whose members were prominent in public life in nearly every

FOUR MILE TREE, JAMES RIVER

generation. William Browne, the last of the name who owned Four Mile Tree, died, in 1799, leaving an only child, Sally Edwards Browne, who married, in 1813, John T. Bowdoin, and dying, in 1815, left also an only child, Sally Elizabeth Courtney Bowdoin, who married Gen. Philip St. George Cocke, and they lived there until General Cocke built Belmead, on upper James River.

In the graveyard may be seen—still in perfect condition—the oldest tomb in Virginia having a legible inscription, that of Mrs. Alice Jordan, who died in 1650. Her husband,

* Browne: *William and Mary College Quarterly Historical Magazine*, xvi, 227 *et seq.*

George Jordan, at one time Attorney General of Virginia, long survived her, and in his will, made in 1678, directed that he be buried beside his wife and children in Major Browne's orchard.

GREEN SPRING

Some distance back from the river, and four miles from Jamestown, was Green Spring, the home of Sir William Berkeley (1606–1677), the famous Cavalier Governor of Virginia. The place derives its name from " A very fine green spring that is upon the land," whose water was " so very cold that 'tis dangerous drinking thereof in summer-time."

The estate of nearly a thousand acres was granted to Governor Berkeley in 1643,[1] and here he built him a home consisting of a central building containing six rooms and a large hall, with a commodious wing on either side. The fireplaces were over four feet wide and nearly as deep, and there was a central chimney seven feet wide. There were a terraced lawn and flower gardens, and hot-houses in which orange trees and other tropical shrubs grew and bore fruit, and there were great stables filled with fine horses.

Here Sir William kept open house for the Cavaliers who took refuge in Virginia during the banishment from England of his Majesty, Charles II; here Nathaniel Bacon, on the march to Jamestown, where Sir William was entrenched, rested, and made one of his ringing speeches to his " hearts of gold," and here he returned after besieging and burning Jamestown, and took up his headquarters. Here, too, on account of the destruction of the State House at Jamestown, the first Grand Assembly after Bacon's Rebellion met.

After Sir William Berkeley's death, his widow, the fair and fascinating Lady Frances, married the Honorable Philip Ludwell I (becoming his second wife), and Green

---

[1] Hening, *Statutes at Large . . . of Virginia*, ii, 319.

Spring passed to the Ludwell family.[2] Three successive Philip Ludwells owned it—wealthy and prominent men, all of them, and members of his Majesty's Council. In taking a second husband Lady Berkeley could not bring herself to part with the title her first had given her, and not only did she continue to be called by it the rest of her days, but "Lady Berkeley" was the name inscribed on her tomb. Her cousin Lord Culpeper, who was made Governor of the Colony in 1680, rented Greenspring from the Ludwells and lived there in state.

Finally Green Spring passed to the Lees, by the marriage of Hannah Philippa, daughter and co-heiress of the third Colonel Philip Ludwell, with Honorable William Lee, Minister of the United States at the Courts of Vienna and Berlin, who in his latter days retired to the famous old plantation and lived there in style and splendor.

An advertisement in a Richmond newspaper of 1816 for the sale of Green Spring—at that time 2934 acres—shows that the house then standing (the ruins of which now remain) was built by William L. Lee, son of William Lee.

CLAREMONT

In the same county with Four Mile Tree—at its upper end—is Claremont, best known as the home of the Allen family, which has been identified with it for two centuries and a quarter. Part of this handsome estate of 12,000 acres was granted as early as 1649 to Arthur Allen, Justice of Surry—for several years a burgess and in 1688 Speaker of the House of Burgesses—who married Catherine, daughter and heiress of Burgess Lawrence Baker, of Surry, and left a number of children. The manor plantation was first inherited by the eldest son James and after his death by his brother, Arthur Allen, third of the name. This Arthur married Elizabeth Bray. His daughter Catherine married

[2] Ludwell: An account of the Ludwell family may be found in E. J. Lee's *Lee of Virginia*.

Benjamin Cocke, and his son James died unmarried, leaving his unentailed estate to his sister and her children and in case of their death without heirs, to Southwark Parish, for founding a school to be called " Allen's School." Upon James Allen's death the manor plantation at Claremont passed to his cousin, Colonel William Allen, of Claremont —a member of the Convention of 1788 and of the Virginia Legislature. He left one son, Colonel William Allen, Jr., of Claremont—a member of the Legislature, Colonel of Militia in the War of 1812 and one of the largest land and slave owners in Virginia.

CLAREMONT, SURRY COUNTY

Colonel William Allen, Jr., left his estate to his great-nephew, William Orgain, who took the name of Allen. He served as a major of artillery in the Confederate Army and was known as Major William Allen, of Claremont. At one time he owned the largest landed estate in Virginia —his possessions including the plantations of Claremont, Kingsmill, Jamestown Island, Neck of Land, Curle's Neck and other valuable lands to the number of thirty or forty thousand acres. He also owned some seven or eight hundred slaves. With his death, in 1875, the Allen tenure at Claremont ceased, and the great estate has been since cut up into small farms—part of it being now the town of Claremont.

An interesting incident in the Allen family history is furnished by the will of Mrs. Elizabeth Bray Allen, who upon the death of her husband, Colonel Arthur Allen, third, married Colonel Arthur Smith, of Isle of Wight, and founded a free school at Smithfield. In her will she left fifty pounds for the purchase of " an altar piece for the Lower Church of Southwalk Parish," Surry, upon which Moses and Aaron were to be represented holding between them the Ten Commandments, while upon either side was to hang a small tablet, one of them containing the Lord's Prayer and the other the Apostles' Creed.[3]

TEDINGTON

The Sandy Point estate on James River, in Charles City County, was for several generations the home of that branch of the Lightfoot family in Virginia which descends from Honorable Philip Lightfoot (grandson of Richard Lightfoot, rector of Stoke-Bruerne, Northamptonshire, England), who was in the colony as early as 1671. He held various offices of trust and honor, among them collector for the Upper District of James River and surveyor general of the colony.[4]

Philip Lightfoot owned a large acreage at Sandy Point, where, by the way, was, at the settlement of Virginia, seated the Indian town of " Paspahegh."

The house at Sandy Point, says Tyler in his *Cradle of the Republic*, is said to have been built in 1717, and is called " Tedington," the name of a place in London. This

[3] Allen genealogy, *William and Mary College Quarterly Historical Magaz'ne*, viii, 110–115.

[4] Lightfoot family: *William and Mary College Quarterly Historical Magazine*, ii, 91–97, 204–207 and 259–262; iii, 104–111, 137.

house has massive walls of brick and from the first floor is weather-boarded over the inside brick casing, known in Colonial days as a stock brick building and supposed to be indestructible.

At Sandy Point are buried several of the older generations of the Lightfoot family, beneath tombs bearing the family arms.

TEDINGTON, CHARLES CITY COUNTY

From the Lightfoots, the estate passed to the Minges and Bollings and from the latter, by sale, to Baylor.

Charles Campbell, the Virginia historian, published a fascinating account of Tedington in the *Southern Literary Messenger* for March, 1841, called, " Christmas Holidays at Tedington."

BRANDON

Separated only by Upper Chippokes Creek from the great Claremont estate and extending like it along the James, is historic Brandon.

Its approach from the river-front is through the loveliest old garden in Virginia, and every flower and shrub known to Virginia gardens has a place there, from the violet, the cowslip and the lily-of-the-valley underfoot, to the mimosa and the magnolia shedding sweetness in the upper air.

The garden is open to the river at the end but is enclosed on each side by a box-hedge walk. Entrance is from a corner where box-walk and river bluff meet, through a bower of honeysuckle. A short path along the bluff leads to a broad grass-walk, bordered on either side with flowering shrubs of every description, which cuts the garden in two and provides a most beautiful approach to the house. In the spaces between this central walk and the box-walks the flowers in their respective seasons make a variety of color. In midsummer numberless hollyhocks set in formal rows and in beds are in their glory, while through spring, summer, and fall roses in splendid variety show what roses can be at their best.

The grass-walk ends in a smooth green lawn stretching away on either side to the box-hedges, upon which stands the hoary mansion, its tempest-stained and bullet-scarred walls presenting a striking contrast to the gay garden, for no attempt has ever been made to cover the fact that during the War between the States the house was used as a target by Northern soldiers, who also burned the barns and outbuildings, pried off some of the wainscoting inside of the house in hope of finding treasure, and broke some window-panes upon which had been scratched with diamonds the names of visitors to the house for a hundred years or more —many of them persons of note. The Southern poet John R. Thompson made these panes the subject of a quaint bit of verse, " The Window-panes of Brandon."

The house consists of a square central building with square porches at both back and front, and this central building is connected by one-story passage-ways with a wing at either side. Crossing the threshold we find ourselves within a spacious hall, wainscoted to the ceiling and relieved midway by triple arches supported upon fluted columns. After two hundred years the Harrisons still own

BRANDON, PRINCE GEORGE COUNTY

THE HALL AT BRANDON

and occupy Brandon, with the household gods accumulated during that period around them. These gentle and companionable deities will prove as full of inspiration as the flower garden, for they make the home as redolent with memories as the garden is with bloom.

Upon the walls of drawing-room and dining-room which open upon the hall from either side hang the famous collection of Byrd portraits from Westover—brought hither when the daughter of the third Colonel William Byrd married Benjamin Harrison. Some of these are by such distinguished artists as Godfrey Kneller, Vandyke and Sir Peter Lely. Here is, also, rich old mahogany worthy to be used by the stately ladies and gentlemen who look down upon it, and picturesque old cabinets filled with Colonial silver, every piece of which has its own story.

Here is a gown of pink brocade and a painted fan which once belonged to the fair Mistress Evelyn Byrd.

A round of the treasure-filled rooms finally brings us out into the porch at the opposite end of the hall from that by which we entered, and here the eye is surprised by the contrast the grounds on this side of the house make with the river-front. Instead of the brilliant garden is an open lawn, and beyond a sunlit space of unbroken green spreads a park where wide-spreading oaks and elms make shadowy vistas.

Brandon plantation was first granted to John Martin, who came over with John Smith and was a member of " his Majesty's first Council in Virginia," and its earliest name was " Martin's Brandon." One of the most interesting relics in Virginia is the original grant to John Martin still preserved at Brandon. Later Martin must have either sold or abandoned the estate, for in 1635 it was granted to John Sadler and Richard Quiney, merchants, and William Barber, mariner. Richard Quiney's brother, Thomas Quiney, married Judith, daughter of William Shakespeare. Richard Quiney left his share of the property to his son, who left it to his great-nephew, Robert Richardson, who sold it in 1720 to Nathaniel Harrison[5] (1677–1727) of "Wakefield," Surry County, son of Honorable Benjamin Harrison (1645–1712) of "Wakefield," who was second of the name in Virginia. He had evidently already bought the rest from the Sadlers, for the records show that he owned "the tract called Brandon, containing 7,000 acres."

The new owner of Brandon was a burgess and a councillor, naval officer of the Lower James, county lieutenant of Surry and Prince George and finally auditor general of the Colony. He married a widow, Mrs. Mary Young, née Cary, and had seven children—among them Nathaniel Harrison II, eldest son, who inherited Brandon and built the present house. Nathaniel Harrison, of Brandon, was like his father a prominent man in the colony and a member of the Council of State. He married first Mary, daughter of Colonel Cole Digges (1692–1744),[6] and secondly, Lucy, widow of Henry Fitzhugh and daughter of Honorable Robert Carter, of Corotoman. His first wife was the mother of his eldest son and the heir of Brandon, Benjamin Harrison, whose portrait is among those upon the walls.

Benjamin Harrison was twice married, and the portraits of his two exceeding fair ladies hang amicably in the same room at Brandon. His first wife was Anne Randolph, of Wilton, who left no children, and the second, Evelyn Taylor Byrd, daughter of Colonel William Byrd III, of Westover—of an entirely different type from her namesake and aunt, the famous Evelyn, but second only to her in beauty. By his marriage with her, Benjamin Harrison had two sons, between whom the plantation was divided—George Evelyn, the elder son, of course, inherited the lower part, upon which the family-seat stands, and

[5] The Harrison family has been very thoroughly worked out by Keith in his *Ancestry of Benjamin Harrison* . . . Philadelphia, 1893, and in *The Critic* (Richmond, Va.), June 23, July 7 and 21, 1889.

[6] Digges family: *Pedigree of a Representative Virginia Planter*, in *William and Mary Quarterly*, i, 80–88, 140–154, 208–213.

William Byrd Harrison, the younger son, received the part upon which Upper Brandon was built.

George Evelyn Harrison was a prominent man in his time and a member of the House of Delegates from his county—Prince George. He married Isabella Ritchie, daughter of Thomas Ritchie, the distinguished Virginia editor, and had two children, George Evelyn and Isabella. He died in 1839, aged 42, and from that date until her own death, in 1898, Brandon was owned by his widow, Mrs. Isabella Ritchie Harrison, who was affectionately known throughout Virginia by the name her servants gave her, "Old Miss," and who reigned supreme, not only over Brandon but its vicinity for miles around, for over a half-century. In doing the honors of her hospitable home she was always assisted by her daughter "Miss Belle," who was widely known and admired for her loveliness and charm of person and character, but who, electing to remain unmarried, never left the Brandon roof-tree.

George Evelyn Harrison, Jr., married Miss Gulielma Gordon, of Savannah, Georgia. He died young, leaving several children, and upon the death of "Old Miss," his widow, Mrs. Gulielma G. Harrison, succeeded to the distinguished post of mistress of Brandon. Since her death, the estate is owned by her sons and daughters.

UPPER BRANDON

Upper Brandon, a handsome and spacious mansion, flanked on either side by commodious wings, stands in a box-bordered lawn, completely screened from the view of passers-by on the James by the grove of superb oaks between it and the river. It was built early in the nineteenth century by William Byrd Harrison, son of Benjamin Harrison and the beautiful Evelyn Taylor Byrd, his wife.

Mr. Harrison was one of the most prominent gentlemen and planters in Virginia. He was twice married, first, in 1827, to Mary Randolph, daughter of Randolph Harrison of Elk Hill, Goochland County, and secondly to

Ellen Wayles, daughter of Colonel Thomas Jefferson Randolph, of Edge Hill, Albemarle County. Three of his sons were gallant officers in the Confederate Army and one of them, Captain Benjamin Harrison, of The Row, Charles City County, was killed at the Battle of Malvern Hill.

After the death of Mr. Harrison, Upper Brandon was sold and passed into the possession of his nephew, Mr. George H. Byrd, of New York, whose son now owns the place and lives there.

There were formerly at Upper Brandon a number of interesting portraits—among them one of Miss Blount, said to have been a sweetheart of the poet Pope.

WEYANOKE

Weyanoke, which lies on the north side of the river, not many miles above Upper Brandon, first appears in history during the exploring voyage of Captain Christopher Newport, Captain John Smith and others, up the James, in 1607. They found seated at this place the Weyanoke Indians—a tribe governed by a queen subordinate to Powhatan. In the writings of the early colonists there is frequent reference to the Queen of Weyanoke.

Governor Sir George Yeardley acquired an estate at Weyanoke which was afterwards sold to the rich planter and merchant Abraham Piersey. On account of the destruction of the county records, we have no knowledge of the ownership of the plantation for a time, but toward the end of the seventeenth century it became the property of the Harwoods [7]—long a prominent family in Charles City County.

In 1740, William Harwood built in place of an earlier dwelling the spacious frame house which still stands at Weyanoke. Toward the close of the eighteenth century,

---

[7] Harwood notes: *Virginia Magazine of History and Biography*, ii, 183–185.

UPPER BRANDON, PRINCE GEORGE COUNTY

Agnes, daughter and co-heiress of Major Samuel Harwood, of Weyanoke, married Fielding Lewis, a son of Colonel Warner Lewis, of Warner Hall, Gloucester County, and inherited the old homestead. Mr. Lewis was noted as a scientific planter, and his portrait was in the collection of the Virginia Agricultural Society, and now hangs in the Virginia State Library. His daughter, Eleanor, who likewise inherited the homestead, married Robert Douthat, and had several children. One of these, Major Robert Douthat, was the next master of Weyanoke,

WEYANOKE, CHARLES CITY COUNTY 1785

which he sold in 1876. Another son, Fielding Lewis Douthat, inherited part of the estate. He married Mary Willis Marshall, a descendant of the great Chief Justice, who with her children now lives at Lower Weyanoke.

SHERWOOD FOREST

"Sherwood Forest" is situated on the north side of James River in Charles City County, Virginia, opposite to the famous Brandon estates in Prince George County. The tract originally consisted of 1200 acres, and the manor house is a building of framed timbers facing a ten-acre grove of primeval oaks, and in the rear is a circular descending park of choice trees originally from the Washington Botanical Gardens. The main building is two stories and a half high with dormer windows. On each side is a wing consisting of a story and a half, and to each wing is attached a long enclosed colonnade, ending in two framed buildings, also of a story and a half—the eastern wing containing the laundry and kitchen, and the western the library and overseer's office. It is the longest connected dwelling in Virginia—being upwards of 100 yards in

SHERWOOD FOREST, CHARLES CITY COUNTY

length. The place was formerly known as "Walnut Grove," and was bought by President John Tyler of Collier Minge in 1842. At the time of the purchase, there was standing a house of Revolutionary age. President Tyler duplicated the structure and added the colonnades and houses at the ends. On his retirement from the Presidency, in 1845, he came there to live with his bride, the second Mrs. Tyler, whose maiden name was Julia Gardiner.

The President was very fond of poetry and romance, and, in view of his outlawry by the Whig Party, he likened himself to Robin Hood and named his new home "Sherwood Forest," after the scene of action, in England, of the bold Englishman. Although everything was destroyed on the farm, the house passed safely through the Civil War, and is now the residence of President Tyler's oldest son by his second marriage—D. Gardiner Tyler, Judge of the 14th Judicial Circuit of Virginia.

Three miles away is Greenway, the residence of Governor John Tyler, Sr., and the birthplace of the President.

FLOWER DE HUNDRED

The fantastic name of Flower de Hundred (whose origin is wrapped in mystery), the setting of green lawn and foliage and the view of the river with its " firm, sandy shore, its bluff beyond, its fringe of trees and tangle of lilies," give the long, white, cottage-like homestead " a charm rare even in the enchanted region of James River."

The plantation is one of the oldest and most historic on the river. Its first owner was Sir George Yeardley, the Governor who called and presided over the famous Assembly of 1619—the first free legislature convened in America. In this Assembly, Flower de Hundred was represented by Governor Yeardley's nephew, Edmund Rossingham, and John Jefferson, an ancestor of Thomas Jefferson. Governor Yeardley himself lived at Jamestown, but, in 1621, he built, at Flower de Hundred, the first wind-mill in America. In the massacre of 1622, the Indians murdered six persons at Flower de Hundred. A few years later the plantation was sold to the rich " Cape Merchant " and councillor, Abraham Piersy.

In 1633, Thomas Paulett was Burgess for Flower de Hundred and his heir was his nephew, Sir John Paulett. After that there were several changes of ownership until 1725, when it was bought by Joseph Poythress and has been owned by his descendants ever since. In 1804 it passed to the Willcox family by the marriage of Susan Peachy Poythress to John Vaughn Willcox, a resident of Petersburg. Mr. Willcox built the oldest part of the present house something over a hundred years ago; this consisted of three rooms which he used while superintending the cultivation of the plantation. The house, as it stands to-day, was completed by John Poythress Willcox (son of John Vaughn Willcox).

Like most old Virginia homes, Flower de Hundred has its war history. In 1862, its " new wharf " was burned by order of the Confederate Government to prevent the landing of Northern soldiers on the south side of the James. " Before its embers were cold the first Federal gunboat ever seen that high up the river came in sight to disturb a peaceful stretch of waters which after this became a ' forest of masts.' " Two years later, in June, 1864, General Grant on the march to Petersburg, made his famous crossing of the James, 130,000 strong, from River Edge, opposite Flower de Hundred. " The feat was accomplished in two

FLOWER DE HUNDRED, PRINCE GEORGE COUNTY

days—a glorious sight as described by his generals—under a brilliant sky, in fields of sunshine," but to the gentle mistress of Flower de Hundred, " along with her aged mother and a few faithful servants, the picture had a reverse side. She watched the landing at Windmill Point, the tramping through her standing corn, the bivouac about her house, the place swarming with soldiers and covered with tents, batteries, horses and wagons, and when they went away there were floors torn up and mahogany hacked to pieces, and marble hearths broken to bits and the memory of one trooper disappearing up the road decked in the bridal veil and orange blossoms of a newly married daughter of the house. Long afterward the broken marble was gathered up as a sacred relic and became a hearth again—this time a mosaic."

The Flower de Hundred plantation has undergone as many changes of size and shape as of ownership. It contains at present upward of a thousand acres.

This interesting old homestead has been made the scene of three published romances.

MERCHANT'S HOPE CHURCH, PRINCE GEORGE COUNTY 1657

MERCHANT'S HOPE CHURCH

Not many miles from Flower de Hundred, in the same county—Prince George—stands, within a beautiful grove, the quaint old brick church known as Merchant's Hope, which took its name from a plantation established at a very early date by some London merchants. It is supposed to have been built in 1657, as that date was found upon timbers inside the roof.

This church, sixty feet long and twenty-six feet wide, is still in a fair state of preservation—the pulpit and chancel furniture destroyed during the War between the States having been replaced by new ones. The original floor of stone flagging is still there, as is the ponderous Bible printed in 1625.

Not far from the church, on the same side of the river, is " Jordan's Point," which was so long the plantation and home of the distinguished family of Bland. The old mansion house disappeared long ago. At an early period of our history it was the home of Mrs. Cicely Jordan, a too fascinating widow, whose coquetries induced the Governor and Council to issue a stern edict against women who engage themselves to two men at the same time.

There is no record in Virginia indicating that this edict was ever revoked.

WESTOVER[8]

From a deep green setting of shade-tree and turf, Westover, deep red, tall, stately and serene, gleams upon James River. Its high and steep roof is unrelieved save by dormer windows and towering chimneys. Its formal red-brick walls are unencumbered by porch or ornament, but foot-worn gray stone steps rise in a pyramid to a white portal of exquisite taste. Above a fan-light a massive cornice, supported by Corinthian pilasters, is capped by a carved pineapple—emblem of hospitality—within a broken pediment.

---

[8] For full histories of the Byrds and their estates see *The Writings of Colonel William Byrd of Westover in Virginia, Esqr.*, edited by John Spencer Bassett, New York, 1901, the Introduction and Appendix; *The Critic* (Richmond, Va.), December 14 and 16, 1888; *The Title to Westover* in *William and Mary Quarterly*, iv, 151–155.

WESTOVER, CHARLES CITY COUNTY C.1730

The row of wonderful old tulip poplars, with their gnarled and twisted arms, in front of the house is believed to have stood guard there for a century and a half, and the green carpet that stretches to the edge of the bluff is as old as the trees.

The main entrance to the grounds is at the rear where noble iron gates bearing the Byrd arms swing between square, brick piers ten feet high, surmounted by brass falcons standing with wings spread as if for flight. The interior of the mansion—with its great central hall and

WESTOVER GATES

stairway, its panelled rooms, whose ceilings are adorned with medallions and garlands in relief, its deep fireplaces and tall carved mantels, its massive doors with their huge brass locks—is in perfect keeping with the stateliness of the exterior, and proclaims it at once as the home of culture and elegance.

About the year 1674 William Byrd (1653–1704), first of the name in Virginia, and his wife, Mary—descendants, both, of good old English families—came to Virginia and settled at the Falls of James River, where they called their home Belvidere. In 1688 Byrd bought from

Theodorick Bland the plantation of Westover, and took up his abode there. About the year 1730 his son and heir, William Byrd II (1674–1744), built the mansion which so fittingly crowns that fair plantation.

In the young master of Westover were met such an unusual number of happy gifts, so well improved by cultivation, that he was dubbed the " Black Swan " of Virginia. He was not only born to " an ample fortune "—as

THE PARLOR AT WESTOVER

his epitaph informs us—but with a brilliant mind, a courageous spirit and a kindly disposition. Besides, he was handsome, graceful, and fascinating. He was liberally educated abroad, where he travelled much and was in the best society. He was in demand everywhere, for he was at once the most elegant of gentlemen and the best of good fellows. He was a man of many resources, with a special leaning toward literature, and collected, at Westover, the finest library of Colonial times in America. He did not write for publication, but left diaries which have been printed under the title of "The Westover Manuscripts" and are models of pure English—fresh, sparkling and picturesque.

He took an active and leading part in public affairs, and filled many important offices—among them that of President of "his Májesty's Council."

He was twice married—first to Lucy, daughter of Colonel Daniel Parke (1669–1710), Marlborough's aide-de-camp; and after her death to Maria Taylor, of Kensington, a wealthy and attractive young widow. The first wife was the mother of Evelyn (1707–1737) and Wilhemina Byrd; and the second, of Anne (1725–1757), Maria (1727–1744), William (1729–1777), and Jane. His daughters were noted belles, especially Evelyn—the eldest—whose fame as a beauty spread to England. She was presented at Court at the age of eighteen and was the toast of noblemen—the King himself expressing pleasure at finding his Colonies could furnish such "beautiful Byrds." According to tradition, she was wooed and won while in England by the Earl of Peterborough, but her father would not hear of the match and hurried her back to Virginia, where the "beautiful Byrd" gradually faded away and, at the age of twenty-seven, died a spinster, of a broken heart. A fine portrait which now adorns the walls at Brandon preserves her flower-like loveliness.

Her sisters, whose portraits show that they were close seconds to her in beauty, became the wives: Wilhemina, of Thomas Chamberlayne; Anne, of Charles Carter of "Cleve"; Maria, of Landon Carter of "Sabine Hall"; and Jane, of John Page of "North End"; and her only brother, Colonel William Byrd III (1729–1777), heir of Westover, married: first, Elizabeth Hill, daughter of John Carter, of Shirley, and, secondly, Mary, daughter of Charles and Anne Shippen Willing, of Philadelphia. The descendants of the "Black Swan" of Virginia are legion.

Colonel William Byrd III was, like his father and

grandfather, a distinguished member of the Virginia Council and served gallantly as a colonel of a Virginia regiment during the French and Indian War. His spirit and liberality in this service were highly commended by the English Commander-in-Chief in America. He was a man of talent and cultivation, but was, unhappily, possessed

WESTOVER DURING THE WAR 1861-1865

by an incurable passion for gaming, which finally wrecked his superb estate. He died in 1777, leaving, at Westover, a widow and several daughters, who, like the "beautiful Byrds" of the former generation, were noted for their charms. They especially attracted some of the French officers who had taken part in the siege of Yorktown, and the Marquis de Chastellux declared in his memoirs that Westover was the most beautiful place in America.

Westover was twice visited by the British army during the Revolution. Arnold was there in 1781, and Cornwallis crossed the river there, with his forces, in April of the same year. Mrs. Mary Willing Byrd had many Tory connections and was at one time so strongly suspected of corresponding with the enemy that her papers were seized by the Virginia officers. The splendid library at Westover and the family plate were sold during her lifetime and after her death the estate passed from the Byrd family. It was long the property of the Seldens and passed from them, by sale, to Major Augustus Drewry and from him, in the same manner, to Mrs. Clarice Sears Ramsay, the present owner, who has done much to restore both house and grounds to their early beauty.

Many interesting traditions linger about Westover. The room of the lovely Evelyn Byrd is still pointed out and it is said that the tap of her high-heeled slippers and swish of her silken gown may be sometimes heard on the broad stair, in the watches of the night. Not far from the house, at the site of the old Westover Church, may be seen her tomb, together with those of her grandfather, William Byrd I, Theodorick Bland and other worthies of an earlier time. Her father's ashes rest under a handsome tomb in the garden.

Westover had its taste of the war of 1861–1865 as well as of the Revolution, for there McClellan's army camped after the retreat from Richmond.

WESTOVER CHURCH

WESTOVER CHURCH

Was built about 1740, after the site close to Westover house was given up. It has had a checkered career, having been, during the general depression of the Episcopal Church, at the beginning of the nineteenth century, used as a barn, and, during the War between the States, used by Federal troops as a stable. It has now been thoroughly restored.

BERKELEY

Berkeley, which adjoins the Westover estate, and Brandon have been called the "cradles" of the Harrison family in Virginia. Berkeley house stands a quarter of a mile back from the river. It is a square brick building, two stories high, with gable roof and dormer windows, and a wide porch, added in later times, running around it. Within there are panelled rooms, a wide arched hall and carved mantels and cornices of unusual beauty. In historic interest it is second to that of none of the James River mansions.

Its story begins before the Harrisons came to Virginia, when, in 1618, the London Company granted Berkeley plantation to Sir William Throckmorton, Sir George Yeardley, Richard Berkeley and John Smith of Nibley.[9] On December 4, 1619, the ship *Margaret,* of Bristol, arrived at Jamestown, bringing, under care of Captain John Woodlief, thirty-five settlers for the Town and Hundred of Berkeley, which then contained about 8,000 acres. In 1621, Reverend John Paulett, a kinsman of Lord Paulett, was minister at Berkeley Hundred. In 1622, the year of the great Indian massacre which nearly wiped Virginia out of existence, Mr. George Thorpe, formerly a gentleman of the King's Privy Chamber, who had been appointed by the Virginia Company head of the

---

[9] Papers relative to settlement, etc., Berkeley Hundred, are published in *Bulletin of the New York Public Library,* iii, Nos. 4–7 (April to July, 1899).

BERKELEY, CHARLES CITY COUNTY

proposed college, was one of the nine residents of Berkeley Hundred murdered by the Indians. After the massacre the plantation was abandoned for a time. Later, it became the property of John Bland,[10] a London merchant, whose son Giles Bland lived there until he was hanged, in 1676, by Sir William Berkeley, for his part in Bacon's Rebellion. After this Berkeley passed into the hands of the Harrison family, who owned and occupied it through five generations, during which it was the birthplace of a governor of Virginia and signer of the Declaration of Independence, a Revolutionary general and a president of the United States.

The first of the Harrisons to be master of Berkeley was Benjamin (1673–1710), third of the name in Virginia, who was attorney-general and speaker of the House of Burgesses and treasurer of the Colony. He was the son of the Honorable Benjamin Harrison II (1695–1712), of "Wakefield," Surry County, and brother of Honorable Nathaniel Harrison I, of "Wakefield," whose son, Honorable Nathaniel Harrison II, was the founder of the "Brandon" family. Benjamin III's massive tomb, with its inscription in Latin, with the exception of one line, which is in Greek, remains at the site of old Westover Church. By his side rests his wife, who was Elizabeth, daughter of Honorable Lewis Burwell II, whose tomb bears the coat-of-arms of her family. Upon his death the estate descended to his son Benjamin IV, who was many years a member of the House of Burgesses and who built the present house at Berkeley. He married Anne, daughter of Robert ("King") Carter, and at his death, in 1744, left Berkeley to his son Benjamin Harrison (1726–1791), signer of the Declaration of Independence, and father of William Henry Harrison, President of the United States, who was born at Berkeley.

President Harrison's eldest brother, Benjamin, in-

---

[10] *The Critic* (Richmond, Va.), July 9, 1880.

herited Berkeley, which passed down through a line bearing the same Christian name until it was sold not long before the War between the States.

It is said that every President of the United States, from Washington to Buchanan, was at some time a guest at Berkeley, and that upon the election to this high office of General William Henry Harrison ("Tippecanoe") he went to his mother's room there, to write his inaugural address. The historic room is still pointed out.

The late President Benjamin Harrison, during his administration, visited this historic home of his forefathers.

During the War between the States the house at Berkeley was used as headquarters by General McClellan and his staff after his retreat from Malvern Hill, and his army was camped for miles along the river banks. The cellar is said to have been used by him as a prison for Confederate soldiers, and from the Berkeley Wharf, known to history as "Harrison's Landing," his troops were embarked upon the Northern transports.

In 1882, Berkeley, which now contains 1400 acres, became the property of Judge Henry F. Knox, of New York. To-day the old place has a practical as well as a sentimental interest, for the Berkeley fishing-shore is one of the finest, as well as one of the oldest, on James River, and as many as 22,931 shad and 200,000 herring have been landed there in one season. A visitor there once described the hauling of the seine 500 yards long, by a crew of fifteen men.

"It is a fascinating sight to see a haul on a good day on the Berkeley shore. As the great seine is drawn in shore by the crew the very waters seethe with fish of all varieties, from the luscious roe shad to the insignificant baby perch. As the haul is landed the fish are sorted into baskets and taken to the fish house, where they lie on the cool brick floor until they are shipped to the city markets."

Berkeley has lately become the property of Mr. Jamieson and is in admirable condition.

APPOMATTOX

Upon a green point between two rivers, where the Appomattox meets and joins the James, glimpses of a rambling white house, with dormer roof and huge chimneys, may be seen through the foliage of the ancient trees that embower it—making one of the most charming of the many charming pictures with which old Virginia rewards the exertions of its tourist. This is Appomattox, the home

APPOMATTOX, PRINCE GEORGE COUNTY

of the Eppes family for two hundred and seventy years—a length of tenure unequalled in Virginia, and probably in America.

As early as 1635 Francis Eppes,[11] a member of "his Majesty's Council in Virginia," patented here broad acres, which have ever since been the property of his descendants. They also own goodly estates in the neighboring counties of Chesterfield and Charles City, which are divided from Appomattox by the two rivers, but may be plainly seen across them.

[11] Eppes family: *Virginia Magazine of History and Biography*, iii, 281, 393–401.

Appomattox is now the home of the daughters of Dr. Richard Eppes.

At one time during the siege of Petersburg, in the War between the States, the house was the headquarters of General Grant.

BLANDFORD CHURCH

At the head of tide-water, on the Appomattox River, stands Petersburg. This town has many historic associations, but its chief treasure and pride is old Blandford, the principal church of Bristol Parish.[12] For some years

BLANDFORD CHURCH, PETERSBURG 1787

before the Revolution the town of Blandford (now a part of Petersburg), from which the church gets its name, was a busy port and one of the leading shipping points for tobacco from Virginia to England and Scotland.

The church was built in 1787. According to the articles of agreement, it was to be of brick, sixty by twenty-five feet in the clear, and fifteen feet from the spring of the

[12] Chamberlayne, *The Vestry Book and Register of Bristol Parish, Virginia, 1720–1789*. Richmond, 1898.

arch to the floor. The aisle was to be six feet wide and paved with Bristol stone. There was to be a "decent pulpit and a decent rail around the altar place and a table suitable thereto as usual."

In the year 1737 the great orator, Whitefield, preached at Blandford—an event which made a great sensation.

Some time after the Revolution the old church was abandoned and fell into decay, but the churchyard continued to be, and still is, the town cemetery of Petersburg. As a moss-grown, ivy-draped ruin Blandford became famous and has been the subject of some half-dozen published poems and many a burst of eloquence in prose. The celebrated Irish comedian, Tyrone Power, during a visit to Petersburg, fell in love with this picturesque relic of the past and described it in his "Travels."

To Power, too, has been attributed a much-quoted poem written with pencil upon the whitewashed wall within the church. Its first and last stanzas are as follows:

"Thou art crumbling to the dust, old pile:
Thou art hastening to thy fall;
And round thee in thy loneliness
Clings the ivy to the wall;
The worshippers are scattered now
Who knelt before thy shrine,
And silence reigns where anthems rose
In the days of 'Auld Lang Syne.'

"Oh! could we call the many back,
Who've gathered here in vain,
Who've careless roved where we do now,
Who'll never meet again,
How would our very hearts be stirred,
To meet the earnest gaze
Of the lovely and the beautiful,
The lights of other days!"

Old Blandford was close to the battle-fields in the War between the States, and its venerable walls suffered damage from the shells. The famous "Crater" was but a short distance away.

This now restored church has lately become a Confederate Memorial Hall, in which each of the States of the Southern Confederacy has placed a memorial window.

BOLLINGBROOK

The most interesting house in Petersburg is Bollingbrook, the old homestead of the Bolling family.

In April, 1781, when the British first occupied Petersburg, their commander, General Philips, made Bollingbrook his headquarters. On May 10, when they again took possession of the town, General Philips was ill and was carried to Bollingbrook. The Americans under Lafayette were cannonading Petersburg from the other side of the Appomattox and the fire was so severe that the sufferer

BOLLINGBROOK, PETERSBURG *

was carried into the cellar for safety. One cannon-ball went tearing entirely through the house. General Philips is said to have exclaimed, " Why will they not let me die in peace." He did die here on the thirteenth of May.

The Marquis de Chastellux, in his Memoirs, describes a visit to Bollingbrook soon after the surrender of Yorktown. The mistress of the old homestead at that time was Mrs. Mary Bolling, widow of Robert Bolling, of Bollingbrook, and daughter of Colonel Thomas Tabb, of Clay Hill, Amelia County. The son to whom Chastellux refers

* Picture from Lossing's *Field Book of the Revolution*, published 1850, vol. 2, p. 339.

was Robert Bolling, who had served in the Revolution as a captain of volunteer cavalry and who had married on November 4, 1781, Mary, daughter of Robert Bolling, of Chellow.

According to Chastellux, Mrs. Bolling was one of the greatest landholders in Virginia, and proprietor of half the town of Petersburg, including the tobacco warehouses.

He says, " Mrs. Bolling's house, or rather houses, for she has two on the same line resembling each other which

CENTRE HILL, PETERSBURG
One of the Bolling homes, now owned by Mr. C. H. Davis

she proposes to join together, are situated on the summit of a considerable slope which rises from the level of the town of Petersburg. This slope and the vast platform on which the house is built are covered with grass which affords excellent pasturage, and are also her property. It was formerly surrounded with rails, and she raised a number of fine horses there, but the English burned the fences and carried away a great number of the horses. On our arrival we were saluted by Miss Bolling, a young lady of fifteen, possessing all the freshness of her age; she was followed by her mother, brother, and sister-in-law. The mother, a lady of fifty, has but little resemblance to her country-women. She is lively, active and intelligent, knows perfectly how to manage her immense fortune and, what is yet more rare, knows how to make good use of it. Her son and daughter-in-law I had already met in Williamsburg. The young gentleman appears mild and polite, but his wife, of only seventeen years of age, is a most interesting ac-

COLLECTING CHICKEN FEED IN THE OLDEN DAYS

quaintance, not only from her face and form, which are exquisitely delicate, and quite European, but from her being also descended from the Indian Princess Pocahontas, daughter of King Powhatan."

In about 1850, one of the wings of the Bollingbrook house was destroyed by fire.

BATTERSEA

Just above Petersburg, on the banks of the Appomattox, is Battersea. Of this imposing villa—the home of the Banister family—the Marquis de Chastellux, who visited it during the Revolution, writes: " It is decorated in the Italian rather than in the English or American style, having three porticoes at the three principal entrances, each of them supported by four columns." He says the house was occupied by " an inhabitant of Carolina, called Nelson, who had been driven from his country by the war, which followed him to Petersburg."

The first of the Banisters in this country was the Reverend John Banister,[13] a distinguished naturalist, who was living in Charles City County in 1689, and in the next year received a grant of land in Bristol Parish. While on a botanical excursion, in 1692, he slipped and fell from rocks on the Roanoke River and was killed. His son, John, who was collector for the Upper James, vestryman of Bristol Parish and justice of Prince George County, owned land near the present site of Petersburg, which was doubt-

BATTERSEA, NEAR PETERSBURG

less identical with the Battersea estate. He was the father of Colonel John Banister, of Battersea, who was a burgess from Dinwiddie County, member of the Revolutionary conventions and lieutenant colonel of cavalry in the Revolutionary Army, and in 1778-1779 a member of Congress. Colonel Banister was twice married, first to Martha, daughter of Colonel Theodorick Bland, of "Cawsons," and afterwards to Anne, daughter of President John Blair

[13] Horner, *The History of the Blair, Banister and Braxton Families* (Philadelphia, 1898).

of the Colonial Council. By his first marriage he had three children, but this branch of the family is now extinct. By his marriage with Anne Blair he left two sons, Theodorick Blair and John Monro Banister.

MANSFIELD

Mansfield, near Petersburg, was the home of Roger Atkinson, who emigrated from Cumberland, England,

MANSFIELD, NEAR PETERSBURG

about 1750. He had many prominent descendants of his own name and in the families of Mayo, Pryor, Page, Burwell, Gibson and others.

SHIRLEY

Just above the point where the Appomattox River enters the James is beautiful old Shirley, in Charles City County.

Four square to the world, three stories high it stands, in the midst of a lawn shaded by giant oaks. Rows of many-paned dormer windows look out from all four sides of its high sloping roof and huge chimneys tower above them. The entrances are through square, two-storied, pillared porches, and the massive brick walls are

SHIRLEY CHARLES CITY COUNTY

checkered with glazed "headers." A glance proclaims it the product of prosperity as well as of taste.

To the rear of the mansion are substantial brick outbuildings, at one side lies the flower-garden with its box-hedges, old-fashioned roses and beds of sweet lavender and mignonette, while the front commands a beautiful view of the river. The north porch gives entrance to a great square hall, panelled to the ceiling, from which an exceedingly striking stairway leads to upper regions of airy, white-panelled bedrooms. The architectural details in this hall, and in the two stately drawing-rooms and the dining-room are most attractive. Mantels, door-frames and cornices are enriched with beautiful carving. Over some of the doors are quaint transoms with tiny, odd-shaped panes of glass in them, while above others are mounted ancient hatchments bearing the arms of the Hill family.

The family history of Shirley, like that of Brandon, is illustrated by a splendid collection of old mahogany, portraits, brasses and silver, for, also like Brandon, the estate has never been in the market.

Just when Shirley was built is not known. The plantation was granted in 1660 to Colonel Edward Hill,[14] a leading man in the Colony, a member of the House of Burgesses, of which he was sometime speaker, and of his Majesty's Council. He had lived for a time in Maryland, and in 1646, during the rebellion there, was chosen governor by the insurrectionary party, but was taken prisoner by Governor Calvert. Besides being a law-maker he was a military man and was commander-in-chief of Henrico and Charles City Counties. In 1656, he commanded a force of Colonists and friendly Indians in a battle with some hostile Indians near the Falls of James River and the name Bloody Run, given to a stream now within the limits of Richmond, still remains to testify to the fierceness of the

[14] Hill family: *Virginia Magazine of History and Biography*, iii, 156–159.

conflict.[15] Colonel Hill's forces were badly routed and the "mighty Tottapottomoy," who commanded his Indian allies, was killed. The defeat aroused the displeasure of the Assembly and Colonel Hill was disfranchised and fined, by way of punishment.[16]

Colonel Hill died about 1663 and his handsome estate was inherited by his son Colonel Edward Hill II (1637–1700), of Shirley, "one of his Majesty's honorable Council of State, Colonel and Commander-in-Chief of the Counties of Charles City and Surry, Judge of his Majesty's high Court of Admiralty, and sometime Treasurer of Virginia." He was an adherent of Governor Berkeley's during Bacon's Rebellion and was disfranchised by Bacon's Assembly. His dust lies in a massive tomb bearing the Hill coat-of-arms, in the Shirley graveyard, and his portrait, that of a handsome and elegant gentleman in crimson velvet and lace, and flowing peruke, adorns the walls of the house, along with those of many of his family and kindred—Carters, Byrds, Randolphs, Lees and others. His wife, who was the daughter of Sir Edward Williams, of Wales, is represented as a young, rarely beautiful dame, and her daughter, Elizabeth (who married Honorable John Carter II), is strikingly like her—a lovely girl, with her arms filled with flowers.

Especially interesting is this young girl, Elizabeth Hill, for the death of her brother, Colonel Edward Hill III, without male descendants, made her the heiress of Shirley, and it was by her marriage, in 1723, with John Carter (who died in 1742), of Corotoman, eldest son of Robert ("King") Carter, that Shirley passed from the Hill to the Carter family, in which it has ever since remained. About a year before his marriage the new master of Shirley had been appointed secretary of Virginia, and as "Secre-

---

[15] Campbell, *History of the Colony and Ancient Dominion of Virginia*, pp. 233–234.

[16] "Defence of Colonel Edward Hill," in *Virginia Magazine of History and Biography*, iii, 239–252, 341–349; Hening, *Statutes at Large . . . of Virginia*, ii, 364–365.

tary Carter" he was known for the rest of his days. He has been described as "a man of integrity and ability, managing large domestic affairs with prudence and skill and filling ably high political offices." His portrait, too, in velvet and lace, is to be seen at Shirley, as is also that of his son and heir, Charles Carter (1732–1806) of Shirley, in the quieter, though still picturesque, garb of a generation later.

Charles Carter was a burgess and member of Revolutionary Conventions. Twice married—first to his cousin Mary Carter, daughter of Charles Carter, of Cleve, and after her death to Anne Butler Moore, daughter of Bernard Moore and Katherine, daughter of Governor Alexander Spotswood—he was the father of twenty-three children, who inter-marrying with the Randolphs, Lees, Braxtons, Burwells, Nelsons, Fitzhughs, Berkeleys, and other families of the old régime in Virginia, left numerous descendants, who hold Shirley in tender regard. One of his daughters—Elizabeth—was the grandmother of Bishop Alfred M. Randolph, and another, Anne, became the wife of "Light Horse Harry" Lee, and the mother of General Robert E. Lee. General Lee was a frequent visitor at Shirley, and in his letters [17] makes affectionate allusions to this noble old homestead.

The last master of Shirley, Captain Robert Randolph Carter, a gallant officer in the United States Navy and afterward in the Confederate Navy, went to Maryland for a bride—Miss Louise Humphreys, of Annapolis. By her many charms of mind and character "Miss Lou," as she was called far and near, early made a large place for herself in the heart of Virginia—and kept it throughout her life. Like "Old Miss," of Brandon, she was a notable personage, and many there are who, when making the trip up and down the James, miss her familiar figure and sweet, strong face from among those in the group on the landing,

---

[17] Lee, *Recollections and Letters of General Robert E. Lee* (New York, 1904).

and the opportunity to step ashore for a moment for a grasp of her hand and the word of cheery, cordial greeting always so ready on her tongue. Upon her death, in 1906, her daughters, Mrs. Bransford and Mrs. Oliver, became mistresses of Shirley.

MALVERN HILL

Not far above Shirley lies the Malvern Hill plantation where formerly stood one of the most attractive as well as one of the oldest homesteads in Virginia.

MALVERN HILL, HENRICO COUNTY

It was built by Thomas Cocke, son of Richard Cocke (*circa* 1600–1665), the first of that name in Virginia.[18]

This estate derives its name from the Malvern Hills in England. Toward the close of the eighteenth century, the estate was sold, by James Powell Cocke, to Robert Nelson.[19]

---

[18] Cocke family: *Virginia Magazine of History and B'ography*, iii, 282–292, 405–414; iv, 86–96, 212–217, 322–332, 431–450.

[19] A younger son of Honorable William Nelson and Elizabeth Burwell.

It has been the fate of this old plantation to be often the scene of war. Lafayette camped there during the Revolution; in the War of 1812 Virginia Militia was there; and as the field of battle between Generals Lee and McClellan, in the War between the States, Malvern Hill will always have a place in history.

The Malvern Hill house was destroyed by fire about 1905.

WILTON

Wilton,* just below Richmond, is referred to in some very early records as " the land's end "—which shows how remote it seemed to the first settlers. The present house, a fine old brick mansion, stands upon a green terrace overlooking the James, nearly opposite the beautiful and historic " Falling Creek." As is usual in Virginia houses of its class and period, the walls of its wide hall and great square rooms are enriched with handsome woodwork, and the windows are so deeply recessed that persons occupying the window-seats would be entirely hidden by the curtains.

Wilton house was built about the middle of the eighteenth century by William Randolph III (died 1761), a younger son of William Randolph II (1681–1742), of Turkey Island.[20] Upon his death it was inherited by his son Peyton, who married Lucy Harrison, daughter of Benjamin Harrison, signer of the Declaration of Independence. The Randolphs owned it until about the beginning of the War between the States, when the heiress of the family married Edward C. Mayo, of Richmond, Virginia. Since then the estate has frequently changed hands.

During the Randolphs' time at Wilton a large collection of their family portraits hung on the panelled walls. These are now the property of Mr. Edward C. Mayo, Jr., of Richmond. Among them is one of Anne Randolph,

---

* See illustration, page 107.

[20] Randolph family: *William and Mary Quarterly*, vii, 122–124, 195–197; viii, 119–122, 263–265; ix, 182–183, 250–252.

daughter of William Randolph, the builder of Wilton house, called "Nancy Wilton," to distinguish her from a cousin who bore the same name. She was noted for beauty and charm and had many suitors. She finally accepted Benjamin Harrison and became mistress of Brandon, but died young, leaving no children. Thomas Jefferson was one of her contemporaries and admirers, and she is referred to in some of his youthful letters. In one of these he says, "Ben Harrison has gone courting to Wilton."

During the excitement the rumored approach of the United States steamer *Pawnee* to Richmond caused in the early part of the War between the States, earthworks were thrown up at Wilton, and part of the plantation lies opposite Drewry's Bluff, so well known during the war.

AMPTHILL

Just across the river from Wilton stands an old mansion whose chief characteristics are dignity and strength. This is Ampthill—a big square house with massive brick walls, a square white porch and a steep Dutch roof flanked on either hand by a square brick out-building as massive as itself. Within, the high-pitched rooms are also big and square, and they and the wide hall are panelled from floor to ceiling with solid oak. The windows are protected by panelled inside shutters of the same wood, while huge brass locks and hinges make fast the thick oak doors.

It was built in 1732 by Henry Cary (1675?–1749),[21] who superintended the building of the Governor's Palace and the State House in Williamsburg, and also the rebuilding of William and Mary College when it was destroyed by fire. Upon his death, in 1750, Ampthill passed to his son Archibald Cary (1721–1787),[22] the celebrated Revolutionary patriot, and chairman of the committee in the Virginia Convention of 1776, which brought in the resolution

---

[21] Cary family: *The Critic* (Richmond, Va.).

[22] For an excellent sketch of Archibald Cary, see Grigsby's *The Virginia Convention of 1776* (Richmond, 1855), p. 90 *et seq.*

WILTON, HENRICO COUNTY
The River Front.

POWHATAN, HENRICO COUNTY

AMPTHILL, CHESTERFIELD COUNTY

FALLING CREEK MILL, CHESTERFIELD COUNTY

directing the Virginia members of Congress to move for entire independence of Great Britain. From his force of character and determination he was known as " Old Iron."

Ampthill has since had various owners—the families of Temple and Watkins having enjoyed the longest tenure.

Within the original bounds of the Ampthill plantation was beautiful Falling Creek, with its arched stone bridge and its quaint old mill, where the first iron-works in America were established, under John Berkeley, in 1619. The works were abandoned in 1622, after the Indian massacre in which Berkeley and all of his men were murdered, and during the Revolution the furnaces were destroyed by Tarleton and his troopers.

EPPINGTON

The early history of the Eppes family has been told in connection with "Appomattox." Lt-Col. Francis Eppes, a brother of John Eppes, ancestor of the "Appomattox" line, was killed in battle with the Indians in 1678 and was succeeded by his eldest son, Col. Francis Eppes (1659–1718), long a member of the House of Burgesses for Henrico. His son, a third Col. Francis Eppes, who died in 1734, was also a Burgess for Henrico, and owned large landed property where Eppington was afterwards built. Richard Eppes, son of the last named, who was for several terms a Burgess for Chesterfield County, died in 1765, and was succeeded by his son Francis Eppes, of Eppington (1747–1808), two of whose daughters, Lucy and Mary, married, respectively, Archibald and Richard N. Thweatt, while his son John Wayles Eppes (1773–1823) was U. S. Senator and married a daughter of Thomas Jefferson. Eppington was inherited by the Thweatts, and since it was sold by them has passed through several hands.

The following is an extract from a letter, written in 1856, by Francis Eppes, son of John W. Eppes, to Henry S. Randall, the biographer of Jefferson:

"You ask me for a description of Eppington, but such an impression, as I can now give, must be considered an imperfect sketch. The mansion-house itself, an old-fashioned, two-story building, with a hipped roof in the centre, and wings on the sides, with a long hall or passage in front, running from one wing to the other and opening on the offices, and with piazzas in front and rear, was placed at the extreme side of a large level or lawn, covered with green sward, extending to a considerable distance in front, and declining on the left side as you entered, and in the rear of the house to the low grounds of the Appomattox, a mile off. In front, and over the neighborhood road which skirted the lawn, was situated the garden, long famous in the vicinity for its fine vegetables and fruit; and to the right of the lawn, as you entered, was an ex-

EPPINGTON, CHESTERFIELD COUNTY

tensive orchard of the finest fruit, with the stables between, at the corner and on the road. The mansion, painted of a snowy white, with green blinds to the windows, and its rows of offices at the end, was almost imbedded in a beautiful double row of the tall Lombardy poplar—the most admired of all trees in the palmy days of old Virginia—and this row reached to another double row or avenue which skirted one side of the lawn, dividing it from the orchard and stables. The lawn in front was closed in by a fence with a small gate in the middle and a large one on either extremity, one opposite the avenue of poplars, and the other at the end of the carriage-way which swept around it.

"The plantation was quite an extensive one, and in the days of my grandfather, Francis Eppes, Sen., was remarkably productive. Indeed, it could hardly have been otherwise, under such management as his; for he was eminent for his skill both in agriculture and horticulture; and I have heard Mr. Jefferson, who knew him intimately, say of him, that he considered him not only 'the first horticulturist in America,' but, 'a man of the soundest practical judgment on all subjects that he had ever known.'"

POWHATAN

When Captain John Smith, Christopher Newport, and others, made their first voyage of exploration up James River from Jamestown, in June, 1607, they found, upon a hill near its north bank and a little below the present site of Richmond, a palisaded Indian town named Powhatan. The Colonists were so charmed with its situation and surroundings that they purchased it from the red men and Captain Smith named it "None Such." It was more than one hundred years after this that Joseph Mayo, who came to Virginia from the Island of Barbadoes about 1727, bought the estate, restored it to its original name, and built himself a commodious brick house overlooking the river.* Either he or his descendants surrounded the house with beautiful flower-gardens, remembered by persons still living. Suggestions of these gardens may still be seen in the mock-orange bushes and other old-fashioned shrubs which in the months of May and June bloom between the dusty railroad tracks and brickyards which have now encroached upon the old place, with a resolution to live above their surroundings that is most praiseworthy. Here, too, were until very recently to be seen two boulders, one of which was, according to a long since exploded tradition, the stone upon which Captain Smith's head lay when he was rescued by Pocahontas, the other the gravestone of

* See illustration, page 107.

Powhatan. Upon one of these boulders is cut the letter M and the date 1741.

Powhatan descended through many generations of Mayos, its last owner of the name being Mr. Robert A. Mayo, father of Mr. Peter H. Mayo, of Richmond.

Of late years modern progress has swept away old Powhatan, and it has even been necessary to remove the bodies of those that slept in the family burying-ground, some of whose graves were marked by Colonial tombs bearing the Mayo arms. These are now to be seen in the Mayo section in Hollywood Cemetery, Richmond, Virginia.

BROOK HILL *

The dwelling at Brook Hill, the home of Robert Williamson, who married his cousin Susanna Williamson, was built prior to 1735, and five generations of the family, as follows in direct line, were born in the same house—most of them in the same room: Robert Williamson, 2d (1735–1796), who married Anne Coxe; their son Robert Carter Williamson (1796–1871), who married Lucy Parke Chamberlayne; their daughter Mary Amanda Williamson (1822–1910), who married John Stewart, a native of Rothesay, Scotland; their daughter Isobel Stewart (1847–1910), who married Joseph Bryan, of Eagle Point, and their son John Stewart Bryan.

In 1842 Brook Hill was purchased by Mr. John Stewart, who enlarged the house and made of a portion of the grounds a most beautiful park.

This home has always been celebrated for its hospitality and Mr. Stewart and his descendants for their philanthropic interest in everything that pertains to the welfare of the community.

The dwelling No. 707 E. Franklin Street, which was occupied by General Lee from 1861 to 1865 as his war-time residence, was in 1892 given by the Stewart family to the Virginia Historical Society and has since that time been the home of that Society.

---

* See illustration at head of Contents.

PART III

RICHMOND, MANCHESTER AND THE UPPER JAMES

RICHMOND

IN June, 1607, Captain Christopher Newport, Captain John Smith and others set out from Jamestown in the pinnace, *Discovery*, to explore the James. Upon the tenth they reached the highest point of navigation, where they named the shallow waters racing and tumbling over a bed of stones and boulders " The Falls,"

MARKETING TOBACCO IN THE OLD DAYS

and where they " set up a cross " which much puzzled the Indians. This was the white man's first appearance at the site of the present capital of Virginia.

In 1733, Colonel William Byrd II, of Westover, laid

RICHMOND IN 1800

out a town at the Falls of James River, named Richmond—probably because of the resemblance of the site to Richmond on the Thames. In 1742 the town was incorporated; in 1779 it supplanted Williamsburg as the capital of the State, and from 1861 to 1865 it was the capital of the Confederacy.

It is situated upon a number of hills—popularly estimated as seven—and stretches around a beautiful bend of

THE HOME OF THE LATE GENERAL JOSEPH R. ANDERSON, RICHMOND

the river. It was pronounced by Thackeray, during his visit some years before the war, " the most picturesque place in America " as well as " the merriest." In April, 1865, war desolated it and a large section of it was burned, but it stands to-day one of the most prosperous and progressive, as well as one of the most interesting, cities in this country.

ST. JOHN'S CHURCH

Crowning what was first known as Richmond Hill—afterward as Church Hill—stands, in the midst of a walled graveyard occupying an entire block, old St. John's Church.[1]

The graveyard is shady and green. It is thickly tenanted, and mouldy and moss-grown tombstones tell in prim, old-fashioned phrase of the virtues of those that " rest in peace " beneath them, or remind the reader of the shortness of life, in metre, whereof the following is a characteristic sample:

> " Stop my friend as you pass by,
> As you are now so once was I,
> As I am now you soon shall be;
> Prepare my friend to follow me."

The oldest part of the church was built in 1740. It is of wood, painted white, and has a pretty spire and a sweet-voiced bell. Some time after the Revolution it was enlarged and made into the shape of a cross. Within, the quaint sounding-board and shell-shaped font are still to be seen, as in its earliest days. When it was the only church and largest public building in Richmond, St. John's was sometimes used for political as well as religious gatherings; and so it happened that within its hallowed walls the patriots who made up the Virginia Convention of 1775 assembled and heard Patrick Henry's immortal speech ending with the words, " Give me liberty or give me death."

The pew in which the orator stood is still pointed out.

THE VAN LEW HOUSE

Also on Church Hill, and not far away from St. John's, was the Van Lew House,* best known of late years as the home of the famous " Miss Van Lew." It was perhaps the stateliest of the Richmond mansions of its time. Certainly it adorned the most charming site in the city. It

---

[1] Moore, *History of Henrico Parish and Old St. John's Church, Richmond, Va., 1611–1904.* The inscriptions on tombstones in St. John's Church yard are printed in this book, pp. 413–529.

* See illustration, page 123.

ST. JOHN'S CHURCH, RICHMOND

was built when ample grounds and roomy porticoes overlooking picturesque "falling" gardens were the fashion, and it was situated in a section which became unfashionable before the days of cutting up handsome grounds into twenty-foot building lots.

And so the old garden terraced back to the brow of the hill, overhanging, and commanding a superb view of James River, with its sunny spaces and shady nooks, its hundred leaf roses and cool, sparkling spring, was long preserved.

The house was built (probably near the end of the eighteenth century) by Dr. John Adams, son of Mr. Richard Adams.[2] Both father and son were gentlemen of large fortune and also of large heart, whose pet hobby was the advancement and beautifying of Richmond. Dr. Adams married Peggy, one of the charming daughters of Mr. Geddes Winston, and their home had a brilliant social history. It was noted for hospitality and was one of the houses in which Lafayette was entertained during his visit in 1824.

After Mr. Adams' death the house was bought by a Mr. Van Lew, a northern gentleman, who settled in Richmond and became a prominent merchant. He and his family mingled in the "high society" of Richmond Hill until the War between the States, when their sympathy with the invading army cut them off. A young daughter of the house became noted as a friend of Federal prisoners, many of whom she helped to escape. For many years after all of her family had passed away "Miss Van Lew" lived alone and friendless in the old mansion to which the presence of a solitary, hoary dame lent a weird interest. With her bent form, thin, clear-cut features, framed in gray curls, and her piercing eyes that seemed made for peering into hidden mysteries, she might have passed for the reincarnation of some ancient sybil.

---

[2] Adams family: *William and Mary College Quarterly Historical Magazine*, v, 159–164.

She was accustomed to thrust herself upon public notice just once a year—the day on which she paid her taxes. Upon that day she always published in the local papers, under her signature, an emphatic protest against taxation without representation. In 1900 she died, full of years, in this old house, which has since been pulled down and a public school built on its site.

OLD MASONIC HALL, RICHMOND 1785

OLD MASONIC HALL

Coming down Franklin Street into the valley that lies between Church Hill and Shockoe Hill, the tourist finds between Eighteenth and Nineteenth Streets an old frame house standing back from the public highway. This is the oldest building in America, still in use, erected for Masonic purposes exclusively. It dates from 1785, when

VAN LEW OR ADAMS HOUSE, RICHMOND (FRONT C. 5 or 9 or 18C.

VAN LEW OR ADAMS HOUSE (REAR)

its cornerstone was laid, and has been the scene of many interesting incidents in the Masonic history of Virginia.

At a reception given to General Lafayette in this unpretentious old "temple," in 1824, that favorite hero was, amid great enthusiasm, made an honorary member of the lodge.

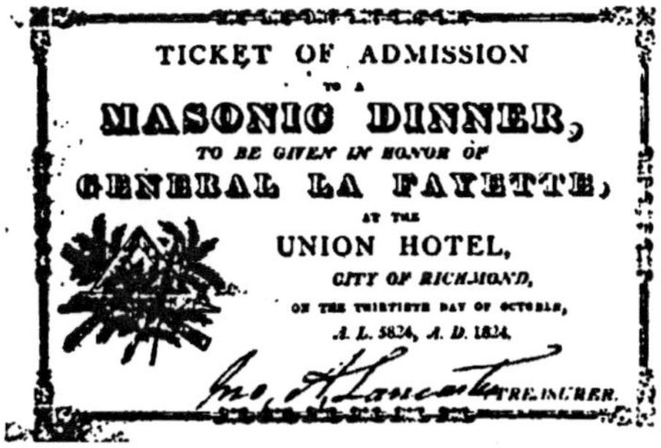
TICKET OF ADMISSION
TO A
MASONIC DINNER,
TO BE GIVEN IN HONOR OF
GENERAL LA FAYETTE,
AT THE
UNION HOTEL,
CITY OF RICHMOND,
ON THE THIRTIETH DAY OF OCTOBER,
A. L. 5824, A. D. 1824.
TREASURER.

TICKET FOR MASONIC DINNER GIVEN IN HONOR OF GENERAL LAFAYETTE

MONUMENTAL CHURCH

On the night after Christmas of the year 1811, Richmond suffered a disaster which put the whole town into mourning and caused the building of a church which has always been not only one of the chief factors for good, but one of the most appealing objects of interest in the city. Upon that awful night the elite of Virginia's Capital, including the governor, George William Smith (1762–1811), had gathered in the fashionable theatre on Broad Street, between Twelfth and Thirteenth, to witness the tragedy of "The Bleeding Nun," as presented by a popular actress and her company. When interest was at its height the cry of "fire!" was heard above the voices of the actors and in a few minutes the house was in flames, and panic reigned. The destruction of the building was complete and sixty human beings—among them Governor Smith and others prominent in official and social life—were burned to death.

Many were painfully injured, while many more had hair-breadth escapes and were made famous by their heroic work in saving the lives of others.

The impression made by the disaster was tremendous. The whole country stood aghast. Resolutions and letters of sympathy poured into Richmond from every quarter. Legislatures and councils all over the United States took formal action and churches held memorial services and offered prayers for those in affliction. Of course Virginia and Richmond were given over to mourning. In Richmond there was a marked decline in theatre going and increase in church going, which was noticeable for years afterward to such a degree that the city became proverbial among theatrical managers for its poor support of their offerings. Immediately after the fire, the citizens met in the Capitol Building to arrange for a suitable monument to those who had perished in the flames, and the Monumental Church, upon the site of the burned theatre, was the result. All creeds and classes were subscribers to the building fund, and it was decided by vote that the monument should take the form of an Episcopal church. The ashes of those who perished in the fire lie under the building and upon a marble cenotaph in the porch their names are recorded.

The " Old Monumental," as it is familiarly called, is a noble specimen of architecture—plain, but dignified and impressive. Within, its air of solemnity and sacredness compels reverence. From the beginning, it has been one of the most influential churches in Virginia and many prominent men in both Church and State have been intimately connected with it. Bishop Richard Channing Moore was its earliest rector—serving at the same time that he was Bishop of Virginia—and Chief Justice Marshall was one of its earliest pew-holders. Edgar Allan Poe often worshipped there as a youth. Bishop Dudley, of Kentucky, was a pupil in its Sunday-school when a boy, and Bishop Newton, of Virginia, was called to the Episcopate while its rector.

MONUMENTAL CHURCH, RICHMOND 1811

ARCHER HOUSE, RICHMOND

THE CRUMP HOUSE

Upon Twelfth Street, diagonally across Broad Street from the Monumental Church, and upon the site now occupied by the Memorial Hospital, stood the Crump House, built toward the end of the eighteenth century, by Mr. Samuel Myers—grandfather of the late Major E. T. D. Myers—and during its latter years the home of Judge W. W. Crump, who bought it in 1850 and occupied it for about a half century.

During the time of Mr. Myers, who was a naval officer, he planted in the grounds an acorn which he brought from Africa and from which sprang a notable tree. The gardens were extensive and beautiful. "It represented," wrote Mrs. Sally Nelson Robins, in an article on the Crump House, "as no building now recalled, the ante-bellum establishment—mansion, kitchen, laundry, servants' quarters, stable, carriage-house, smoke-house, and big yard where children played and box-bushes and flowers grew, where ladies in morning dresses sat in the rose-clad summer-house and read or did embroidery, while other ladies called and chatted of house-keeping and books and perhaps of their neighbors."

Upon the night of the theatre fire—December 26, 1811—many of the victims of that tragedy were brought to the Myers home and laid upon the parlor floor and stains could be traced upon the boards for years afterwards.

Judge Crump, with his greatness of soul and intellect, his striking personality and charm of manner and conversation, with his books around him, and with the woman who was his helpmate in the highest sense of the word at his side, would have made any house notable.

This massive old homestead with its spacious rooms, its high carved mantels, its big open fires whose light played upon old silver and mahogany and rare pictures, made an ideal setting for the great lawyer, the ripe scholar, the gracious host. His home was a centre of intellectual life, a resort of cultured, Christian gentle-folk.

No one who ever heard Judge Crump talk could fail to deplore the fact that he never put his observations and reminiscences upon paper. Many were the distinguished men he had known, many the important events he had witnessed, and his conversation about them made a series of clear, bright pictures. When Charles Dickens visited Richmond, the Judge was one of the committee appointed to give him a fitting welcome, and his impressions of the novelist and his wife, as they appeared at the banquet given in their honor, would have made an interesting chapter in a book of " recollections."

THE WHITE HOUSE OF THE CONFEDERACY

With Twelfth Street we reach the eastern boundary of what was known in the stately days of yore as the " Court End " of town. Following this thoroughfare northward as far as Clay Street, one sees a large, gray stucco mansion with a double pillared portico. This is the beautiful " White House of the Confederacy." It stands upon the brink of a deep ravine and those who remember it " as it used to be " tell of a " falling garden " whose terraces ran a good way down the hill, and of bright spaces of old-fashioned flowers and potted shrubs from foreign climes —conspicuous among which were fruitful hazelnut bushes.

The house was built in 1818 for the residence of Dr. John Brockenbrough,[3] long president of the Bank of Virginia, and his wife, who was Mrs. Gabriella Harvie Randolph, daughter of Colonel John Harvie and widow of Thomas Mann Randolph, of " Tuckahoe." Dr. Brockenbrough had been one of the committee of three appointed to direct the building of a church as a memorial to the victims of the theatre fire and in planning his home he chose for the architect, Mr. Mills, whose design for the Monumental Church had won great praise. Long before this the intimacy between Dr. Brockenbrough and John Randolph,

[3] Brockenbrough family: *Virginia Magazine of History and Biography*, v, 447–449; vi, 82–85.

CRUMP HOUSE, RICHMOND

THE WHITE HOUSE OF THE CONFEDERACY, RICHMOND 1818

of Roanoke, which continued to the end of Randolph's life, had begun, and when the new house was completed Randolph was a frequent visitor there, and often for weeks at a time "the most agreeable and interesting inmate you can possibly imagine," wrote Dr. Brockenbrough to a friend.

The acquaintance began during the famous Aaron Burr trial in 1807, when Dr. Brockenbrough was a member of the jury and John Randolph its foreman, and from that time on the friendship between these two men, as it appears in the letters that passed between them and in those of Randolph to other friends, published in the *Life of John Randolph,* runs like a bright thread through the sombre history of that fascinating personality. John Randolph's sweetheart, the fair and engaging Maria Ward, was also intimate at the Brockenbrough home, and when her affair with Randolph was broken off, she entrusted his letters in a sealed packet to the care of Mrs. Brockenbrough, with the request that after her death that lady should burn them without breaking the seal. As Mrs. Brockenbrough was a woman who could keep a secret even from herself, the contents of the interesting packet will never be known.

It was said that Dr. Brockenbrough built his house with an especial view to entertaining, and it seems to have become a centre of both intellectual and gay society. Chief Justice Marshall and other distinguished members of the Bar and of the famous "Barbecue Club" were intimate there and were fond of discussing politics and the classics with Mrs. Brockenbrough, whom Blennerhassett, writing in 1807, of affairs and people in Richmond, described as "the nearest approximation to a savant and bel-esprit." The lovely Randolph girls, Mrs. Brockenbrough's nieces, and later on, the beauties and belles of the Seddon and Morson connections, may not have cared for politics and the classics, but many of the most distinguished men of the time, in Richmond and out of it, came to the old house to dance with and pay court to them. In one of John

Randolph's letters to his friend he says, " Mr. Speaker related to me that you had given a splendid party; for so I interpreted the word *fandango* used by him;" and many were the occasions when the music of the " many twinkling feet" held full sway.

Dr. Brockenbrough finally sold the house to Mr. James M. Morson, who after a few years' residence in it sold it to his cousin and law-partner, Honorable James A. Seddon, member of Congress from Virginia and secretary of war of the Confederate States. Mr. Morson and Mr. Seddon married sisters, the lovely Bruce girls, Ellen and Sally, and during their time the house continued to be a centre of all that was best and brightest in the Virginia of the old régime. Says a beau of the period, still living, " My impressions of the White House of the Confederacy before the war make a poem in my memory." Not long before the war Mr. Seddon sold the house to Mr. Lewis D. Crenshaw, who occupied it for a brief period, during which he added the top story.

The curtain was rung down on the brilliant drama which the social history of *ante-bellum* Richmond made, to rise on the tragedy for which the city lent itself as a stage during four years of civil warfare. Again the house at the corner of Twelfth and Clay Streets occupied a conspicuous place in the setting. Echoes of viol and wedding-bell were now lost in the alarums of rifle and cannon. The stately rooms of that house where so bright the lights had " shone o'er fair women and brave men," were become the council chambers of war and government. In place of the procession of carriages filled with ladies and gentlemen arrayed for a fête, filing up the street toward the house, might occasionally be seen a very different pageant—President Davis and General Lee riding side by side, in earnest conversation, and clattering behind them their staff officers.

In the room to the right of the entrance hall, where many a time a fair girl had waited the coming of gallant lover, the President's wife now sat night after night and

RICHMOND IN 1833

listened with strained ear and anxious face for the sound of horses' hoofs on the street outside, for mayhap a courier would come in the night with dispatches for her husband, indulging in uneasy sleep in the room above. When the capital of the Confederacy was moved from Montgomery, Alabama, to Richmond, the city bought the house, spent $8,000.00 furnishing it and tendered it to Mr. Davis, who agreed to accept it only upon condition that the Confederate Government should pay full rent for it. The house now began to be known by the name which added the crowning touch to its glory—the White House of the Confederacy—and now the dames and the squires, the belles and the beaux who had danced and feasted there bent their steps that way to pay court to the President and his lady.

Upon the evacuation of Richmond, United States troops under General Weitzel took possession of the White House of the Confederacy for headquarters, and held it until September, 1870, when it was restored to the city. In June, 1884, it became the property of the Confederate Memorial Literary Society, and as the home of a priceless collection of Confederate relics the "Confederate Museum" is to-day one of the centres of interest in the city.

THE VALENTINE MUSEUM

Tom Moore, the loved Irish poet, writing of his sojourn in Richmond, in 1803, says that the most agreeable gentlemen he met were "some Whig lawyers, one of whom, Mr. John Wickham, was fit to adorn any court." Mr. Wickham's residence, built in 1812, now the home of the Valentine Museum, stands upon Clay Street, just one block above the White House of the Confederacy, and, like it, was planned by Benjamin Mills, the architect of Monumental Church. Thanks to the artistic sense of the Valentines, so long its owners, this superb old mansion has been perfectly preserved. To the stranger in the street it presents a front reserved, dignified, plain. But a touch of the brass knocker admits one to the handsomest interior possessed by any house ever built in Richmond. From a perfectly proportioned hall, winding mahogany stairs lead to a beautiful gallery. Polished mahogany doors with silver knobs and hinges open from this hall into the stately rooms built around it. Striking details of these rooms are sculptured marble mantels brought from Florence; frescoed walls; carved door and window frames—white enamelled with the delicate relief-work gilded with gold leaf; great mirrors in Florentine frames, chandeliers of burnished brass.

At the rear of the mansion, a pillared portico, with a gracefully curved outline, embowered in honeysuckle, Virginia creeper, and purple and white wistaria, looks upon an old garden, surrounded by a high, ivy-covered brick wall. A fountain makes music in the midst of the garden, and through a rose-garlanded arch we may have such glimpses as the vine-clad trellises and shrubbery will permit of figures in white marble of the goddesses of Beauty, Flowers, and the Harvest, peeping out among the green. Every olden-time flower is to be found in the trim parterres divided by narrow brick walks, and many goodly fruit trees and grape vines on trellises and latticed arbors vie with the flowers in making the garden a place of delight. In one corner a century-old magnolia tree makes June fragrant.

In the Wickhams' time the house was the scene of brilliant festivities; for in those days of plenty and of good servants Virginia hospitality was in full flower in Richmond, and it was Mr. Wickham's pleasure to entertain in honor of " men of parts " visiting the city.

In the year 1807 the famous trial of Aaron Burr, for treason, drew the attention of all America upon Richmond and upon Mr. Wickham. The prominence of the prisoner at the bar, the political excitement at the time and the brilliant legal talent employed united in bringing throngs of people to the city. John Marshall was the presiding judge, Wickham the leader in the defence, and John Randolph, of Roanoke, foreman of the jury. Among the witnesses were General Wilkinson, of the Army, and Andrew Jackson, afterward president of the United

THE HALL AT VALENTINE MUSEUM, RICHMOND

VALENTINE MUSEUM, FORMERLY WICKHAM HOUSE, RICHMOND 1812

States. Burr's acquittal was generally supposed to be chiefly due to the eloquence and ability of Mr. Wickham. After the trial Burr dined with Mr. Wickham and his beautiful wife, who was noted as a tactful and charming hostess.

In course of time the Wickham residence became the property of the Ballard family, and many of the beautiful features of its interior are said to have been added by Mr. Ballard. Its next owner was Mr. Alexander Brooks.

In later years it was long the residence of Mr. Mann S. Valentine, during part of which period Mr. Edward V. Valentine, the sculptor, made his home there. At Mr. Valentine's death he generously bequeathed this residence with his valuable collections, and an endowment for maintenance as a museum, to the city of Richmond, and there may now be seen, in addition to many other objects of historical and artistic value, one of the finest collections of Indian relics in the world.

THE McCANCE HOUSE

One of the principal show places of the " Court End " of town stood upon the corner of Leigh and Eighth Streets. This house was built about a hundred years ago by the widow and son of Mr. John Hayes, of the " Falls Plantation," just below Manchester—a gentleman of large wealth and owner and publisher of the *Virginia Gazette*. The house was commodious and handsome and a Greek portico at the rear overlooked a garden which extended to Clay Street. From the Hayes family the property passed, by purchase, to Mr. Thomas Green, a successful lawyer and familiar figure in Richmond society in the first half of the nineteenth century.

Mr. Green at once turned his attention to the beautifying of his home, making the flower-garden his chief pride. Across the garden ran a deep ravine with a stream flowing through it. Mr. Green terraced the ravine and by checking the flow of the brook with a stone dam made a little lake, which was spanned by a rustic bridge. Upon the lake a small boat floated, and near the shore stood a tiny chalet-like cottage, covered with bark. In another part of the grounds was a bear-pit, containing several black bears, while here and there among the shrubbery and flowers gleamed pieces of white marble sculpture from Italy. Among these was a fountain representing the birth of Venus from the waves of the sea. A marble scallop shell rested upon the backs of two dolphins which spouted water over a life-sized figure of the goddess, as she stood poised on the edge of the shell. Other figures represented "The Seasons," "Flora," "Ceres," "Ganymede," etc. Some of these are now preserved in the garden of the Valentine Museum.

One of the attractions of the garden was a fine spring which was a favorite drinking place. In later years the charming old mansion was long the home of the McCance family. When the emigration of fashion to the West End reached high tide, it gave way to a row of tenements which now occupies the site of house and garden.

THE MARSHALL HOUSE

Upon the corner of Marshall and Ninth Streets stands a plain, but massive and dignified old brick mansion, the home of Richmond's greatest citizen and the most famous of American judges—Chief Justice John Marshall (1755–1835).[4]

To his neighbors "the old Chief," as he was affectionately called, was as much beloved for his domestic and social gifts as he was admired for his ability and learning. As a member of the "Barbecue Club," made up of the leading men of Richmond, and joining with the zest of a boy in his favorite game of throwing quoits, we see the intellectual giant at play, and it is a pleasant sight. Over this old home he presided as a tender husband and father, kind master, gracious host.

Until the last few years the house was owned and occupied by his descendants, who also sat Sunday after Sunday

---

[4] Paxton, *The Marshall Family.* Cincinnati, 1885.

McCANCE HOUSE, RICHMOND

GAMBLE HOUSE, RICHMOND

in his pew in Monumental Church; but it has since been bought from his granddaughters, by the city, and turned over to the Association for the Preservation of Virginia Antiquities. Its stately rooms, with their beautifully carved mantels and cornices, contain many memories of the " Old Chief " and his family and has become a mecca to visitors of Richmond.

THE STATE CAPITOL

About two blocks away from the Marshall House stands the old Capitol in the midst of its ten-acre " square " —the chief attraction of the city still, in spite of the prosperous West End. Indeed, with its appealing natural beauty and its associations it must for all time be a centre of interest to the visitor in lovely and historic Richmond.

The plan for the building was furnished by Thomas Jefferson when he was minister to France and was taken from the Maison Carree, at Nismes. It was begun in 1785 and finished in 1792, when the Legislature had been meeting within its walls for some years. The chaste beauty of its classic outlines and proportions has been warmly admired by persons of taste. It stands upon the brow of a hill with the green square sloping away from it and ancient trees arching the walks that lead to it from all directions. Nearby stands the splendid Washington monument, one of the noblest groups of statuary in America. The equestrian statue of Washington, which is its central and crowning figure, and most of the other figures on the monument, were modelled by Thomas Crawford, of New York, but as he died before the work was finished, those of Thomas Nelson and Andrew Lewis were made by Randolph Rogers. Other figures in the group surrounding Washington are Patrick Henry, Thomas Jefferson, George Mason, and John Marshall. The monument was unveiled in 1858. The statues of Henry Clay, " Stonewall " Jackson, Governor William Smith, and Dr. Hunter McGuire also adorn the Square. The Virginia State Library stands within the Square some distance to the rear of the Capitol, while on a line with the library and to the north of it stands, at the head of a shady avenue, also within the Square—the governor's mansion—a serene, dignified and beautiful, but unostentatious Virginia home.

Much of the history of Virginia has been made within the walls of this old Capitol. The Hall of the House of Delegates, especially, teems with associations. Within this hall at least a part of the celebrated trial of Aaron Burr was held; within it met the famous Constitutional Con-

GOVERNOR'S MANSION, RICHMOND

vention of 1829–1830, of which Madison, Monroe, Marshall, John Randolph and many other eminent men of the time were members; within it met the "Secession Convention" of 1861; and within it, during the war that followed, were held the sessions of the Confederate Congress.

Soon after the Revolution, Houdon, the most famous sculptor of the time, came from Paris to Mount Vernon for the purpose of making a statue of General Washington. This masterpiece of portraiture in white marble, declared by Lafayette to be "a *fac-simile* of Washington's person,"

STATE CAPITOL, RICHMOND

HOME OF CHIEF JUSTICE MARSHALL, RICHMOND

stands in the centre of the Rotunda and is the Capitol's chief treasure.

In 1906 the Capitol was enlarged by the addition of two wings harmonizing in architecture with the design of the main building. The assembly halls of the House of Delegates and State Senate may now be found in these new wings, but the historic " Hall of the House " has been preserved and is now used as the State Agricultural Museum.

In the Capitol basement is the State Land Office where may be seen records of land-grants and patents going back as far as the year 1628.

On April 27, 1870, the Capitol was the scene of a frightful disaster. The Court of Appeals was sitting in a room in the northeast corner of the building, and a case of unusual interest had drawn a crowd which packed the apartment to the doors. Suddenly the floor gave way under the unaccustomed weight and went crashing down into the hall of the house below, carrying with it a panic-stricken mass of humanity. The number of persons killed was sixty-five, while two hundred others, more or less, were seriously injured. Among the victims were many of Richmond's leading citizens.

THE WESTMORELAND CLUB

A short walk up Grace Street from the main entrance of Capitol Square brings the tourist to one of the gracious old roof-trees of former days, which has been preserved by becoming the home of the Westmoreland Club. The house was begun about 1837, by Mr. James Gray, a wealthy tobacco merchant, but was sold by him before it was completed, to Judge Robert Stanard, of the Virginia Court of Appeals, who finished it and occupied it until his death. It was elegantly equipped, as befitted its stately rooms, with furniture from Paris and carved mantels from Italy.

Judge Stanard had formerly lived in a house on Ninth Street, opposite the Capitol Square, where the youthful

Edgar Allan Poe had been a frequent visitor, as a friend of the Stanard boys. Mrs. Stanard won the heart of the poet-to-be, by her kindness and sympathy, and to her afterwards were addressed the lovely lines, "To Helen," which helped to make Poe famous and caused her to be known as "Poe's Helen."

She did not live to accompany her husband and children to their new home. Though he remained a widower, Judge Stanard's entertainments were famous—his friend Mr. James Lyons often assisting him in doing the honors.

Upon his death his son, Robert C. Stanard, a dis-

WESTMORELAND CLUB, THE STANARD HOUSE, RICHMOND

tinguished member of the Richmond bar, the State Senate and the Constitutional Convention of 1851, inherited the house. Mr. Stanard married a beautiful and brilliant daughter of Kentucky, and with her as hostess the traditions of the house were amply sustained. The brightest men of the time flocked to her salon, and Thackeray was one of the many men of note entertained by her husband and herself.

After the Stanards' time, their home was owned successively by Mr. William H. Macfarland and Mr. James Lyons, prominent gentlemen, both of them, and lavish hosts.

RICHMOND IN 1848

The Westmoreland Club was organized at a meeting held January 29, 1877. It assembled first at its own home, 707 E. Franklin Street, formerly the residence of General R. E. Lee, on May 1st of the same year. In 1879 the Club purchased its present home, which was then the property of Mr. James Lyons. Extensive additions and improvements have since been made to the building and the Club, now in its 38th year, is one of the most prosperous and noted in the United States.

THE ARCHER HOUSE *

So small a number of the few of Richmond's old mansions that remain are still homes that the mere fact of being the residence of a private citizen gives a distinction all its own. One whose air of quiet and dignified homelikeness proclaims it to be the possessor of this distinction may be seen just a square below the Westmoreland Club at the corner of Franklin and Sixth Streets. It makes a charming picture and its interior is equally charming. It was built early in the last century by Mr. Cunningham, a merchant, from plans drawn by Mr. Mills, the architect of the Monumental Church, the White House of the Confederacy, and the Valentine Museum. Mr. Cunningham sold it to Dr. George Watson, a distinguished physician of the time, and it is still owned and occupied by his descendants, the Archer family. Upon its door hangs the polished brass knocker that responded to the touch of the gentle guests of nearly a hundred years ago, and a high brick wall around the yard still secures to the premises the privacy so dear to the heart of the modest old-time folk.

THE CASKIE HOUSE

Two squares further on, upon the corner of Main and Fifth Streets, stands the quiet and attractive Caskie home, which was built by Mr. Tate, Mayor of Richmond, and after his death descended to his nephew, who was a second "Mayor Tate." Since the time of the Tates, the house has been successively the home of the Neilson, Gray and

* See illustration, p. 127.

Caskie families. It is as interesting architecturally within as without, a striking feature being a beautiful octagon-shaped drawing-room.

The tourist, finding himself suddenly face to face with the Archer and Caskie homes, upon their busy corners, has a pleasant sense of having stumbled upon a bit of reposeful yesterday in the midst of bustling, strenuous to-day.

THE ALLAN HOUSE

Diagonally opposite the Caskie House on the southeast corner of Main and Fifth Streets, now occupied by brick tenements, once stood an old mansion famous for its social history, and as the home, for a brief period, of Edgar Allan Poe.

The house was built in 1798 by David Meade Randolph, United States Marshall for Virginia. According to the contract, Mr. Randolph was to pay for the construction of his home "£100 worth of corn, £50 worth of oyster shells, delivered at Rocketts, £100 worth of goods (£25 of which to be in wet goods) and the remainder in money, to be paid by Christmas Day, 1800." It was far enough up town, in those days, to be almost in the country, and must have been very like a country place, with its spreading lawn shaded with pine trees and, at the rear, its "falling garden" filled with fruits and flowers. Like a country place too, it had a name, for Mr. Randolph quaintly combining his own name—David—with that of his wife—Molly—called it "Moldavia," and as "Moldavia" it was long known.

Mrs. Randolph was noted as a wit and also as a housekeeper. In her prosperous days she was called "the queen" by the guests who thronged her hospitable home, and when reverses came she showed she could be queen of the kitchen as well as the drawing-room, for she opened upon Cary Street a boarding house which achieved immediate success, and whose "board" became as famous as that at "Moldavia" had been. She published her recipes in a cook-book which is still an authority in many an old Virginia home.

In 1805 " Moldavia " was sold to Mr. Joseph Gallego, owner of the Gallego Mills, who occupied it for twenty years and then sold it to Mr. John Allan, whose brilliant adopted son, Edgar Allan Poe, was then about seventeen years old. There is a great uncertainty as to just how long Poe lived at the Allan house, for soon after Mr. Allan bought it, Poe entered the University of Virginia and later went to Boston to live. He seems, at least, to have un-

ALLAN HOUSE, RICHMOND 1798

doubtedly made his home there during a good part of the year 1826.

The Allans made the beautiful interior of their house the background for superb furniture and artistic ornaments brought from Europe. They had the social gifts of true Richmonders, and their home was famous for its brilliant entertainments. Among notables from across the water who enjoyed its hospitality at different times were Charles Dickens, Lord and Lady Napier, Lord and Lady Lyons, and the Honorable Miss Murray. The old *Richmond Enquirer* contains an elaborate account of a fancy ball given at the Allan House, with the initials of the belles and beaux present, and the characters they represented, and detailed descriptions of their costumes.

Long after the Allans' day their home was once more the scene of festivity when the citizens of Richmond, in 1881, gave there a grand ball to the distinguished delegations sent over by the governments of France and Germany to represent those countries at the Yorktown Centennial.

THE GAMBLE HOUSE

A few of those who enjoy the charms of Gamble's Hill—its green terraces, its sweet breezes and its superb view of the river, town and country—remember the Gamble mansion which gave the hill its name.*

The house was built in the year 1800, by Colonel John Harvie, a Revolutionary patriot, and member of the Convention of 1775 and of Congress, but was barely finished when he died, and Mrs. Harvie sold it to Major Robert Gamble (1754–1810),[5] a Revolutionary officer and commander of the first company to enter the fort at the storming of Stony Point.

Major Gamble came to Richmond from Augusta County, where he had married Catherine, daughter of Major John Gratton, who had made herself as famous for courage as she was for beauty by riding through the country at night warning the settlers on the "border," in the neighborhood of her home, of an impending Indian raid.

This interesting pair was, of course, a welcome addition to Richmond society and made "Grey Castle," as the Gamble House was called, a charming home. Their sons removed to Florida and founded a prominent family there, but their two daughters made brilliant matches in Richmond and continued to live at "Grey Castle." Elizabeth, after a long courtship, became the wife of the distinguished William Wirt, while Agnes made choice from her many

* See illustration, page 143.

[5] For an account of Colonel Gamble and his family see Brown, *The Cabells and Their Kin*, p. 255 *et seq.*

suitors of Judge William H. Cabell, of the Court of Appeals of Virginia and Governor of the State. As the roof-tree of these two distinguished couples "Grey Castle" naturally continued to be one of the notable homes of Virginia. In the course of time the Wirts moved away, and Judge and Mrs. Cabell became sole master and mistress of the house and dispensers of its hospitality. Tom Moore was once entertained there, when Miss Maria Mayo, a famous beauty and belle and afterwards the wife of General Winfield Scott, paid him the pretty compliment of singing to him and the assembled company, "Believe Me If All Those Endearing Young Charms."

After the time of the Cabells, "Grey Castle" had various owners. For some years the celebrated McGuire's School was taught there. It was afterward pulled down and a row of tenements was built upon its site.

THE RUTHERFOORD HOUSE

The first resident of Richmond to see that the future of the city lay to the westward was Mr. Thomas Rutherfoord,[6] a native of Scotland, who, over a hundred years ago, established his family in a handsome residence in the country, but near enough to town for him to go to and from his business. This earliest of West End homes stood upon the northeast corner of the present Franklin and Adams Streets, but has given place to the row of modern houses that now occupies that site. In the words of one who remembers it, the Rutherfoord House was "a noble specimen of colonial architecture," one of the last of its kind. The roof was in keeping with the style built by the rich aristocratic class, lofty and peaked, and flanked by tall chimney stacks which stood out in relief against the sky, towering above the loftiest trees. The body of the house was broad and ample, and afforded a typical example of simplicity and strength characteristic of the structures of the Colonial period. The grounds occupied an extensive area and were

[6] Rutherfoord family: *The Richmond Standard*, ii, Nos. 25–28.

laid off into lawns, kitchen and flower gardens, orchard and vineyard. A massive brick wall enclosed many acres of what is now First Street, occupied by orchards of every variety of fruit known at that day.

Mr. Rutherfoord married the lovely Sallie Winston, daughter of Mr. Geddes Winston. After his death and when his goodly band of sons and daughters had scattered into homes of their own, the Rutherfoord House changed hands several times, but from first to last the mansion, and those that lived in it, held a prominent place in the social life of Richmond. It was at one time the home of the Honorable John Y. Mason, Secretary of the Navy, Attorney General of the United States, and United States Minister to France. Colonel A. S. Buford was its last owner.

BULLOCK HOUSE, RICHMOND

THE BULLOCK HOUSE

Upon the site now occupied by the Commonwealth Club once stood, in the midst of spacious grounds shaded by splendid old elms, a commodious brick mansion known as the Bullock House. It was begun by Mr. Peyton Drew and finished in 1814 by Mr. John Mutter—prominent citizens of Richmond, both of them—and in 1830 was sold to Mr. David Bullock, mayor of the city, who made his home in it for many years. Later it became the home of Mr. George Palmer.

The Commonwealth Club was organized March 3, 1890, and practically succeeded the old Richmond Club, situated at Third and Franklin Streets, which was organized soon after the War between the States. The Commonwealth Club is one of the largest and most influential in the South.

SWAN TAVERN

Swan Tavern, at the northwest corner of Broad and Ninth, was long the favorite stopping place of prominent visitors to Richmond. It was built soon after the Revolution. Its most noted guest was Edgar Allan Poe, who boarded here during his last visit to Richmond.

SWAN TAVERN, RICHMOND

MANCHESTER

THE GRAY AND CLOPTON HOUSES

Manchester (now South Richmond), lying just across the river from Richmond, in the county of Chesterfield, had, under its Colonial name of Rocky Ridge, almost as early an origin as its larger neighbor. During the period when it was a flourishing tobacco market, a number of handsome homesteads, most of which have now disappeared, were built there. Among those that remain are the Gray House, the floor of whose hall still bears the mark of the effort of the British soldiers to burn it; and the Clopton House, built by Robert Graham, a Scotch merchant, who

GRAY HOUSE, MANCHESTER, SOUTH RICHMOND

was arrested and sent to the interior during the War of 1812. This house was afterward the home of the distinguished jurist John Bacon Clopton.

BLACK HEATH

Thirteen miles above Manchester, on the edge of the village of Midlothian, in Chesterfield County, once the centre of the famous coal-mining district, stands, in a state of rapid decay, Black Heath, for several generations the home of the Heth family.[7]

---

[7] Heth family: *The Critic* (Richmond, Va.), Sept. 17, 1888.

The most important of the Heths of Black Heath was Lieutenant General Henry Heth of the Confederate Army, or " Harry " Heth, as he was affectionately called. His soldierly instincts were inherited, for the brother of the first of his name at Black Heath was Colonel William Heth, of the Continental Line.

The house, a large, rambling old mansion, part brick and part frame, was in its early days surrounded by all the appurtenances of a home of wealth and taste. There were a flower garden, oak grove, a great circular pigeon

BLACK HEATH, CHESTERFIELD COUNTY

house, a barn, stables, and other outbuildings; but many years ago coal pits were sunk practically all around the house, and tunnels, or drifts as they were called, run beneath the grounds, and, it is said, beneath the house itself.

Coal was mined at Midlothian as early as 1730 and for miles around may be seen the remains of the pits owned and operated by the Wooldridges, Clarkes, Cunliffes and other Chesterfield families.

After the time of the Heths, Black Heath was occupied by Mr. Gifford, an Englishman, and later by the family of Colonel William B. Ball.

CHESTERFIELD COURT HOUSE

Chesterfield Court House was built in 1749–50 and was ordered by the County Court to be a copy of the then Henrico Court House. In 1779 Hamilton, the British governor of Detroit, who had been captured by G. R. Clark, was confined here for a time. In 1781 the British forces under General Phillips burned the Court House, but its substantial walls remained intact, and when

CHESTERFIELD COURT HOUSE

the house was restored it must have been made like it was at first. Many celebrated trials have been held here. At the rear there is a wing (not shown in the picture) almost as large as the front part of the house.

SALISBURY

A few days after the election of Patrick Henry as governor of Virginia, in November, 1784, he left the capital in order to arrange his affairs in Henry County and removed his family to a farm called Salisbury, in Chesterfield

County, near Richmond. The house chosen by the famous patriot as a residence during his term as governor was no palace or mansion, but a charmingly quaint, frame homestead, with big, bright, airy rooms, only a story and a half high, which had been built some time during the eighteenth century by the Randolphs, as a hunting lodge. Governor Henry rented it from Thomas Mann Randolph.

Salisbury is only fourteen miles from Richmond and but a little way from the village of Midlothian, but its situ-

SALISBURY, CHESTERFIELD COUNTY

ation seems lonely and remote by reason of the deep woods lying between. Cloistered among splendid old oaks, the house makes a pretty picture, with its dormer windows, its great chimneys and its square, white porches.

In 1789, while Salisbury was the home of Henry, Mr. Randolph sold it to Doctor Philip Turpin, a native of Virginia, who was a graduate of medicine and surgery of the University of Edinburgh, Scotland. During the Revolution Dr. Turpin attempted to return home, but was taken prisoner and held by the British Government as surgeon on board ship until the close of the war. The cry of

"Tory" was raised against him, but friends and officers in the British Navy bore witness that he was an unwilling prisoner, and, through the influence of Thomas Jefferson, an unconditional release of his property, which included Salisbury and had been placed under confiscation, was granted. At his death Doctor Turpin bequeathed Salisbury to his daughter Caroline, the wife of Doctor Edward Johnson, who left it to her sons Edward and Philip Turpin Johnson.

Edward Johnson was a gallant officer in the United States Army and a distinguished major-general in the Confederate Army. At the close of the War between the States he made Salisbury his home and died there, leaving no descendants. After the death of Philip Turpin Johnson the estate passed from this family.

NORWOOD, POWHATAN COUNTY

NORWOOD

On James River, in Powhatan County, not far above the Chesterfield line, is Norwood, an old home long the property of the Harris family. It was sold by Mr. Baratier

Harris to Mr. Beverley Randolph, formerly of Eastern View, Fauquier County, who owned it as early as 1835, and who added the wings.

At the death of Mr. Randolph, Norwood passed to his son Doctor Charles H. Randolph, who left it to Mrs. Nancy Randolph Kennon, and her husband Lieutenant William H. Kennon, U. S. N., for life, and at their death to their eldest son Charles Randolph Kennon, at whose death it passed to his brother William H. Kennon.

BEAUMONT POWHATAN COUNTY

BEAUMONT

Higher up the river, in Powhatan County, is Beaumont, formerly the beautiful home of Mr. William Walthall Michaux, father of Doctor Jacob Michaux, of Richmond.[8] Though adjoining other large family estates which were inherited by Mr. Michaux, the house dates from before this time. It was the home of Mr. Edward Walthall, who, dying childless, left it to his relative and adopted son, William Walthall Michaux.

The descendants of Abraham Michaux, one of the

[8] Michaux family: *The Critic* (Richmond, Va.), May 19, 1889.

Huguenots who settled at Manakin Town in 1700, gradually acquired lands in this neighborhood until their holdings comprised many thousand acres. Though Beaumont has been sold, some of the ancestral lands are still owned by the Michaux family.

Michaux's Ferry has long been a well-known crossing place on James River.

PAXTON

Dr. Ennion Williams Skelton, son of Josiah Skelton, came to Virginia about 1802 from New Jersey. He was a Master of Arts of Princeton and received a medical edu-

PAXTON, POWHATAN COUNTY

cation at the Medical College of Pennsylvania. He settled at Genito, which was at that time a thriving village. Bateaux on the Appomattox were carried as far up as Genito Mill. This mill was owned by Dr. Skelton, who had an extensive practice. He married, in 1823, Catherine Waldron Gifford, of Newark, New Jersey, and lived in the village while his home Paxton was being built. Upon its completion, in 1824, Dr. Skelton's parents went there to live with him and, as will be seen further on, five generations of this family lived at Paxton between 1824 and 1865.

After the death of Dr. Skelton and his wife, the property was inherited by their son, Dr. John Gifford Skelton, who graduated in medicine at the University of Pennsylvania. He lived at Paxton, where he practised medicine until soon after the War between the States, when he moved to Richmond and was one of the most prominent physicians in that city. He married, as his first wife, in 1841, Charlotte Foushee Randolph, daughter of Peyton Randolph and his wife Maria Ward, and granddaughter of Edmund Randolph, Secretary of State of the United States. The only child by this marriage was Maria Ward Skelton. His second wife was Marianne Meade, by whom he had ten children. Maria Ward Skelton married at Paxton, in 1864, John Langbourne Williams, of Richmond, and their oldest son, John Skelton Williams, was born there July 6, 1865, being the fifth generation of the family to live at Paxton.

The place was celebrated for its hospitality. The location, being at the intersection of two public roads, made it a convenient stopping place for the soldiers during the war, and for the friends of the family at all times.

POWHATAN COURT HOUSE AND TAVERN

Powhatan Court House stands upon the site of an older building erected in 1777. Near it was fought, some time in the forties, the famous duel between Doctor Branch T. Archer and Doctor Otway Crump. Doctor Crump fell at the first fire. Doctor Archer removed to Texas, where he became prominent in the affairs of the then republic.

At Powhatan Court House still stands, though now used for other purposes, one of the large old Court House Taverns, once so famous as gathering places, and for jovial hospitality.

BELMEAD

Belmead, also in Powhatan County, was built by Philip St. George Cocke (1808–1861), son of General John Hartwell Cocke (1780–1866), of Bremo, Fluvanna County. Philip St. George Cocke was a graduate of West Point and was a brigadier general in the Confederate Army.

The great size and striking architecture of the Belmead house make it one of the most imposing mansions on James River. It is now the property of the Roman Catholic Church.

TUCKAHOE

On the north side of the river opposite Powhatan County is the County of Goochland, at the lower end of which stands Tuckahoe, the oldest of the James River mansions west of Richmond.

Tuckahoe was a frontier settlement established at a time when, on account of the Indian terror, the law required for every five hundred acres, " One Christian man, perfect of limb, provided with a well-fixed musquett or fuzee, a good pistoll, sharp simeter and tomahawk," to live upon the land. The house stands upon the brow of a steep, wooded hill and is approached through an avenue of beautiful elms. To the left may still be seen the curious old " box-labyrinth," with its twisting and winding walks, and traces of the flower-garden, where rose-bushes, bridalwreath, lilacs, sweet william, and other old-fashioned flowers flourished in prim beds and borders.

The mansion, built in part of Colonial brick and in part of wood, is of unique design. There are two wings, each 25 feet deep and 40 feet long, connected by a hall 24 feet wide and 40 feet long, with arched doorways opening at either end into the wings—giving the house the shape of the letter H.

A visitor to Tuckahoe, writing in 1779, says, " it seems to be built solely for the purposes of hospitality," and that the family lived in one wing while the other is " reserved solely for visitors." The rooms and hall are panelled from

TUCKAHOE, GOOCHLAND COUNTY before 1779

BELMEAD, POWHATAN COUNTY

floor to ceiling with black walnut. A fine stairway of the same wood, with hand-carved balustrade, adds to the beauty of the hall. This hall was furnished with four sofas, two on each side, " besides chairs," and served the double purpose of a " cool retreat " in summer and " an occasional ball-room."

Upon several of the tiny panes of glass in the windows may be seen the names of some of the Randolphs and their friends, scratched with diamonds before the Revolution.

Tuckahoe was built by Thomas Randolph (1689–1730), of Turkey Island, who was a burgess for Henrico and commander-in-chief of Goochland at the time that county was formed. He married Judith Fleming and was the father of Judith Randolph, who married Reverend William Stith (1689–1755), president of William and Mary College and historian of Virginia, and of Mary Randolph, who became the wife of Reverend James Keith (and was the grandmother of Chief Justice Marshall). Thomas Randolph died in 1730, leaving Tuckahoe to his only son, William Randolph, who married Maria Judith, daughter of Honorable Mann Page I, of Rosewell. William Randolph was for several years, and at the time of his death, a burgess for Goochland. He died in 1745, possessed of a large estate. He left £1200 sterling, a handsome fortune in those days, to each of his two daughters. His will directed that a tutor should be employed to teach his only son, Thomas Mann Randolph, and also his daughters. At the time of his death this only son was a child, and in response to a request in the will, Peter Jefferson (whose wife was Jane, a daughter of Isham Randolph, of Dungeness, who was great-uncle to the said Thomas Mann) came to Tuckahoe, bringing with him his son Thomas, and took the estate and the family under his charge. It thus befell that Thomas Jefferson, when a lad, went to school with his cousins, the Randolph children, in the tiny school-house still to be seen in the yard at Tuckahoe.

Thomas Mann Randolph, of Tuckahoe, was a member of the House of Burgesses, and, after the Revolution, of the Virginia Legislature. By his first marriage with Anne, daughter of Archibald Cary, of Ampthill, he was the father of (among several other children) Thomas Mann Randolph, of Edge Hill, Albemarle County, governor of Virginia, and by his second marriage, with Gabriella Harvie, of another Thomas Mann Randolph, who inherited Tuckahoe, but who sold it in 1830 to Edwin Wight, of Richmond. Mr. Wight sold it twenty years later to Joseph Allen, from whom it passed to Major Richard Allen and

SCHOOL-HOUSE AT TUCKAHOE
Where Thomas Jefferson went to school

his wife, who was Miss Virginia Mitchell, a famous beauty and belle of Richmond. In 1898 the old place again changed hands, this time becoming once more the property of those of Randolph blood—the Coolidge family of Boston, descendants of Governor Thomas Mann Randolph, who still own it.

The social history of Tuckahoe has been brilliant. Colonel William Byrd in his *Progress to the Mines* describes a visit there in 1732 and from that time on many distinguished men have been sheltered by this famous old roof-tree. The house was divided in opinion during the

Revolution and both Washington and Cornwallis are said to have enjoyed its hospitality.

Of course Tuckahoe has its ghosts. Creepy stories are told of the shade of a murdered pedler which haunts the southeast chamber and a distressed bride, with flowing locks and wringing hands, who paces the east walk.

In a vault screened from view by grape arbors and shrubbery, about two hundred yards distant from the mansion, sleep the Randolphs of Tuckahoe.

OAKLAND [9]

On June 26, 1731, about fifteen years after Governor Spotswood's trip of exploration to the Blue Ridge Mountains had caused the gradual movement of the settlements, from the head of tide-water on the James and other rivers towards the foot of the mountains, a Land Patent, covering the site of Oakland, was issued in the name of George II, King of Great Britain, by Governor William Gooch, to " Bowler Cocke, Gentleman." This patent or grant was made in consideration of 12 pounds, for 2400 acres of land on the south side of the James on Muddy Creek, formerly in Henrico County, at that date in Goochland County, and now in Cumberland County (Virginia Land Office, Land Patents, Vol. 14, p. 187).

Bowler Cocke, to whom the grant was made, was the son of Richard Cocke, 3d, son of Richard, 2d, son of Richard 1st, who came to the Colony of Virginia prior to 1632 (as his name appears in the list of Burgesses of the "Grand Assembly" for that year), and settled at "Bremo," the original home of the Cocke family in Virginia, near James River, about twelve miles east of Richmond (*Virginia Magazine of History and Biography,* III, 282). On the death of Bowler Cocke, 1st (1771), Oakland passed to his son, Bowler Cocke, 2d. On the latter's death (1772), it passed to his son, William Cocke. On William's death (1825), it passed to his son, Wm. Armistead Cocke,

[9] This account was written by a member of the Cocke family.

who was the great-great-grandson, through his mother, Jane Armistead, of Colonel William Byrd, 2d. And on the death of Wm. A. Cocke (1855), who married Elizabeth Randolph Preston, of Lexington, Va., it passed to their four sons, William Fauntleroy, Thomas Lewis Preston, Edmund Randolph, and John Preston Cocke, all of whom were in the Confederate Army. Oakland is now owned by Edmund R. Cocke.

Though Oakland has been owned by the Cocke family for more than 175 years, it seems that it was not occupied as a home until about 1788, when William Cocke moved there from Bremo.

Oakland is about forty miles west of Richmond, and about six miles south of Cartersville. It is a typical old Virginia tobacco plantation, though it also produces wheat, corn and oats and an abundance of vegetables and fruit. Its greatest attraction is its large yard of about twelve acres, which, during the last century, contained some fifty-five or sixty gigantic oaks, white and red, chiefly the former, and a large number of other kinds of beautiful shade trees. The largest of these oaks are said to be some twenty feet in circumference, casting a shade at mid-day of over a hundred feet in diameter. It is not probable that such a collection of oaks can be found, within such a limited space, anywhere else in this country. The writer, who has visited many parks and other places noted for their fine forest growth, has never seen such a collection of large trees except on the Pacific Coast.

The following incident, related by a Virginia authoress, which occurred shortly after the Civil War, illustrates very fully the surpassing grandeur of these trees:

> Oakland was not by any means among the handsomest of the old Virginia houses, but in one respect it surpassed them all. I remember on one occasion driving back to the home from service at the country church with Bishop Whittle, when a member of the family said to him, " Bishop, this is not your first visit to Oakland; you were here, sir, 20 years ago, when you were just Mr. Whittle." It was evident that the Bishop did not recall the visit, and the

OAKLAND, CUMBERLAND COUNTY

OAKLAND, SHOWING THE GROVE

conversation was deftly changed to save embarrassment. But when the open carriage swept around the edge of the woods, and brought the 12-acre lawn to view, with its 80 or more trees, 50 of them primeval oaks, measuring several feet in diameter, and spreading out into vast sanctuaries of shade, the Bishop stood up in the carriage and took off his hat. "You are mistaken, Captain Cocke," he said; "I might have been graceless enough to forget the kindest host, but not these monarchs. I have never seen Oakland before." [10]

An interesting description of the "old days" at Oakland is given by Mrs. Allan in her *Life of Mrs. M. J. Preston;* and of "War Times" by Mr. E. A. Moore, in *The Story of a Cannoneer Under Stonewall Jackson.*

While Oakland was visited by many persons of note during the last century, it was especially honored by a visit from General R. E. Lee, just after the close of the Civil War. At the invitation of Mrs. Elizabeth R. Cocke, the mistress of Oakland from 1835 to 1889, General Lee came to Oakland in June, 1865. He was accompanied by Mrs. Lee, Miss Agnes, Miss Mildred and General Custis Lee. General Lee and the ladies came by the "packet boat" on the old James River and Kanawha Canal, and as the berths were very close and uncomfortable, the General preferred sleeping on the open deck of the boat with his cloak wrapped around him. This is probably the last occasion on which he ever bivouacked.

After a week spent here (Oakland), General Lee removed with his family to "Derwent" (the home of T. L. P. Cocke, adjoining Oakland). There he spent several months of quiet rest, only interrupted by the calls of those who came in all honesty and sincerity to pay their respects to him. Old soldiers, citizens, men and women, all came without parade or ceremony.[11]

In August, 1865, while at Derwent, General Lee was visited by Judge John W. Brockenbrough, Rector of the Board of Trustees of Washington College, Lexington,

[10] *Life of Mrs. M. J. Preston,* by Mrs. Elizabeth P. Allan, p. 102.

[11] *Recollections and Letters of General Robert E. Lee,* by Captain Robert E. Lee, pp. 171–172.

Va., who offered him the Presidency of that College. After several weeks of deliberation, General Lee accepted that position, and in September removed with his family to Lexington.

Oakland, unlike most old Virginia homes, was not overrun by the Federal troops during the Civil War; its inaccessibility alone saved it. But in August, 1900, a mouse and a match caused a greater loss than the Federals would probably have inflicted, by destroying the delightful home represented in the accompanying picture, and by damaging the large oaks which flanked it both east and west. Mrs. Elizabeth P. Allen, after alluding to the great loss of such a home and its contents, some of which possessed an incalculable sentimental value, adds, " Surely there must be a spiritual immortality for such a home."

SABOT HILL, GOOCHLAND COUNTY

SABOT HILL AND DOVER

A short distance above Bendover, in the same county, Goochland, and also overlooking the James, are two beautiful houses, which on account of the intermarriages of the families of their builders are closely associated—Sabot

DOVER, GOOCHLAND COUNTY

Hill, the old homestead of the Seddons, and Dover, of the Morsons.

Sabot Hill was built in 1855 by James Alexander Seddon, afterward Secretary of War of the Confederate Government. It is now the property of Mr. W. E. Harris.

Dover was built by Mr. Arthur Morson and is one of the fairest of old Virginia's fair mansions. Its long pillared portico is an especially striking feature. It, too, has changed hands, but its present owner, Mr. C. Boice, has beautifully restored it.

HOWARD'S NECK, GOOCHLAND COUNTY

HOWARD'S NECK

The dwelling here was built by Edward Cunningham in 1825, whose son, Dr. Francis Cunningham, was a prominent physician in Richmond many years ago. The property was purchased from the Cunninghams, in 1842, by John B. Hobson, who married Martha Bland Selden, of Westover. Now owned by Mr. Saunders Hobson.

ROCK CASTLE

Rock Castle, in Goochland County, for the past half century the hospitable home of Mr. John Coles Rutherfoord and his family, takes its name from the high rocky bluff overlooking James River, upon which the house is perched. The simple cottage with vine-covered porch and sloping dormer roof bears little likeness to a castle, but it is well worthy of consideration, for it has its place in the social history of Virginia and has suffered from two wars. It is one of the oldest homesteads in this section. The plantation was seated nearly two hundred years ago by Mr. Tarleton Fleming (according to tradition, a descendant of the Earl of Wigton, in Scotland), whose wife was Mary Randolph, of Tuckahoe. Colonel William Byrd in his *Progress to the Mines* (1732) mentions a visit to Tuckahoe, where he met Mrs. Fleming, "on her way to join her husband at Rock Castle, thirty miles farther up the river in a part of the country little settled, and but lately redeemed from the wilderness."

ROCK CASTLE, GOOCHLAND COUNTY

Upon the death of Tarleton Fleming, Rock Castle passed to his son, Thomas Mann Fleming. Upon his death it was bought by Colonel David Bullock, a prominent lawyer, of Richmond, who kept open house, and liberally dispensed old-fashioned Southern hospitality there, for years. Some time after the death of Colonel Bullock,

Governor John Rutherfoord bought the estate as a summer home, and it finally became the residence of his son, Mr. John Coles Rutherfoord, of Richmond, who modernized the front of the house. However, the quaint architectural features of the Colonial period may still be seen at the rear.

During the Revolution, Rock Castle was visited by a raiding party under General Tarleton, who angrily cut down and bore away the coat-of-arms of Tarleton quartered with Fleming from the wall of the panelled parlor.

Years later, during the raid around Richmond, a party of Sheridan's soldiers sacked the house and were only prevented from firing it by the entreaties of the faithful colored servants.

Rock Castle is now the property of the distinguished surgeon, Dr. Geo. Ben Johnston, whose wife is a daughter of John Coles Rutherfoord.

BOLLING HALL, GOOCHLAND COUNTY

BOLLING HALL

From the early eighteenth century the Bollings of Cobbs, in Chesterfield County, owned much land in Goochland, and various members of the family made their homes in that county at times. But the first to abandon the original homestead and settle permanently in Goochland was Colonel William Bolling, of "Bolling Hall," a militia officer in the War of 1812, and a man of prominence in his community. He was a philanthropist as well as a soldier, and after removing to Bolling Hall established at his old home, Cobbs, the first institution for the education of deaf mutes in America.

Upon the walls of Bolling Hall long hung one of the most complete collections of family portraits in the State of Virginia. In it was represented every generation of Bollings from Robert, the emigrant, down. It is now the property of Mr. Richard Bolling, of Richmond, who has loaned it to the Virginia Historical Society.

"UNCLE" ASA AND "AUNT" JINSEY AT BOLLING ISLAND
This old couple lived to be more than 100 years old.

BOLLING ISLAND

Colonel William Bolling left the valuable plantation Bolling Island to his son Thomas, who built the homestead.

Later the estate was purchased by Mr. A. Y. Stokes, of Richmond, and is still the property of his descendants.

BOLLING ISLAND, GOOCHLAND COUNTY

UNION HILL, CUMBERLAND COUNTY

UNION HILL

Union Hill, in Cumberland County, was the home of John Cary Page (1789–1853). One of Mr. Page's daughters, Harriet Randolph, married, in 1857, Coupland Randolph, of Maryland, and they removed to New Hampshire about 1865.

CLIFTON

The Clifton estate in Cumberland County seems to have been settled by Carter Henry Harrison, of "Berkeley"—a brother of Benjamin Harrison, the signer of the Declaration. The master of Clifton married Susannah,

CLIFTON, CUMBERLAND COUNTY

daughter of Colonel Isham Randolph, of "Dungeness." After his death the homestead passed to his son Randolph Harrison, who married his first cousin, Mary, daughter of Thomas Isham Randolph, of "Dungeness."

Randolph and Mary Harrison, of "Clifton," had fourteen children, and their descendants, now widely scattered, form an influential social connection.

BELLMONT

Tradition says that quaint Bellmont, in Buckingham County, was the first frame dwelling in that section of the country—the pioneer settlers there having, hitherto contented themselves with log-houses. Its dormer windows, little square porch and big chimneys are indications of its age. Ancient trees form an arch high above the house which looks sedately forth from a yard filled with old-fashioned shrubs and flowers.

Bellmont was built by Colonel Archibald Cary for his sister, Judith, who married Colonel David Bell, a native of Scotland and a member of the House of Burgesses for

BELLMONT, BUCKINGHAM COUNTY

Buckingham County. It was inherited by Colonel and Mrs. Bell's daughter, Mrs. Harrison, who left it to her daughter, Mrs. Ligon. The Ligons sold it to Mr. I. C. Gannaway.

THE BREMOS

Near each other in Fluvanna County are the three homesteads and estates known as Bremo, Lower Bremo, and Bremo Recess.

General John Hartwell Cocke (1780–1866), of Surry County, a gentleman of prominence and fortune, removed, about 1803, to Fluvanna County, where he owned large tracts of land. He built Bremo Recess, and lived in it while he was erecting the handsome mansion which he named Bremo, in honor of Bremo in Henrico County, which was the home of the Cocke family at a very early date. Bremo House, with its great stone barns and other outbuildings, is one of the notable places on James River.

General Cocke was devoted to the cause of temperance and as a temperance memorial he had placed on the bank

BARN AT BREMO

of the James River and Kanawha Canal, at Bremo, a huge iron vase, pitcher-shaped, which was constantly filled to overflowing with water introduced by pipes from a spring. This unique fountain was long a famous sight to travellers up and down the canal.

After the death of General John H. Cocke the property was inherited by his son, Dr. Cary C. Cocke, and at his death it passed to his two daughters, Misses Mary and Lelia, who are the present owners.

Lower Bremo was built in 1843 and belonged to Dr.

BREMO, FLUVANNA COUNTY (FRONT)

BREMO (REAR)

Cary C. Cocke until 1855, when he and his father, General Cocke, exchanged homes. It is now the property of Mrs. W. R. C. Cocke.

LOWER BREMO, FLUVANNA COUNTY

OLD "MARSHALL" PACKET BOAT

The old *Marshall* was the last packet boat used on the James River and Kanawha Canal and the one on which the body of Stonewall Jackson was carried from Richmond to Lexington. Dr. George W. Bagby in his writings has an interesting chapter on Canal Reminiscences, and the following account is condensed therefrom:

"Those were the 'good old days' of bateaux,—picturesque craft that charmed my young eyes more than all the gondolas of Venice would do now. If ever man gloried in his calling, the negro bateaux-man was that man. His was a hardy calling, demanding skill, courage and strength in a high degree. I can see him now striding the plank that ran along the gunwale to afford him a footing, his long iron-shod pole trailing in the water behind him. Now he turns, and after one or two ineffectual efforts to get his pole fixed in the rocky bottom of the river, secures his purchase, adjusts the upper part of the pole to the pad on his shoulder, bends to his task, and the long, but not ungraceful bark mounts the rapids like a sea-bird breasting the storm. His companion on the other side plies his pole with equal ardor, and between the two the boat bravely surmounts every obstacle, be it rocks, rapids, quicksands, hammocks, what not. A third negro at the stern held the mighty oar that served as a rudder. A stalwart, jolly, courageous set they were, plying the pole all day, hauling it to shore at night under the friendly shade of a mighty sycamore, to rest, to eat, to play the banjo, and to snatch a few hours of profound, blissful sleep.

"The packet-landing at the foot of Eighth Street presented a scene of great activity. Passengers on foot and in vehicles continued to arrive up to the moment of starting. I took a peep at the cabin, wondering much how all the passengers were to be accommodated for the night. At last we were off, slowly pushed along under the bridge on Seventh Street; then the horses were hitched; then slowly along till we passed the crowd of boats near the city, until at length, with a lively jerk as the horses fell into a trot, away we went, the cut-water throwing up the spray as we rounded the Penitentiary hill, and the passengers lingering on deck to get a last look at the fair city of Richmond, lighted by the pale rays of the setting sun.

"As the shadows deepened, everybody went below. There was always a crowd in those days, but it was a crowd, for the most part, of our best people, and no one minded it.

"Supper over, the men went on deck to smoke, while the ladies busied themselves with draughts or backgammon, with conversation or with books. But not for long. The curtains which separated the female from the male department were soon drawn, in order that the steward and his aids might make ready the berths. These were three deep, 'lower,' 'middle,' and 'upper;' and great was the desire on the part of the men not to be consigned to the 'upper.'

"The ceremony of ablution was performed in a prim-

WIND-POWER GRIST MILL IN MATHEWS COUNTY

THE OLD "MARSHALL," THE LAST PACKET BOAT RUN ON JAMES RIVER AND KANAWHA CANAL

itive fashion. There were the tin basins, the big tin dipper with the long wooden handle. I feel it vibrating in the water now, and the water a little muddy generally; and there were the towels, a big one on a roller, and the little ones in a pile, and all of them wet.

"Of all the locks from Lynchburg down, the Three-Mile Locks pleased me most. It is a pretty place, as every one will own on seeing it. It was so clean and green, and white and thrifty-looking. To me it was simply beautiful. I wanted to live there; I ought to have lived there. I was built for a lock-keeper—have that exact moral and mental shape. Ah! to own your own negro, who would do all the drudgery of opening the gates. Occasionally you would go through the form of putting your shoulder to the huge wooden levers, if that is what they call them, by which the gates are opened; to own your own negro and live and die calmly at a lock! What more could the soul ask?"

POINT-OF-FORK, FLUVANNA COUNTY

POINT-OF-FORK

Point-of-Fork, in Fluvanna County, was for years the home of the Galts. William Galt, first of this family in

Virginia, was born in 1755, in the parish of Dundonald, Ayrshire, Scotland, and emigrated to Virginia in early youth and later became associated in business with his nephew, John Allan (Edgar Allan Poe's foster-father). He died in Richmond in 1823. His nephew, James Galt, of Point-of-Fork, a native of Irvine, Scotland, died April 26, 1826, in his seventy-second year.

During the Revolution there was a State arsenal and armory near Point-of-Fork.

In latter years it has been owned by General Lindsay Walker, Mrs. Hartwell Cabell, who was a daughter of General T. M. Logan, and now by Mr. James Alston Cabell.

CUMBERLAND COURT HOUSE

CUMBERLAND TAVERN

The county seat of Cumberland still possesses one of the large old taverns, formerly called the Effingham Tavern, so full of suggestions of bygone days. John Randolph, of Roanoke, was often a guest at this tavern and made political speeches in the Court House.

EFFINGHAM TAVERN, CUMBERLAND COURT HOUSE

AMPTHILL, CUMBERLAND COUNTY

AMPTHILL

Ampthill, in Cumberland County, is said to have been built by Randolph Harrison, who married, in 1790, Mary Randolph of Dungeness. Their daughter Mary Randolph Harrison married, in 1827, William Byrd Harrison, of

Upper Brandon, and was the mother of Colonel Randolph Harrison, a gallant soldier of the Confederate Army, who inherited Ampthill and long made it his home.

LIBERTY HALL

When, in 1724, Doctor William Cabell, of Union Hill, came from Wiltshire, England, and settled in what is now Nelson County, Virginia, his first home was a house which stood on the site now occupied by Liberty Hall. He afterward built nearer the river, where the family graveyard,

• LIBERTY HALL, NELSON COUNTY

shaded by a lofty elm, said to have been planted at the head of his grave, may still be seen.

Liberty Hall was the inheritance of Doctor Cabell's youngest son, Nicholas (1750–1803), passing from him to his youngest living son, Nicholas Cabell, Jr. (1780–1809), thence descending to *his* son Nathaniel Francis Cabell 1807-1891). The last mentioned Mr. Cabell at the time of his first marriage, about 1837, with Anne Blaws (1811–1862), daughter of General John Hartwell Cocke, of Bremo, moved the house to the site of the earliest home of his great-grandfather. About 1848 a wing was added to the house. Liberty Hall is still owned by Mr. Nathaniel Francis Cabell's children.

The dwelling was built by slaves from timber cut from the plantation and the wrought nails used in its construction were made on the place.

UNION HILL

In the County of Nelson may be found a number of estates and dwellings which formerly were, and some of which still are, the homes of the connection aptly styled by

UNION HILL, NELSON COUNTY

one of the most distinguished among its members "the Cabells and their kin." From this group of homes have come representatives who have made their family known in almost every walk of life throughout the country.

Part of the Union Hill estate was granted in 1738 to Doctor William Cabell (1699–1774),[12] the first of the name in Virginia, who in 1763 deeded it to his son, William

[12] For a full genealogy of the Cabells see Brown's *The Cabells and Their Kin.* Houghton, Mifflin Company.

(1730–1798), who made large additions to its acreage. The tract when completed extended for about ten miles along James River, and contained at least 25,000 acres of land. The building of the homestead began about 1775, and as the Revolution soon cut off supplies from England, the work had to be done almost entirely from materials to be had on the place. The wood was cut and bricks and nails made on the plantation. Save that the shingled roof has been replaced by tin, and repairs made, the house is about as Colonel Cabell left it. It is 60 feet wide by 40 feet deep and has two stories, a basement and an attic, with wainscoted rooms and halls and ample cellars. Around it stood all the numerous outbuildings necessary to a great plantation.

Colonel William Cabell, the builder of Union Hill, was one of the most eminent Virginians of his day. He was for many years a member of the House of Burgesses, was colonel of the Amherst militia and was a member of the Conventions and the Committee of Safety and a leader in the Revolutionary movement. Only a detailed study of his life as given by Doctor Alexander Brown can give an adequate idea of his services to the State. Colonel Cabell married Margaret, daughter of Colonel Samuel Jordan, of Buckingham County, who after her husband's death, on March 23, 1798, continued to occupy Union Hill with her son-in-law, William H. Cabell, afterward governor of Virginia.

Governor Cabell left Union Hill in 1801 and Colonel William Cabell, Jr., whose home at that time was Colleton, went to Union Hill and lived there until his death, in 1822, when he was succeeded by his son Mayo Cabell. Mr. Mayo Cabell married first Mary, daughter of Judge William Daniel, and secondly Caroline, daughter of Christopher Anthony, who surviving him at his death, in 1869, continued to live there.

In 1873 Union Hill was bought by Alexander Brown, the distinguished Virginia historian, who was twice married, both times to a Miss Cabell. The estate is now owned by Miss Lucy G. Cabell, who is the sister-in-law of Alexander Brown.

EDGEWOOD, NELSON COUNTY

Edgewood's special claim to distinction is as the home of Honorable Joseph Carrington Cabell (1778–1856), a leading member of the Virginia Legislature and a gentleman of rare talent and culture. It was chiefly through his sympathy and aid that Thomas Jefferson's plans for the

EDGEWOOD, NELSON COUNTY

University of Virginia were carried out. Mr. Cabell succeeded Jefferson as Rector of the University and held that office until his death, in 1856.

Edgewood, as may be seen from the picture, was one of the houses that grew with the needs of its occupants, thereby gaining that delightful rambling effect characteristic of so many old Virginia homesteads. The central building is about a century old. It stands upon what was originally a town lot in Warminster, which during Colonial days and for fifty years afterward was a village of a few hundred inhabitants and a shipping point for tobacco by *bateaux* down the James. The old house was built by Mr. Robert Rives, of Oak Ridge, Nelson County, who was then a merchant at Warminster, and was sold by him to Mr. Cabell. Mr. Cabell added the wings and kitchen and enlarged the central building at the rear.

Mr. Cabell married Miss Mary Carter of Lancaster County, and in the Edgewood yard stands a cottage where once lived the Honorable St. George Tucker, and his second wife, who was Mrs. George Carter, the mother of Mrs. Cabell. The mortal remains of all the above named lie in the graveyard to the rear of the house. After her husband's death Mrs. Joseph C. Cabell continued to make Edgewood her home until her death, in 1862. It was bought from Mr. Cabell's residuary legatee by Mr. Philip B. Cabell, whose widow now owns it.

Edgewood boasts of a well-authenticated ghost, for, though there seem to be few who have actually seen the gentle visitor from " beyond the veil," many there are who bear testimony of the light touch upon the shoulder of " Cousin Polly," as Mrs. Joseph C. Cabell was universally called in the connection. This lady was heiress of a goodly portion of the " King Carter " property, in Lancaster County, and left a large estate. Having no faith in lawyers, and determined that they should have nothing to do with her property, she wrote, with her own hand, one of the largest and most remarkable wills on record. In spite of her pains it is said that the lawyers got three-fourths of her fortune, which perhaps accounts for her uneasy rest.

SOLDIER'S JOY

Soldier's Joy, another delightfully rambling old homestead, was built in 1785 by Colonel Samuel Jordan Cabell, a gallant officer in the Revolutionary War and an original member of the Virginia Society of the Cincinnati. Immediately after his marriage to Sally Syme, of Hanover, in 1781, Colonel and Mrs. Cabell lived with his parents at

Union Hill. From 1795 to 1803 Colonel Cabell represented his district in Congress.

An interesting item in the diary of Colonel William Cabell of Union Hill is this entry under date of May 1, 1791: " My son Sam sent us some ice from his ice-house of which I had a Bowl of Punch. The first ice-punch I ever drank."

SOLDIER'S JOY, NELSON COUNTY

Soldier's Joy is now the home of Mr. and Mrs. Charles T. Palmer. Mrs. Palmer was Miss Alice Winston Cabell, a daughter of Doctor Clifford Cabell.

OTTER BURN

This dwelling, built in the early part of the nineteenth century, situated about two and one-half miles north of Bedford City (formerly Liberty), in the County of Bedford, was the home of the late Benj. A. Donald, who was for many years presiding justice of the old county court of that county. He married Sally Camm, of Amherst County, and at her death she devised Otter Burn to her sister, Mrs. Elizabeth Patteson, of Buckingham, the widow of Dr. David Patteson. It has now passed out of the family, but is well kept up.

Before the War between the States Otter Burn was one of the noted Virginia homes. It is not many miles from the Blue Ridge Mountains, with the famous Peaks of Otter in full view. The dwelling, which is situated about a mile from the public road, is an old styled four-gabled house built of brick, with broad porches running the entire length at the front and more than half way at the back, supported by double columns extending up to the eaves. This construction gives a most imposing effect. All of the rooms have large French windows opening out on the porches. The driveway in the front yard is

OTTER BURN, PATTESON, BEDFORD COUNTY

around a circle which brings the visitor up to the circular stone steps at the front porch. The front yard is covered with a great variety of trees and evergreens, and is surrounded by hedges of althea, boxwood and lilac. Adjoining the front yard is a beautiful old-fashioned flower garden, artistically divided into sections by boxwood hedges, where one could find growing in the utmost luxuriance roses, flowers and evergreens.

The old place still retains its homelike appearance of restfulness far from the interminable jangle of bells and the roar of modern town life.

OAK RIDGE

Robert Rives,[13] a native of Sussex County, Virginia, became a leading and wealthy merchant, and married, in 1790, Margaret, daughter of Colonel William Cabell, of Union Hill. From 1791 to 1803 Mr. and Mrs. Rives lived at Edgewood. In 1798 Mrs. Rives inherited from her father part of the Oak Ridge plantation, Mr. Rives later purchasing the remainder from the other heirs, and in 1801–1802 built the mansion, which he occupied

OAK RIDGE, NELSON COUNTY

until his death, in 1845. He left a large estate, including much land in Albemarle, and from ten to fifteen thousand acres in Nelson County. After Mr. Rives' death Oak Ridge was the home of his daughter Margaret Jordon Rives, who died unmarried in 1862. One of his sons was the distinguished statesman, William Cabel Rives, of Castle Hill, Albemarle County.

Oak Ridge is now the property of Mr. Thomas F. Ryan, the well-known financier, and is, with its beautiful mansion, a splendid estate. One of the greatest attractions

---

[13] Rives family: Brown, *The Cabells and Their Kin.*

of the house is the large collection of life-sized portraits of Englishmen associated with the settlement of Virginia, copied for Mr. Ryan and exhibited by him in the History Building at the Jamestown Exposition.

MASSIE HOMES IN NELSON COUNTY

LEVEL GREEN AND PHARSALIA

In Nelson County, in the neighborhood of Massie's Mills, there remained, until several years ago, three old mansions of the Massies: "Level Green," "Blue Rock" and "Pharsalia." "Level Green" has passed out of the possession of the family. "Blue Rock" was burned to the ground about ten years ago, and "Pharsalia," though having passed out of the family, is the only one which retains anything of its former beauty.

Major Thomas Massie, the founder of the Massie family in Nelson County, was born in New Kent County, August 22, 1747; was educated at William and Mary College; a captain in Revolutionary service and was promoted Major in the Northern campaigns, 1776–1779, generally on detached or particular service. At the Battle of Monmouth he delivered Washington's order of attack to General Charles Lee. He was Major, and for a time acting Colonel, of the 2d Virginia Regiment, 1778–1779; aide-de-camp to General Nelson, winter of 1790–1791 to the fall of Yorktown; after the war he received $5333\frac{1}{3}$ acres of land in the States of Ohio and Kentucky for his services as Major, etc.; and was a member of the Society of the Cincinnati. He moved from St. Peter's Parish, New Kent County, about 1780, to Frederick County, and thence to old Amherst, to property which is in the present County of Nelson, of which county he was one of the first Magistrates from 1808. He married, about 1780, Sarah Cocke. He died at "Level Green," his seat in Nelson County, February 2, 1834. His father, William Massie, who married Martha Macon, who afterwards married Colonel Theodorick Bland, was a son of Captain Thomas Massie, of St. Peter's Parish, New Kent County, who died about 1740. The Massies came from Cheshire, England.

Sarah Cocke (wife of Major Thomas Massie) was born at "Turkey Island," March 8, 1760, and died at "Level Green," April 20, 1838.

While seeking a home Major Massie visited the wild and beautiful upper valley of the Tye River, in that time in Amherst County and then almost uninhabited. Much taken with the magnificent scenery, the richness of the

PHARSALIA

rough land and its accessibility to the markets—being only twenty miles from the James (then considered a short distance)—he bought from John Rose, the original patentee, 8111 acres on the upper Tye River.

This gently rolling plateau, between 900 and 1000 feet above the sea and lying at the foot of the "Priest" Mountain, was selected by Major Massie as the site of his new home.

The first small house was completed in 1798, the larger one begun in 1799 and finished about 1803. They both face the east and overlook the little valleys of Castle Creek and Rocky Run, and, behind, the big " Priest " towers up 4084 feet above the sea.

The plan of the second and larger house is simple. The first floor was one long line, only broken by a porch covered with a large climbing rose and honeysuckle, and contained four rooms and a quaint square panelled hall. From the back of this hall a long passage extended to another large room, built originally for a dining-room. The floors in the house were of hardwood and the wooden mantels very quaint and high, those in the upper rooms almost reaching the ceiling. In the back yard were the kitchen and smoke-house. Until the place was sold the front door bore a large brass knocker in the form of an eagle with " T. M." on its breast. Back of the house was the orchard and garden and near them the old family graveyard, in which lie buried Major Massie, his wife and many of his descendants.

" Pharsalia," the residence of Hon. William Massie, the third and youngest son of Major Massie, is about two miles from " Level Green " and is situated on a spur of the " Priest " about 1000 feet above the sea. It commands a wide and extensive view of hills and mountains, those of Buckingham and Campbell melting into the horizon.

" Pharsalia " was planned by and built under the direction of Major Massie. It was commenced early in 1818 and completed in the autumn of 1814, just before the first marriage of Hon. William Massie.

The house has a long front, only relieved by the high pillared portico, with flagged floor. Mounting the broad stone steps and crossing the porch one enters the large hall. On the right is the parlor and joining it by two small entries (one each side the chimney) a guest chamber. On the left of the hall is the large dining-room and beyond it another guest chamber similar to the one on the right. Just back of the dining-room is a large pantry and from its porch a flagged walk leads to a big brick kitchen. Back of the front hall is another containing the stairway.

Every room on the ground floor has its own private outdoor entrance, a fashion necessary in those days of many servants and slaves. Over the whole of the front runs a long garret. The rear portion is, however, built higher, and contains three medium-sized bedrooms.

Mr. Massie was an exceedingly progressive and energetic man. He brought water to the yard by underground pipes from a spring higher in the mountain, and a constant flow of pure cold water gushes from a hydrant near the kitchen.

Mr. Massie was married four times: first, to Miss Sally Steptoe, of Bedford County; second, to Miss Wyatt, of Lynchburg; third, to Miss Clark, of Campbell County, and fourth, to Miss Maria C. Effinger, of Harrisonburg, Virginia. He died at " Pharsalia " and is buried at " Level Green."

Though in the mountains and out of the general track, it suffered greatly from raids during the War between the States. Fire was put under " Pharsalia " house in three places, but the cook discovered and extinguished the flames. Fortunately most of the silver was buried. Much of it remained so long buried that the exact spots were forgotten, and some of it was not unearthed until several years after the war.[14]

IONIA

Ionia, the home of Major James Watson, in the fertile and beautiful " Greenspring neighborhood," in Louisa County, was built about the year 1770. The Virginia author, Doctor George W. Bagby, while a guest at Hawkwood, the Morris home a few miles away, visited Ionia with his hostess (Mrs. R. O. Morris, Major Watson's granddaughter), leaving for future generations a charming pen-picture of this old homestead.

Says Doctor Bagby, " At Mrs. Morris's suggestion we made a hurried visit to Ionia, a gem, the cunningest old

[14] Massie family: *William and Mary Quarterly Magazine*, vol. xiii, pp. 196–203; also vol. xv, pp. 125–129.

country-house a heart could wish. Hidden away in a deep yard, filled with ancient trees, a story and a half high, it is a nest in which I could be very happy. Inside are corner cupboards and other quaint furniture, including a rare old claw-footed mahogany table and the two oldest mirrors in Virginia. At Ionia Mrs. Morris knew the roses and gladness of life. No wonder she exclaimed as we drove off:

IONIA, LOUISA COUNTY

'I would not exchange it for a palace.' Nor would I, for nowhere in all Virginia have I found so quaint and dear a house."

In 1845 Doctor George Watson, a distinguished physician of Richmond, inherited Ionia. He long made it his summer home, and at his death bequeathed it to his daughter, Mrs. Robert S. Archer, also of Richmond, who still owns it.

BRACKETT'S

Not far from Ionia is Brackett's, whose name came from an early owner of the land who, having built a small house there, sold his holdings to Major James Watson, of Ionia. Major Watson gave Brackett's to his son, Major David Watson, about 1800. The latter greatly enlarged and improved the house, for years making his home there.

David Watson was a person of note: a man of letters and very public spirited. He represented Louisa County in the Legislature and was an early member of the Board of Visitors of the University of Virginia. It is said that he walked with Jefferson, Madison and Monroe at the head of a procession at the opening of the university. His name appears among those of "the Visitors" signed to the

BRACKETT'S, LOUISA COUNTY

minutes of their meetings between the names of Jefferson and Madison.

David Watson married Sally, daughter of Garrett Minor, a person so capable as to warrant her description as a "Napoleon of a woman." She reared at Brackett's not only a large family of her own but also many orphans of her connection.

Brackett's passed from David and Sally Watson to their son Thomas, who was not unlike his father in his literary taste. He, too, made additions to the house, and, marrying his cousin Elizabeth Morris, of "Sylvania," had a number of children. At his death, however, there was but a single surviving son, and as he lost his only child, this branch of the house of Watson is destined to become extinct.

In the War between the States scions of this race covered their name with glory. David Watson was a major of artillery in the Confederate Army, and received a death wound in the Battle of Spottsylvania Court House. The Magruder brothers, five in number, entered the Confederate Army, only one of them surviving the war, and he had lost an arm. These gallant soldiers were grandsons of David and Sally Watson.

At the death of Thomas S. Watson, Brackett's was sold to Mr. H. C. Beattie, of Richmond, who sold it to Mr. Carl Nolting, the present owner.

WEST END

West End was the conception of Mrs. Susan Dabney (Morris) Watson, widow of Dr. James Watson, the eldest son of Major David and Sally (Minor) Watson. Dr. and Mrs. Watson lived at Brackett's, Major David Watson's home, during the years of their married life, while Mrs. Watson and her two children continued to reside there after her husband's death until she went to Richmond for the purpose of educating them.

West End was finished in 1840. The site of the plantation was a portion of Brackett's inherited by Dr. Watson, with additions made by purchase of adjoining land. The site was only a field when Mrs. Watson undertook the work of laying off the grounds and building the attractive home. The trees which beautify the lawn, in pleasant variety, were planted under her direction and the lawn was enclosed with an osage orange hedge. Around the house were set innumerable rose bushes and other shrubs. Mrs. Watson designed and planted a pretty flower garden and beyond that a vegetable garden in which grape vines, fruit trees, currant and gooseberry bushes and the like were effectively arranged.

Mrs. Watson, reserving the homestead and grounds for herself, divided this estate after the marriage of her daughter Mary Minor Watson to Henry Taylor, of Westmoreland County. The divisions were called East End and West End. The former was allotted Mrs. Taylor, the latter to David Watson, the only son. The condition under which Mrs. Watson gave the parts of the estate to her children was that they should furnish her with various supplies.

The War between the States came on and David Watson enlisted in the Richmond Howitzers. He was a gallant soldier and had reached the rank of major when

WEST END, LOUISA COUNTY 1840

he received a fatal wound in the Battle of Spottsylvania Court House. Suffering a great shock from his tragic death, Mrs. Watson survived him only a few years.

After David Watson's death, Mrs. Taylor went to live at East End with her mother and there most of her family of nine children were born and reared. The property still belongs to the Taylor family.

SYLVANIA

Anne Watson, or Nancy as she was called, daughter of Major James Watson, of Ionia, married William Morris, known as "Creek Billy," son of William Morris, of Taylor's Creek, Hanover County. "Creek Billy" built

Sylvania in the Greenspring neighborhood, in Louisa County, about 1790, naming it in honor of his grandfather, Sylvanus Morris.

William and Anne (Watson) Morris had many children, and their descendants are to be found in every part of the United States. Among the most notable of these are William Fontaine, James W. Page and Thomas W. Page, all three professors of the University of Virginia; United States Naval Constructor Rear Admiral D. W. Taylor, and Reverend James W. Morris, rector of Monumental Church, Richmond, Virginia.

James Morris, youngest son of William and Anne, inherited Sylvania and enlarged the house. His wife was

SYLVANIA, LOUISA COUNTY

Caroline Smith, granddaughter of Governor James Pleasants of Virginia. From them Sylvania descended to their youngest son.

"In ante-bellum days," says one who knows, "and especially during the trying war times, Sylvania was noted for its hospitality and many are the Southern soldiers who will remember pleasant times spent under its roof."

PART IV

Gloucester and the York River Country

TO ONE familiar with the history, the geography and social life of Virginia, there is a fascination about the very name of Gloucester. A near neighbor of Jamestown, Williamsburg, and Yorktown, the old county is second only to them in memories of stirring scenes and days. Settlement in

OLD WINDMILL, MATHEWS COUNTY

Gloucester and in Mathews County, which was cut off from Gloucester after Colonial times, began before the Indian Massacre of 1644, but the country north of York River, then a part of Charles River or York County, was abandoned for a time through fear of further trouble from the Indians, and the actual period of settlement began about 1646. Not long after the middle of the seventeenth century the line of settlement passed to the head of York River and gradually extended up its tributaries, including the present counties of New Kent, King William, King and Queen and Hanover, which with Gloucester and Mathews are included in this chapter.

Gloucester is bounded upon one side by the York River, while from another, broad inlets, known as the North, the Ware and the Severn Rivers, run like fingers up into the land from Mobjack Bay—an arm of the Chesapeake. Though the county is one of the oldest in Virginia, very few of its Colonial houses remain; many of them have been replaced by simple modern cottages, and others by more imposing, but still frankly modern residences. But the soil is sacred, and even the least ambitious of these homesteads nestling among beautiful old trees, upon lawns that slope down to blue waters broken now and then by the gleam of a snowy sail and ruffled on breezy days with white caps, make pictures whose charm can neither be caught by the camera nor described in words.

These rivers place the homes within easy reach of each other by sailboat or launch, and this accessibility to one another, together with remoteness from the rest of the world, has kept the characteristics of pleasant hearty "old Virginia" days alive in Gloucester, and has developed in the people a passionate loyalty to home and section.

TIMBERNECK

Upon the Gloucester shore, opposite Ringfield, an ample, rambling, old homestead gazes upon the York.

This is Timberneck, where in an earlier house the Mann family lived. Mary Mann, born at Timberneck in 1672, the only child and heiress of John Mann (1631–1694) of England and Virginia, married Mathew Page (1659–1703), son of Colonel John Page (1627–1691–2), the first of his family in Virginia, and the couple took up their abode at Timberneck. They named their only surviving son Mann, and the name has been handed down in the Page and related families ever since, so that though the family name of these Manns died out with the immigrant, as a surname, more than two hundred years ago, it has been borne as a Christian name by many descendants in every generation since.

After the Revolution the Timberneck plantation passed to the Catlett family, who built the present house and have

TIMBERNECK, GLOUCESTER COUNTY

occupied it for five generations. They are descended from Mary (1698–1703–4), wife of John Mann, by her first marriage with Edmund Berkeley, of Gloucester County. Tombs, bearing arms of John Mann and Mary, his wife, may still be seen at Timberneck.

POWHATAN'S CHIMNEY

Upon the Timberneck estate, just across Timberneck Creek, from the homestead, long stood a huge old, massively built, stone chimney. Tradition from so early a date that the memory of man runneth not to the contrary has insisted that here was the site of Werowocomoco, the favorite residence of Powhatan; that here the Princess Pocahontas saved the life of Captain John Smith, and that this chimney belonged to the house which the English colonists sent Dutchmen to Werowocomoco to build for the Indian king.

The accuracy of this tradition has been lately disputed by some writers, but the chimney was evidently of great age, and was, to say the least, a striking and interesting relic. Both Bishop Meade and the historian Campbell

POWHATAN'S CHIMNEY, TIMBERNECK CREEK

visited it and described it in their works. Campbell says: "The chimney stands on an eminence and is conspicuous from every quarter of the bay, and itself a monumental evidence of no inconsiderable import... In the early days of the annals of Virginia, Werowocomoco is second only to Jamestown in historical and romantic interest; as Jamestown was the seat of the English settlers, so Werowocomoco was the favorite residence of the Indian monarch, Powhatan." He adds, "Werowocomoco was a befitting seat of the great Chief, overlooking the bay, with its bold, picturesque, wood-crowned banks, and in view of the wide, majestic flood of the river, empurpled by transient cloud-shadows, or tinged with the rosy splendor of a summer sunset."

Bishop Meade, who carefully examined the chimney, was satisfied that it was the one built for Powhatan. He says: "The fireplace was 8 feet 4 inches wide, that is the opening to receive the wood, and 4 feet deep and more than 6 feet high, so that the tallest man might walk into it and a number of men might sit within it around the fire. I inspected the only crack which was to be seen outside of the wall, something which showed that the material was of no ordinary kind of stone, but like that of which the old church of York was built—viz., marl out of the bank, which only hardens by fire and exposure, a particular kind of marl composed of shells which abound on some of the high banks of York River.... It is impossible to say how many generations of log and frame rooms have been built to the celebrated chimney."

Massive and stout as this relic of the far past seemed, and many as had been the storms which had beat upon it and left it unharmed, it has within the past few years tumbled to the ground, but the Association for the Preservation of Virginia Antiquities has on foot plans looking toward its restoration.

ROSEWELL

Upon the left bank of York River, across Carter's Creek from Werowocomoco, stands, in a state of partial decay, Rosewell, the lordliest mansion of the time when Colonial Virginia was baronial Virginia.

Some time after the marriage of Honorable Matthew Page (1659–1703),[1] of the King's Council, to Mary Mann, of Timberneck, the couple removed to Rosewell, where

[1] Page, *The Genealogy of the Page Family.*

they lived in a simple wooden dwelling that then stood upon that plantation. In 1725 their only son, Mann Page I (1691–1730) of Rosewell, whom the combined fortunes of the Page and Mann families had made extremely rich, built the present mansion. It was constructed in the most massive style, of brick with white marble casements. There was a great square, thick-walled, high-chimneyed, central building, flanked by wings—since torn down—which formed a court and which gave the house a frontage of two hundred and thirty-two feet. The central building stands three stories above a high basement and is capped by a cupola. It contains three wide halls, nine passages, and twenty-three rooms and the wings had six rooms each. Externally Rosewell house is severely plain, but with its ample proportions and its splendid brickwork, the absence of ornament makes it the more impressive.

In striking contrast to this outside simplicity, was the interior, where, upon crossing the threshold of the main entrance, the visitor found himself at once in a great hall panelled with polished mahogany into which swept down, with generous and graceful curve, the grand stairway which eight persons could comfortably ascend abreast, and whose mahogany balustrade was carved by hand to represent baskets of fruits and flowers.

Not long did the builder of this princely Virginia castle live to enjoy it. Five years after it was begun, and before it was entirely finished, his body lay in state in the hall which he had so gorgeously adorned and the mansion designed for a pleasure house was a house of mourning. Bishop Meade, in his *Old Churches and Families,* quaintly comments upon what he conceived to be the vanity and wickedness of a man's "misspending" his fortunes upon so magnificent an abode for himself and family, and suggests that Mann Page's untimely death was direct punishment from Heaven for such folly.

The first master of Rosewell had been twice married: first to Judith (1694–1716), daughter of Honorable Ralph

ROSEWELL, GLOUCESTER COUNTY 1725

Wormeley (1650–1700) of "Rosegill," Middlesex County,[2] who is described, in Latin, upon the "Monument of grief" erected by her husband in the Rosewell burying-ground, "as a most excellent and choice lady . . . a most affectionate wife, the best of mothers and an upright mistress of her family, in whom the utmost gentleness was united with the most graceful suavity of manners and conversation."

After Mann Page's own death a splendid tomb of carved marble emblazoned with the Page arms was "piously erected to his memory by his mournfully surviving lady"—his second wife, who was Judith, daughter of Robert ("King") Carter, of Corotoman, and who was the mother of his son, Mann Page II—the heir of Rosewell.

This second Mann Page, of Rosewell, was also twice married: first to Alice Grymes,[3] and after her death to Ann Corbin Tayloe. His first wife, Alice (1724–1746), who was the daughter of Honorable John Grymes (1693–1748), of the Council, was the mother of the next master of Rosewell—John Page (1744–1808), scholar, Revolutionary patriot, member of Congress and governor of Virginia, and one of the best as well as one of the most distinguished men of his time. His contemporaries were so impressed with his lofty character and earnest piety, that it is said they wished to make him bishop of Virginia, though he had never studied for the ministry.

While a student at William and Mary College, Governor Page formed an intimacy with Thomas Jefferson, which continued throughout his life, and it was to his chum John Page, of Rosewell, that the letters of the love-lorn Jefferson were addressed, describing the hardness of heart of his fair "Belinda." Doubtless Jefferson often enjoyed the hospitality of Rosewell and tradition says that it was in the cupola on the top of the house that he drafted the

[2] Wormeley family: *Virginia Magazine of History and Biography*, vii, 283–284; viii, 179–183.

[3] Grymes family: *The Critic* (Richmond, Va.), August 18 and September 1, 1889.

Declaration of Independence, reading and discussing it with his host, before going to Philadelphia. Truly an inspiring place for the composition of a great state paper, with its wide view of sky, river and country, and if the story be true, there is something poetic in the thought that from this little observatory the author of the Declaration of Independence could descry the soon-to-be historic Nelson House at Yorktown, fifteen miles away.

In a letter from Governor Page, attending Congress in New York, to his son "Bobby," at Rosewell, the proud metropolis is thus described:

"This town is not half so large as Philadelphia, nor in any manner to be compared to it for beauty and elegance. Philadelphia I am well assured has more inhabitants than Boston and New York put together. The streets here (N. Y.) are badly paved, very dirty and narrow as well as crooked, and filled up with a strange variety of wooden, stone and brick buildings and full of hogs and mud. The College, St. Paul's Church and the Hospital are elegant buildings. The Federal Hall also, in which Congress is to sit, is elegant." He further says that all the drinking water in New York is gotten from wells—"Four carts are continually going about selling it at three gallons for a copper: that is a penny for every three gallons of water."

Governor Page died in 1808, after which time, though Rosewell was still owned by the Pages, it was very seldom occupied by them. In 1838, it was sold to one Booth, whose chief object in becoming the owner of the proud old pile seemed to be to bring humiliation upon it and to make as much money as possible out of it. The venerable cedars that formed the avenue from the door to the river were sold to make tubs. The mahogany wainscoting was stripped from the walls and sold, as also the lead that covered the roof. The carved mahogany stairway was whitewashed. Even the bricks from the graveyard wall and from the tombs themselves were converted into cash. This Booth, who had paid $12,000.00—a mere song for such an estate—for Rosewell, after making about $35,000.00 by the work of demolition, sold it for $22,000.00. It became the property of the Deans family of Gloucester, in 1855, and is now the residence of Judge Fielding Lewis Taylor and his wife, who was Miss Deans.

SHELLY

Shelly plantation, adjoining Rosewell and originally a part of it, is still owned by the Pages. Its pretty and unique name was suggested by the great bed of oyster-shells upon its shore, which, says Bishop Meade, " indicate it to have been a great place of resort among the natives." Shelly was long believed to have been the site of Powhatan's residence, Werowocomoco.

CARTER'S CREEK

About two miles above Rosewell, upon Carter's Creek, stood until a few years ago, when it was, unhappily, destroyed by fire, the early seat of the Burwell family [4] of Virginia. Its original name was Fairfield, but it was later called after the stream that washed its shores, and as Carter's Creek it was longest known.

Architecturally, Carter's Creek House was unique among Virginia mansions. Instead of the eighteenth century type which, though with many variations, was almost universal among brick dwellings in the colony, it followed the fashion of an earlier date and resembled the smaller English manor houses of the sixteenth or seventeenth century. It consisted of a main building with a wing extending back at right angles at each end. One of these wings was burned, or torn away, long ago, though its foundation can still be traced; the other contained a very large room known traditionally as " the ball room."

There was a spacious basement whose ceiling was supported by heavy brick arches. In the middle of this basement, entirely detached from the outer walls, was a small, thick-walled room, something like a modern bank vault,

[4] Burwell family: *William and Mary Quarterly*, vii, p. 44 *et seq.*

which was doubtless used as a safe for valuables. How handsomely some of the rooms in the house had been finished was shown by fragments of marble mantels found in the basement when the deserted old house was in a state of decay. The small windows and clustered chimneys were unlike those in most houses to be seen in Colonial Virginia and contributed largely to the extremely quaint appearance of the house.

Carter's Creek was undoubtedly the oldest looking, though not the oldest mansion in Virginia. Upon one of its gables was in iron figures the date 1692 and, also in iron, the letters L. A. B.—the initials of Lewis and Abigail Burwell. In the year 1648, Lewis Burwell, first of his family in Virginia, patented 2350 acres on the south side of Rosewell Creek, as Carter's Creek was then called. His wife, Lucy, was, according to her epitaph, " the only child of the valiant Captain Robert Higginson, one of the first commanders that subdued the country of Virginia from the power of the heathen."

From this couple, the Carter's Creek plantation descended to their son Lewis (died 1710), who upon his marriage with Abigail Smith (1656–1692), niece and heiress of President Nathaniel Bacon,[5] acquired a great estate in York County, upon which he seems to have lived most of the time, though he probably built the Carter's Creek mansion.

That he was a prominent as well as a rich man is proved by the fact that he was a member of the Council of State. From him Carter's Creek passed to his son, Nathaniel Burwell, who married Elizabeth, daughter of Robert (" King ") Carter, and was the father of Lewis Burwell (1710–1752), third of the name, who was president of the Council and acting governor of Virginia, and was the next heir of the Carter's Creek estate.

President Lewis Burwell was educated at Cambridge,

[5] For an account of the Smiths and Bacons see *Virginia Magazine of History and Biography*, ii, 125–129.

CARTER'S CREEK (FAIRFIELD), GLOUCESTER COUNTY 1692

GREEN PLAINS, MATHEWS COUNTY

and was noted for his learning. His daughter, Rebecca, was one of the belles and beauties of the day, and her charms drew many suitors to Carter's Creek. Thomas Jefferson and Jacqueline Ambler (1742–1798) were desperately in love with her during their college days at William and Mary, and, in spite of Jefferson's ardent wooing, she finally gave her hand to Ambler. Jefferson fantastically called her " Belinda," and by this name refers to her in his letters to John Page. In one of these letters he says: " In the most melancholy fit that ever any poor soul was, I sit down to write to you. Last night, as merry as agreeable company and dancing with Belinda in the Apollo could make me, I never could have thought the succeeding sun would have seen me so wretched as I now am. I was prepared to say a great deal. I had dressed up in my own mind such thoughts as occurred to me in as moving language as ever I knew how, and expected to have performed in a tolerably creditable manner." But he adds, " When I had an opportunity of venting them a few broken sentences uttered in great disorder, and interrupted with pauses of uncommon length, were the too visible marks of my strange confusion."

In another letter to Page, he says, " If Belinda will not accept my services they shall never be offered to another." However, after events prove that he " got over it."

As Mrs. Jacqueline Ambler, the fair Rebecca Burwell, of Carter's Creek, made a charming matron and passed many of her graces on to a bevy of attractive daughters who married prominent men of their day. One of them, Mary Willis Ambler (1766–1831), became the wife of the brilliant young lawyer who was later to win national fame as Chief Justice John Marshall.

President Lewis Burwell's son Lewis, the next master of Carter's Creek, was educated in England at Eton and the Inns of Court, in spite of which he espoused the cause of American Independence in the struggle which began soon after his return to Virginia, and was a zealous member of the Revolutionary Conventions. He married Judith, daughter of Mann Page II, and has many descendants.

In the time of the sons of this Lewis Burwell IV and last, of Carter's Creek, the estate passed from the family that had so long held it and for many years before its destruction was in a state of ruin.

Not far from Carter's Creek House, in the Burwell family burying-ground, was one of the most remarkable collections of tombs in Virginia, one of them dating as early as 1654. After the house was burned it became evident that steps must be taken to preserve these from total destruction. They were already in a sadly dilapidated state, but in 1912, through the efforts of Mrs. Sally Nelson Robins, assisted by members of the Burwell connection, monuments and remains of those to whom they were erected were removed to Abingdon Churchyard, where now this beautiful and impressive group of tombs, rebuilt and restored, may be seen.

ISLEHAM

One of the loveliest of Gloucester's lovely rivers is the North, along each bank of which homesteads lie close upon one another, suggesting the street of a rural Venice.

The first plantation to be passed upon entering this river is Isleham, in what is now Mathews County, the seat of Sir John Peyton (circa 1720–1790), one of the few baronets who made his home in Colonial Virginia.[6] Sir John was an officer in the Gloucester militia during the Revolutionary War and was devoted to the cause of American Independence.

The old house at Isleham has long since disappeared.

GREEN PLAINS

A little farther on, the beautiful Green Plains lawn, cool with the shade of century-old elms, slopes down to the river. The architecture of the mansion is Colonial,

[6] An account of Sir John Peyton and his descendants is given in Hayden, *Virginia Genealogies*, pp. 475–479.

though it dates only to 1802, and its wide halls and spacious rooms, with their high carved mantels and deep window-seats, make it as charming within as without. It was built by James H. Roy, who had married, a few years before, Elizabeth, daughter of George Booth, of Belleville, on the opposite side, and a little farther up the river.

Mr. Roy was the son of Mungo Roy, of Locust Grove, Caroline County, whose father, Dr. Mungo Roy, of Scotland, was the first of the Roy family to settle in Virginia. He represented Mathews County in the House of Delegates in 1818–1819. He was succeeded as master of Green Plains by his son, William Henry Roy, who also represented Mathews County in the Legislature in 1832–1834, and who was twice married: first, to Anne, daughter of Thomas Seddon, of Fredericksburg, and, after her death, to Euphan, daughter of John Macrae, of Park Gate, Prince William County. By his first marriage Mr. Roy was the father of Mrs. John C. Rutherfoord, of Rock Castle, and Mrs Thomas H. Carter, of Pampatike; and by his second, of Mrs. Washington and Mrs. Goldsborough, of Maryland, and Mrs. H. McKendree Boyd, the present mistress of Green Plains.

POPLAR GROVE

Poplar Grove also lies in that part of old Gloucester County which now bears the name of Mathews. It was built over a century ago by Mr. John Patterson,[7] who was an Englishman by birth, but who, during the Revolution, warmly espoused the cause of American freedom. When he planned his house, feeling between the Whig and Tory parties ran high and he beautified the grounds with numbers of Lombardy poplars, the party symbol of the Whigs, and gave the place the name of Poplar Grove.

This charming old homestead was a noted social centre during the time of Mr. Patterson and of his daughters, Mrs. Thomas Robinson Yeatman, of Isleham, and Mrs.

---

[7] Patterson family: *William and Mary Quarterly*, xiii, 174–175.

Christopher Tompkins. Here was born and grew to womanhood the famous "Captain" Sally Tompkins, one of the most beloved and widely known of Virginia's daugh-

POPLAR GROVE, MATHEWS COUNTY

TIDE MILL AT POPLAR GROVE

ters. During the War between the States she devoted her fortune, her time and her strength to nursing the sick and wounded soldiers at the hospitals in the Capital of the Confederacy, and in order that she might go and come with greater freedom and have the authority to order supplies as she needed them for her work, General Lee made her a regularly commissioned captain.

Poplar Grove was long the residence of Judge G. Taylor Garnett.

DITCHLEY

Just opposite Green Plains is Ditchley, built by Dr. J. Prosser Tabb, to succeed an earlier house—the homestead of the Singleton family. Mrs. Tabb was related to the Lees and named her home after the Ditchley owned by them in Northumberland County.

Ditchley is now the residence of Mr. William Ashby Jones.

AUBURN, MATHEWS COUNTY

AUBURN

Next above and adjoining Green Plains, Auburn looks out upon the river from a setting of grassy lawn and spreading elm. It was long one of the homesteads of the Tabb family so numerous and well known in this section, and was built during the last century by Mr. Philip Tabb, of Toddsbury, for his son, Dr. Henry Tabb.

Auburn is now the home of Mr. Charles Heath.

BELLEVILLE

Across the river from Auburn is Belleville, the ancient seat of the Booths, formerly a prominent family of the

BELLEVILLE, GLOUCESTER COUNTY

county, and passing from them to their descendants, the Taliaferros. The house was built by Thomas Booth before the Revolution, but it has been remodelled and enlarged by its present owner, Mr. A. A. Blow. He added a pillared portico.

Some of the old Booth tombs, bearing arms, still remain in the family burying-ground.

DUNHAM MASSIE

Fannie Booth, heiress of Belleville, gave her hand to Warner Taliaferro, and was the mother of the gallant Major General William Booth Taliaferro, of the Confederate Army. Upon General Taliaferro's marriage, his father built for him the attractive home, but a short distance away, which he named Dunham Massie after the ancient seat of his ancestors, the Booths, in England, and which also looks under the boughs of the old trees that shade and shelter it, upon North River.

From the close of the War between the States until General Taliaferro's death, at a good old age, no guest

DUNHAM MASSIE, NORTH RIVER, GLOUCESTER COUNTY

ever crossed the hospitable Dunham Massie threshold but must needs pass under the stars and bars of the "conquered banner," which always hung in the hall just over the front door.

CHURCH HILL

Somewhat back from North River, upon the road to Gloucester Court House and near old Ware Church, stands still another Taliaferro homestead—quaint Church Hill, a relic of early Colonial days. This was the original seat of the Throckmortons,[8] but passed to the Taliaferros by the

[8] Throckmorton family: *William and Mary Quarterly*, ii, 241–247; iii, 46–52, 192–195, 240–242; iv, 128–129; v, 54–55; *Virginia Magazine of History and Biography*, viii, 83–89, 309–312; ix, 192–194.

marriage of Dr. William Taliaferro with two daughters and co-heiresses of the house of Throckmorton.

The Throckmortons, descended from the old family of Throckmorton, of Hail-Weston, Huntingdonshire, England, were long prominent in the social and political life of Gloucester. Their name is now extinct there, though numerously represented in other parts of the country.

Church Hill is now the property of Judge James Lyons Taliaferro. Only one wing of the original house remains.

ELMINGTON

Returning to North River, we find, just above Dunham Massie, Elmington, one of the choicest estates in the old county. The mansion looks upon the river from a setting

ELMINGTON, NORTH RIVER, GLOUCESTER COUNTY

of lovely grounds and within there are spacious rooms and hall, and a wide stairway winding to an upper story capped by an observatory.

During the Colonial period, the Elmington plantation

was the home of the Whiting family, long prominent in Virginia as members of " his Majesty's Council " and of the House of Burgesses and Conventions. The present house was built by Dr. Prosser Tabb.

Elmington has some literary associations. Soon after the War between the States, a Mr. Talbot, who is said to have bought it from the Tabbs for Confederate money, sold it to Colonel George Wythe Munford, author of that quaint and entertaining book, *The Two Parsons;* later Mr. Virginius Dabney made it the scene of his novel *Don Miff,* which was one of the " best sellers " of the year in which it was issued. Later still it was the home of the widely read and discussed novelist, Thomas Dixon, who added a pillared portico to the mansion.

THE EXCHANGE, NORTH RIVER, GLOUCESTER COUNTY

THE EXCHANGE

Adjoining Elmington is The Exchange, the homestead of Dr. Dabney, a distinguished physician of his day. It is now owned and occupied by his descendants, the Misses Dabney, whose mother was a Miss Tabb, of Toddsbury.

ICE-HOUSE AT EXCHANGE

TODDSBURY

Next above The Exchange is Toddsbury, one of the most charming as well as one of the oldest houses in Gloucester. On North River and standing close to the water's edge, amid splendid trees, the homestead, with its gambrel roof, quaint porch-chamber, and other evidences of antiquity, makes a delightful picture. The interior is fully as interesting, with its panelled rooms and arched and deeply recessed windows. Between these windows and the high wainscoted mantels are little cupboards which suggest hidden mysteries and excite the curiosity to a pleasurable degree.

The house was probably built by Thomas Todd,[9] a wealthy merchant and planter, who married Anne

[9] Todd family: *Virginia Magazine of History and Biography*, iii, 79–83. An interesting chart of the English ancestry of Ann Gorsuch, wife of Thomas Todd I, is given *Ibid.*, xvii, 292–293.

TODDSBURY, NORTH RIVER (FRONT), GLOUCESTER COUNTY

TODDSBURY (REAR)

Gorsuch, a niece of the poet Richard Lovelace, and died in 1676. With his great-grandson, Thomas Todd, of Toddsbury, the male line of his branch of the family became extinct and Toddsbury passed to his grandson's nephew, Philip Tabb, who was succeeded by his son, Thomas Todd Tabb, who died in 1835. Later the estate passed from the Tabb family, and is now the residence of the Motts.

The Toddsbury graveyard, where a wonderful old willow keeps guard over the last resting place of numerous Todds and Tabbs and their kindred, is second only to the homestead in interest.[10] It contains more tombstones, perhaps, than any other family burying-ground in Virginia. One of these dates from as early as the year 1703 and one older still is so worn that it is impossible to decipher its inscription.

NEWSTEAD

Upon part of the old Toddsbury estate is Newstead, built in 1856 by John H. Tabb and now the home of the Misses Tabb.

WAVERLY

Next above Newstead is Waverly, a commodious mansion built by Mr. Philip Tabb, of Toddsbury, for his son Edward, at about the time he built Auburn, farther down the river, for his son Dr. Harry Tabb.

Waverly is now the residence of Mrs. Gerard Hopkins.

MIDLOTHIAN

Near the head of North River stands quaint Midlothian, with its steep roof and dormer windows, built by Mr. Josiah Deans a century and a quarter ago. It is now the home of the Davidsons.

---

[10] The inscriptions on the tombstones at Toddsbury are published in *William and Mary Quarterly*, iii, 115 *et seq.*

WHITE MARSH

Inland, but in the midst of ample and picturesque grounds lies fair White Marsh. During the Colonial period a branch of the well-known Whiting family owned this plantation, occupying an earlier homestead. After the Revolution it became the property of the distinguished lawyer Thomas Reade Rootes (1764/5–1824), and at his death, in 1824, passed to his widow (who was his second wife), who had been a Mrs. Prosser, and who left it to her

WHITE MARSH, GLOUCESTER COUNTY

daughter by her first marriage, Evelina Matilda Prosser. Miss Prosser gave her hand and her fortune to John Tabb, son of Philip Tabb, of Toddsbury, who with his wife's estate added to his own became the wealthiest man in Gloucester County.

Mrs. Tabb made at White Marsh a terraced garden, which became famous. Among its unique and beautiful features were arbor-vitae trees planted and trimmed to form summer houses with running roses climbing over them. Mr. and Mrs. Tabb's son Philip was the next master of White Marsh, while their son John fell heir to Elmington, on North River.

Since it passed from the Tabbs White Marsh has had several owners, one of whom, among other changes, gave the mansion a pillared portico.

GOSHEN

Crossing from the North to the Ware River region, we find ourselves at Goshen, a comfortable looking homestead in a pleasant yard, with a beautiful water view. Within, the high mantels and other quaint details give the big square rooms an interesting air and bear witness to a good old age.

Goshen was the original seat of the well-known Tompkins family, of which "Captain Sally Tompkins" is a member, but it is now and has been for a long time the home of the Perrins.

GLENROY

Just opposite Goshen, Ware River circles almost around the grounds of the Glenroy estate, making it a peninsula, and giving it an unusually picturesque site. Tradition says that upon this spot stood the earliest Colonial church in Gloucester County, and the story gains color from the fact that upon opposite sides of the lane leading into the place are two fields known as far back as any one can remember as "the Church field" and "the glebe field," and in "the church field" some ancient tombs may still be seen. In view of this tradition it seems most fitting that the Glenroy plantation should have been the home of a rector of the two remaining Colonial churches of the county, Reverend Armistead Smith, a descendant of the old Smith family of Gloucester, and of Honorable John Armistead of the Colonial Council. He married Martha Tabb, of Seaford, Mathews County, the earliest seat of the Tabb family in this region, and brought her to the old-fashioned homestead that stood upon this river-girt plantation. The house with all the sweet associations that cluster about the rectory of a Virginia country parish was destroyed by fire about half a century ago, and their son and heir, Mr. William Patterson Smith, built the goodly mansion which now stands upon the Glenroy lawn among the spreading elms and towering poplars.

GLENROY, WARE RIVER

Mr. William Patterson Smith married Marian, one of the beauties of the well-known Virginia family of Seddon, and under their rule the new Glenroy kept up the best traditions of the old.

Glenroy is now the residence of Dr. W. R. Jaeger.

WHITE HALL

A short distance higher up, and across the river from "Glenroy," we find a Colonial mansion charmingly embowered in the foliage of ancient trees. This is White Hall, for many years before the Revolution the seat of the Willis family, prominent in Virginia in both social and public life.[11] For several generations past it has been owned and occupied by a branch of the Byrd family, descended from the Westover Byrds, and is at present the home of Captain Richard C. Byrd.

The tomb of the wife of one of the Willises of White

WHITE HALL, WARE RIVER

Hall, bearing her arms impaled with those of her husband, may be seen at old Ware Church, a few miles away.

HOCKLEY

Hockley, a spacious house in attractive grounds, was formerly the home of Colonel Alexander Taliaferro. It is now owned and occupied by Mr. R. P. Taliaferro.

In early times the plantation bore the name of Cowslip Green.

---

[11] Willis, *A Sketch of the Willis Family of Virginia and Their Kindred.* Richmond: Whittet & Shepperson (1900); *William and Mary Quarterly*, v, 24–27, 171–176; vi, 27–29, 206–214.

LOWLAND COTTAGE

Lowland Cottage nestling among venerable trees is one of the oldest homesteads on Ware River, and indeed in the county. It was an early seat of the Gloucester families of Warner, Throckmorton and Jones and is now the home of Major Thomas S. Taliaferro, a gallant officer of the Confederate Army.

AIRVILLE

Airville, a pleasant, roomy old house, commanding a fine view not only of the Ware River, but of Mobjack Bay beyond, was in the early days the seat of the Dixon

AIRVILLE, GLOUCESTER COUNTY

family, descended from the Reverend John Dixon, a Colonial minister.[12] Later it passed to the possession of Major Thomas Smith, and is now the home of Messrs. Thomas G. and Walter C. Harwood.

Nearby, in the graveyard on the Mount Pleasant estate, where traces of a house are still to be seen, are some Dixon tombs.

[12] Dixon family: *William and Mary Quarterly*, x, pp. 272-273.

THE SHELTER

Modest, but exceedingly interesting is The Shelter, with its gambrel-roofed, L-shaped wing and towering, outside chimneys.

In this quaint dwelling, Miss Mollie Elliott Seawell, the distinguished authoress, was born and grew to womanhood. It is now the home of her brother, Mr. J. Hairston Seawell.

WARNER HALL

One of the most famous homes in Gloucester County and in Virginia was Warner Hall, on the banks of the Severn—the old seat of the Warner, Lewis and Clark families [13]—built in 1674. After its almost complete destruction by fire, in 1849, it long lay in ruins, but it has since been restored by Mr. Maynard A. Cheney, and once more the extensive and beautiful grounds of the old plantation are graced by a spacious and handsome mansion.

A son of Mr. Colin Clark, last owner of the original Warner Hall, described the house as " a brick building of three stories and a basement, and together with a two-room addition (and the basement) included eighteen rooms. There were also on either side of the main house two detached brick houses of six and five rooms respectively, used for kitchen, laundry, servants' room, etc." Some time before Mr. Clark's purchase, the five-room house was united with the main building by a two-room addition, so that the whole of the mansion contained twenty-five rooms, and had a front of about 130 feet. First, in 1841, the five-room house was destroyed by fire, and in 1849 the central

---

[13] The Warners are treated in Robinson, *Some Notable Families of America*, and in various notes in *Virginia Magazine of History and Biography* and *William and Mary Quarterly;* for Lewis family see *William and Mary Quarterly*, ix, 191–192, 250–265; x, 48; xi, 39–47; for the Clarks who lived at " Warner's Hall " see Goode, *Virginia Cousins*, pp. 229–373 *et seq*.

part of the mansion burned down, leaving only the six-room wing standing. The second fire, we are told, originated " in the desire of a negro boy to have the family remove from the country to Norfolk, whose joys he had tasted on trips with his young masters."

The Warner Hall estate was patented about the middle of the seventeenth century by Augustine Warner, Senior (1610–1674), long a member of his Majesty's Council and a man who was to have a unique place in Virginia family history, for both George Washington and Robert E. Lee were descended from him. Upon his death, in 1674, Warner Hall passed to his son, Augustine Warner, Jr. (1642–1681), speaker of the House of Burgesses in the famous " reforming " assembly during Bacon's Rebellion, in 1676, and also a member of the Council.

WARNER HALL ON THE SEVERN, GLOUCESTER COUNTY

After the burning of Jamestown when " the prosperous Rebel " went into Gloucester County he made Warner Hall his headquarters for a time, and it was from there that he sent out notices for the people to assemble to take the oath of fidelity to him.

Augustine Warner, Jr., died in 1681, leaving several sons, who died in youth, and three daughters: Mary, who became the wife of John Smith of Purton, Gloucester;

Mildred, who married, first, Lawrence Washington, of Westmoreland (grandfather of General Washington), and, secondly, George Gale; and Elizabeth, the heiress of "Warner Hall," who became the wife of John Lewis, of Gloucester. Lewis, therefore, became master of this estate and was a prominent man in the County and Colony and a member of his Majesty's Council, as was also his son and heir, John Lewis, Jr. (1702–1754).

Warner Hall remained in the possession of the Lewises for generations, sending out in the meantime branches of the family throughout the United States. It was in the last century that the estate was bought by Mr. Colin Clark, who preserved the fame for hospitality that it had always enjoyed, up to the time of its deplorable destruction.

Not far from the restored mansion may be seen the old graveyard containing the ancient tombs of the Warners, Lewises and others. Some of these date from the seventeenth century.

SHERWOOD, GLOUCESTER COUNTY

SHERWOOD

Ample grounds, a fine river view and piazzas of generous proportions make Sherwood, the roof-tree of the

Seldens [14] and Dimmocks, descended from the Lewises of Warner Hall, an ideal country home. Among the charms of the place are the ten-acre lawn, shaded by elms, maples, magnolias, tulip poplars, pecan and other trees, and the old garden equally well furnished with sweet and beautiful flowers and interesting shrubs.

It is now the home of Mr. and Mrs. H. A. Williams.

LEVEL GREEN

Also on the Ware is Level Green, which in the past was long the home of the Robins family,[15] a plantation noted in the political annals of Gloucester as the place where Henry Clay landed during a famous campaign.

EAGLE POINT, GLOUCESTER COUNTY

EAGLE POINT

John Randolph Bryan, who was a namesake of John Randolph of Roanoke and was educated under his care,

[14] Selden family (Sherwood branch): *William and Mary Quarterly*, v, 60–62, 264–267.

[15] Robins family: *Virginia Magazine of History and Biography*, ii, 187–189, 316–317.

married Randolph's greatly beloved niece, Elizabeth Tucker Coalter. This couple made Eagle Point, on the Severn, one of the most noted homes in Gloucester from 1830 until 1862, when it was broken up by the war, and the estate passed out of the Bryan family. It was bought back by the late Mr. Joseph Bryan, of Laburnum, Henrico County, and by him the house was greatly enlarged and beautified and its reputation for genuine old Virginia hospitality re-established.

Full of poetic as well as of antiquarian interest, is the family graveyard, uniquely situated upon a pine-shaded islet in the river, not far from the house.

SEVERNBY

Upon what was once a part of the Eagle Point plantation, Mr. Alfred W. Withers has built Severnby, a delightful home overlooking the river.

LANSDOWNE

Also on the Severn is Lansdowne, the old home of the Thrustons [16] (who still own it), a family resident in Gloucester for many generations.

HESSE

In a remote situation upon the Pianketank, a stream that separates the counties of Gloucester and Middlesex, stands, solitary and alone, Hesse, one of the most venerable brick mansions in Virginia. The Armisteads, who built and long owned it, were among the earliest settlers in Gloucester and were prominent in private and public life during the Colonial period. For many generations "Armistead of Hesse" was as well known as a family designation in Virginia, as "Harrison of Brandon" or

[16] Thruston family: *William and Mary Quarterly*, iv, 31–33, 97–102, 164–171, 226–234; vii, 17–24, 181–186.

"Carter of Shirley." The estate passed out of the Armistead family something like a century ago, and their name, though numerous elsewhere, is not now to be found in the county which was so long their home, but large numbers of persons scattered through the country trace their ancestry to ancient Hesse. A portion of the original mansion was long ago torn down.

HESSE, GLOUCESTER COUNTY

Honorable John Armistead, of Hesse (son of William Armistead, the emigrant), was a member of "his Majesty's Council" in the latter part of the seventeenth century.[17] He was succeeded as master of the estate by his son Henry, who won as his bride, over all other suitors, the fascinating Martha Burwell, daughter of Honorable Lewis Burwell, the young lady with whom Governor Sir Francis Nicholson was so much in love that he vowed that should she marry

[17] Armistead family: *William and Mary Quarterly*, vi, 31–33; 97–102, 164–171, 226–234; vii, 17–24, 181–186.

anyone but himself, he would kill three persons—the bridegroom, the clerk granting the license and the clergyman performing the ceremony. The threat was not carried out, however, for as far as is known, the fair Martha and the husband of her choice, Henry Armistead, " lived happily ever after " at Hesse. One of their daughters, Lucy, married " Secretary " Thomas Nelson (1716–1782), son of Thomas Nelson, the emigrant, and another, Martha, became the wife of Dudley Digges, member of the first Executive Council of the State of Virginia.

Henry Armistead was succeeded as master of Hesse by his son William, who married Mary, daughter of Honorable James Bowles of Maryland, a lady of large fortune, and died about 1755, leaving a son and heir, a second William Armistead, of Hesse, who married, in 1765, Maria, daughter of Charles Carter, of Cleve, by his second wife Anne, daughter of Honorable William Byrd II, of Westover. From letters which have been preserved, written to Mrs. Maria Carter Armistead, or " Molly," as she was familiarly called, she seems to have been a favorite with her friends and family. One of these written by her uncle, William Byrd, 3d, of Westover, upon hearing of her engagement to William Armistead, is as follows:

" My Dear Niece:

I was in great Hopes, as well as your Aunt and Grandmamma, that you would have given us the Pleasure of your Company at Westover e'er now, & should have rejoiced in an Opportunity of convincing you of my Affection. Report informs us you are going to be married very soon; I wish it had been agreeable to you to have given some of your Friends here Notice of it, because we think ourselves interested in your Happiness; for my part I shall always be glad to contribute to it. Mr. Armistead is a young gentleman entirely acceptable to us, & we sincerely wish you both Blessing of the married State. Be pleased my Dear Molly to present my best Compliments to him, & accept yourself of our Love and tender Friendship. I & the rest of your Relations here beg the Favor of you & Mr. Armistead to spend your Christmas at Westover, where many young People are to make merry; & give our Love to your Sisters & bring them with you. Our Coach shall attend you any where at any time.

I ever am
My Dear Niece
Your most affe.
Uncle

WESTOVER Nov: 25th. 1765. W. BYRD."

The only surviving son of William and Maria Carter Armistead was Charles Byrd Armistead, who inherited Hesse, but some time after his death, in 1797, leaving no descendants, the estate, which contained 3879 acres, passed from the Armistead family.

GLOUCESTER CHURCHES

"The history of Gloucester," says Sally Nelson Robins, in her charming sketch of the old county, "is woven in the registers of its Colonial churches. Names faded on the old roll wear a fresher lustre on the parish books of to-day. Where the fathers worshipped the sons still kneel."

The earliest parishes in Gloucester were Petsworth and Kingston, the latter in what is now known as Mathews County. As long ago as 1861 it was written of the former, "Petsworth exists only on paper: its church and worshippers have alike ceased to be." The existence "on paper" as seen in the tattered vestry book is interesting as showing how well cared for was the ancient temple. Under date 1684 we read, "His Excellency the Governor having given to the church one large Bible, one book of Common Prayer, one book of Homilies, the Thirty-nine Articles, and books of Canons of the Church of England, it is ordered that the clerk of the vestry enter the same in the register, to the end His Lordship's so pious a gift may be gratefully remembered." In the same year it was "Ordered that the clerk enter into the register of this parish the generous and pious gift of the Honorable Augustine Warner, deceased, to this church, viz., one silver flagon which though long since given hath not yet been entered." In 1735, "there were great subscriptions made by the present vestry for an organ, to be purchased for the use of the church at Petsworth," also, it was directed that seven hundred gold leaves be ordered for the use of the painter. In 1751 the vestry ordered from England a "pulpit and table cloth and cushion," at cost of £154. 16. 6 current money. The cloth was to be of "crimson velvet with a gold fringe and lace." The rear wall of the chancel rejoiced in an elaborate fresco representing a crimson cur-

WARE CHURCH, GLOUCESTER COUNTY

tain drawn back to reveal an angel with a trumpet in his hand, standing amidst rolling clouds, from which the faces of other angels looked.

Though the glory of old Petsworth, or "Poplar Spring" church, as it was sometimes called, has long since departed, Gloucester still possesses two well preserved and comely Colonial houses of worship—Abington and Ware—where the great-grandchildren of those that sleep in the tombs outside repeat upon Sundays the old liturgy of the early days. Ware church was built in 1693, upon land granted to the parish by the Throckmorton family. A brick in the older part of Abington bears the date 1660, while upon the arch of the door appear the figures 1765. Upon the

ABINGTON CHURCH, GLOUCESTER COUNTY

outer wall of Ware is the tombstone of the Reverend James Black, a native of England and for many years rector of Ware parish, who died in 1723. For the sake of comfort and convenience the interiors of both churches were long since modernized, but Mrs. Robins tells us that as late as 1867 " the flagstones of old Abington echoed the crisp foot-tread of the worshipper. The pews were square, with seats all around, and stiff carpet-covered footstools stood beneath, on which prim children sat and often munched Shrewsbury cakes, drawn from their Mothers' reticule." She adds, " I have heard that excessive wriggling was sometimes summarily checked by a tap from a heelless slipper."

GLOUCESTER COURT HOUSE

In Virginia the court house has always been the business and political centre of the county. In Gloucester as in most other counties the county seat contains a few old dwellings, brick and frame, one or more inns, or taverns as they were generally termed in Virginia, and, of course, the county court house with its appurtenances.

TAVERN AT GLOUCESTER COURT HOUSE

ST. PETER'S CHURCH, NEW KENT

The Pamunkey and Mattapony Rivers joining, form the York. At the meeting point, above old York and Gloucester Counties, lie the newer counties of New Kent (south of the Pamunkey), King William (between Pamunkey and Mattapony), and King and Queen, north of Mattapony and bordering on still another series of counties, those along the Rappahannock.

The tide of emigration entering York River at its mouth flowed up each side of it and spread out along the banks of both the Pamunkey and the Mattapony. In 1654, New Kent, which may be called one of the second generation of Virginia Counties, was formed. It then included the present King and Queen and King William Counties. At a later period, as the settlements went inland, Hanover was formed from King William and King and

Queen, and the stream of emigration coming up from York River mingled, above tide-water, with that which had ascended the James.

The most notable building now to be seen in New Kent County is old St. Peter's Church,[18] within whose walls tradition long persisted General Washington and Martha Custis were married. It is now believed that this interesting wedding was a home affair, taking place at the Custis

ST. PETER'S CHURCH, NEW KENT COUNTY

homestead, the White House, not far away; and St. Peter's is often spoken of as "the church in which Washington was not married."

The church, all but its steeple, which was added later, was built in 1703, at a cost of one hundred and forty-six

[18] *The Parish Register of Saint Peter's, New Kent County, Va.*, and *The Vestry Book of Saint Peter's, New Kent*, were published in Richmond, Virginia, in 1904 and 1905 respectively, by the National Society of the Colonial Dames of America in the State of Virginia.

thousand weight of tobacco. The parish, however, had been in existence some years before. One of its earliest ministers was the Reverend Nicholas Moreau, a Huguenot, who seems to have been a man of deep piety, and so were some others, but the parish was not always so fortunate.

Ministers and laymen expressed themselves forcefully in those days. Pious Parson Moreau wished to have a bishop in Virginia, and, in one of his letters to the Bishop of London, says, " An Eminent Bishop being sent over here will make Hell tremble and settle the Church of England forever." He describes the New Kent fold as " the very worst parish in Virginia and most troublesome," but adds, " God has blessed my endeavors so far already that with his assistance I have brought again to church two families who had gone to Quaker's meeting for three years past."

Reverend David Mossom, who came to Virginia from Massachusetts, and was rector of the parish for forty years, was hardly ideal, but by way of apology for him, Bishop Meade feelingly informs us that he " was married four times, and much harassed by his last wife." Contemporary accounts hint of outbursts of temper on the part of this much-married and much-harassed parson, especially of a quarrel with the clerk of the parish, which was carried so far that one Sunday Mr. Mossom assailed the clerk from the pulpit, threatening to give him a beating, after which the clerk struck back by lining out from his desk the psalm containing the following:

" With restless and ungoverned rage
Why do the heathen storm?
Why in such rash attempts engage
As they can ne'er perform? "

CEDAR GROVE

An interesting New Kent homestead is Cedar Grove, an old roof-tree of the Christian family. Here President

John Tyler was married to his first wife, Letitia, daughter of Robert Christian.

CEDAR GROVE, NEW KENT COUNTY

PROVIDENCE FORGE

The chief interest of the Providence Forge estate is that, as its name suggests, it was the site of Colonial iron-works. It first appears upon record as the property of the Reverend Charles Jeffrey Smith, A.M., a Presbyterian minister from Long Island, who died about 1770. His partner was William Holt, of Williamsburg. At the time of Mr. Smith's death there was a " well-built forge " on the place. Mr. Smith's lands were purchased by Francis Jerdone (1720–1771),[19] a Scotchman, who had acquired a large estate at Yorktown, but who, in 1753, had removed to Louisa County. He died in 1771, and in the *Virginia Gazette* is spoken of as " an eminent merchant, who had acquired a handsome fortune with the fairest reputation."

The estate remained long in the possession of his descendants.

[19] Jerdone: *William and Mary Quarterly*, xi, p. 153 *et seq.*; xii, 32.

Old account books mention bar iron, broad hoes and grubbing hoes as the articles manufactured at Providence

PROVIDENCE FORGE, NEW KENT COUNTY

Forge. There are still some signs of the old forge at the place and there is a deep canal, no doubt cut before the Revolution, for the purpose of the work started by Reverend Mr. Smith and Mr. Holt.

The comfortable old dormer-windowed, frame dwelling, on the estate, still in excellent repair, stands close to the tracks at Providence Forge Station, on the Chesapeake and Ohio Railway.

HAMPSTEAD

The handsomest house in New Kent County is stately Hampstead, long the home of the Webb family. These Webbs were prominent in Virginia from the early eighteenth century. Some of them were members of the House of Burgesses. One of them, George Webb, was treasurer of Virginia during the Revolution and for some time afterward, and other representatives of the name have been distinguished in the United States and Confederate States Navies.

Hampstead was built by Conrad Webb, in 1820, as

the date in gilt figures upon the cornice proclaims. It stands upon the top of a high hill overlooking lovely grounds and gardens, and a wide sweep of country. The front and rear entrances of the mansion are alike. In front the white marble steps descend to a box-hedged walk, from which a circular carriage drive sweeps around a central plot, with a sun-dial in the middle, and filled with shrubs, familiar and rare, some of them brought from Europe. The grounds beyond this circle are set with beautiful and

HAMPSTEAD, NEW KENT COUNTY

interesting trees, many of which, like the shrubs, came across the water to contribute to the charm of a Virginia gentleman's home.

From the rear entrance, the gardens fall away in four terraces, filled with flowers and fruits and vegetables and adorned with summer-houses and trellises, over which old-fashioned roses clamber. Flowering shrubs border the walks and screen from view the squares devoted to the more useful than ornamental purposes of the garden.

The mansion stands four stories high including the English basement and attic. It is divided in the middle by a great hall whose ceiling is supported on one side by columns, and from which a splendid stairway winds to an observatory which affords a view of the country for miles around.

In the high-pitched English basement was the Webb library with its books—in built-in shelves around the walls and up to the ceiling—among them many a "quaint and curious volume of forgotten lore." Also in the basement was the servants' hall and innumerable store rooms and

THE HALL, HAMPSTEAD

lock rooms; the wine cellar and the "fat cellar" (a dark cool room connected with the outer world by a brick-walled passage), in which fresh meats were kept. The basement had its alluring nooks and corners, but it could not vie in charm with the attic, where the ghost of Mr. Conrad Webb dwelt among the trunks and chests filled with wearing apparel of past generations, bundles of old letters and broken toys. One who spent her early days at Hampstead tells how, on rainy days, the children would play in the attic without a qualm all day long, but if dark overtook them in the midst of their games, would stick their fingers in their ears and run for their lives down the winding stair to the safety of lamp-light and grown-up folk, in terror lest the ghost should catch them. The same narrator tells of the great ice-house in the grounds, whose dark chill depths seemed to childish minds to be the abode of unguessed mysteries.

Upon one of the outhouses at Hampstead was a bell-tower in which hung what came to be both " passing bell " and " fire bell," though its main object was to call farm hands to meals from their work in different parts of the large estate. If there was so much as a chimney afire the familiar tones of the bell would at once give the alarm, while when there was a death in the Webb connection anywhere in the neighborhood, a messenger would be sent forthwith to toll the Hampstead bell.

Hampstead is now the property and residence of Mr. W. J. Wallace.

ELTHAM, NEW KENT COUNTY

ELTHAM, CLOVER LEA, AND THE WHITE HOUSE

Before the War between the States New Kent contained other dwellings, which, like Hampstead, were spacious mansions.

Eltham was long the home of the Bassetts, a family whose emigrant ancestor, Captain William Bassett, had served in the Civil War, in England, and in the English garrison at Tangier. He died in 1672 and was succeeded at Eltham by his son, Hon. William Bassett (1672–1723), who was a member of the Council and whose handsome armorial tomb has now been removed to Hollywood Cemetery, Richmond. A third William Bassett, who was a member of the House of Burgesses and died in 1744, was in turn succeeded by his son, Burwell Bassett, who was frequently in the House of Burgesses and died in 1793. This Burwell Bassett was first succeeded by his eldest son, another Burwell Bassett (who was for many years a member of Congress), but as he died without issue, the estate was inherited by his younger brother, John Bassett,

CLOVER LEA, HANOVER COUNTY

who removed to "Farmington," Hanover County, and afterwards built Clover Lea, in the same county, where he died in 1862. Clover Lea was inherited by his son, George Washington Bassett, who was the last of the family to own the property. The house was beautifully wainscoted in black walnut and the stairs are of the same material. The mantels are of carved white marble. This was one of the handsomest houses in Hanover County. Clover Lea still remains, but Eltham was burned in 1876. Fortunately Mr. Herbert A. Claiborne, of Richmond, a descendant of the Bassetts, owns an excellent drawing of Eltham, which he has kindly allowed to be copied.

The White House, on the Pamunkey River, originally an estate of several thousand acres, was owned by the eccentric Counsellor John Custis, of " Arlington," Northampton County, and became the home of his son, Daniel Parke Custis, the first husband of Mrs. Martha Washington. To this house the youthful Colonel went courting and here he married the fair widow. The estate was inherited by her great-granddaughter, Mrs. Robert E. Lee, who, a refugee from Arlington, near Washington, was living at the White House when McClellan's army advanced up the Peninsula. When she left the house she placed a card on the door requesting protection for the home of Martha Washington. The appeal was unhappily not heeded and the old house was burnt. Mrs. Lee's son, General Wm. H. F. Lee, lived on the estate for some years after the War between the States.

CHELSEA

In King William County, which lies between the Pamunkey and Mattapony Rivers, several well-known homesteads are to be found. Perhaps the oldest of these is Chelsea, the venerable home of the Moores, on the Mattapony. It is a spacious brick house bearing many evidences of antiquity and was probably named after Chelsea in England, the home of Sir Thomas Moore, from whom the Virginia Moores claim descent.

Augustine Moore, the first of this family, settled here about the year 1700, and his tomb may still be seen at Chelsea. His son Bernard Moore, a prominent man of his day and long a member of the House of Burgesses, married

Anne Katherine, eldest daughter of Governor Alexander Spotswood (1676–1740). Though her husband was loyal to Virginia during the Revolution, it is said that this fair and spirited daughter of a royal governor disobeyed the official prohibition of tea-drinking and defiantly sipped the tabooed beverage. She was prudent enough, however, to shut herself up in her room for the indulgence.

CHELSEA, KING WILLIAM COUNTY

The Moores owned Chelsea until the extinction of the family in the male line and then it passed, by descent, to the Robinsons, who owned it up to a few years ago, when it was sold by Mr. Lieper Moore Robinson. It is now owned by Messrs. L. P. and Stanley Reed, of Richmond.

ELSING GREEN

Another striking old house in King William County is Elsing Green. This estate was originally owned by Captain William Dandridge, of the British Navy, who was also a member of the Virginia Council.[20] The mansion, a massive brick structure, has been several times burnt out, but the walls are so strong that the fires have not affected the external appearance, though they greatly altered the arrangement of the rooms.

From the Dandridges, Elsing Green passed to Carter Braxton, signer of the Declaration of Independence, who rebuilt the house in 1758. Over the west door may still be seen the initials " C. B." and date " 1758," and on the opposite side, " G. B."—either for Carter Braxton's father or for his brother George Braxton.

From the Braxtons the estate passed, by purchase, to William Burnet Browne, of Salem, Massachusetts, who married Judith, daughter of Charles Carter, of " Cleve," King George County, Virginia, before the Revolution. Mr. Browne was the son of Honorable William Browne, of Salem, and his wife Mary Burnet, who was a daughter

ELSING GREEN, KING WILLIAM COUNTY

of William Burnet, Governor of New York, and granddaughter of the celebrated Gilbert Burnet, Bishop of

[20] For Captain William Dandridge and his descendants see *William and Mary Quarterly*, v, 30 *et seq.*; xii, 126 *et seq.*

Salisbury. Upon their removal to Virginia the Brownes filled Elsing Green with interesting ancestral relics. One room was hung with Gobelin tapestry presented to Bishop Burnet by William of Orange, and among the many portraits was a fine one of the bishop himself.

Formerly each of the wide fireplaces contained a back representing some episode in history. The only one of these now remaining shows the death of General Wolfe.

As William Burnett Browne had no son he left Elsing Green to his grandson, William Burnet Claiborne, provided he should take the name of Browne, which condition was complied with.

The estate finally passed, by sale, from the Brownes to the Gregory family, which has owned it for several generations. It is now the home of the family of Judge Roger Gregory.

HORN QUARTER, KING WILLIAM COUNTY

HORN QUARTER

Stately Horn Quarter, the finest house of its period in King William County, was built in the early nineteenth century by Mr. George Taylor, a gentleman of large estate and son of the celebrated John Taylor (1750–1824), of Caroline County, United States senator from Virginia.[21] The master of Horn Quarter also owned a handsome town home at the corner of Cary and Fifth Streets, in Richmond. He left Horn Quarter to his son, John Penn Taylor, who later sold it.

MATTAPONY CHURCH

Crossing the Mattapony River from King William County we find old Mattapony Church, one of the most striking of the Colonial houses of worship. Soon after the Revolution, the congregation became extinct and the church was abandoned. It suffered much from the ravages

MATTAPONY CHURCH, KING AND QUEEN COUNTY

of time and weather and finally, as there was no congregation, no minister and no vestry, it was regarded as having escheated to the State and was patented as public land by Mr. Pollard of King and Queen County, who conveyed it to a Baptist congregation. Mr. Pollard, however, removed

[21] For Honorable John Taylor and his descendants see Hayden, *Virginia Genealogies*, pp. 682–683.

the handsome baptismal font and presented it to the Episcopal church in Hanover County.

Mattapony is now and has been for many years the home of a large and prosperous Baptist congregation, and is kept in excellent repair. It is a cruciform building of Colonial glazed brick.

HANOVER COURT HOUSE

Above the old Counties of King William and King and Queen is Hanover.

According to a committee appointed to " define the boundary of Hanover County and establish a seat of justice," Hanover Court House was built upon the estate of Francis Meriwether in the year 1735. It is said to be a copy of the King William County Court House. The building's chief claim to distinction is that in it, in December, 1763, Patrick Henry made his maiden oration—the famous speech in the controversy between the people and the clergy, popularly known as the " Parson's Cause." A decision of the court on a demurrer in favor of the claims

HANOVER COURT HOUSE

of the clergy had left nothing undetermined but the amount of damages in the case, which was pending. Soon after the opening of the court, the case was called. The following extract from Wirt's *Life of Patrick Henry* vividly describes what then happened:

"The array before Mr. Henry's eyes was now most fearful. On the bench sat more than twenty clergymen, the most learned men in the Colony, and the most capable, as well as the severest critics before whom it was possible for him to have made his début. The Court House was crowded with an overwhelming multitude, and surrounded with an immense and anxious throng, who not finding room to enter were endeavoring to listen without, in the deepest attention. But there was something still more disconcerting than all this; for in the chair of the presiding magistrate sat no other person than his own father. Mr. Lyons opened the cause very briefly; in the way of argument he did nothing more than explain to the jury that the decision upon the demurrer had put the act of 1758 entirely out of the way, and left the law of 1748 as the only standard of the damages; he then concluded with a highly wrought eulogium on the benevolence of the clergy. And now came the first trial of Patrick Henry's strength. None had ever heard him speak, and curiosity was on tiptoe. He rose very awkwardly, and faltered much in his exordium. The people hung their heads at so unpromising a commencement; the clergy were observed to exchange shy looks at each other; and his father is described as having almost sunk with confusion from his seat. But their feelings were of short duration, and soon gave place to others of a very different character. For now were those wonderful faculties which he possessed for the first time developed; and now was first witnessed that mysterious and almost supernatural transformation of appearance, which the fire of his own eloquence never failed to work in him. For as his mind rolled along, and began to glow from its own action, all the exuviæ of the clown seemed to shed themselves spontaneously. His attitude, by degrees, became erect and lofty. The genius awakened all his features. His countenance shone with a nobleness and grandeur which it had never before exhibited. There was lightning in his eyes which seemed to rivet the spectator. His action became graceful, bold and commanding, and in the tones of his voice there was a peculiar charm, a magic of which any one who ever heard him will speak of as soon as he is named, but of which no one can give you any adequate description. They can only say that it struck upon the ear and upon the heart *in a manner which language cannot tell.* Add to all these his wonder-working fancy and the peculiar phraseology in which he clothed his images; for he painted to the heart with a force that almost petrified it. In the language of those who heard him on this occasion, 'he made their hair to rise on end.'

" It will not be difficult for any one who ever heard this extraordinary man to believe the whole account of this transaction, which is given by his surviving hearers; and from their account, the Court House of Hanover County must have exhibited, on this occasion, a scene as picturesque as has been ever witnessed in real life. They say that the people whose countenances had fallen as he rose had heard but very few sentences before they began to look up; then to look at each other with surprise, as if doubting the evidence of their own senses; then attracted by some strong gesture, struck by some majestic attitude, fascinated by the spell of his eye, the charm of his emphasis, and the varied and commanding expression of his countenance, they could look away no more. In less than twenty minutes, they might be seen in every part of the house, on every bench, in every window, stooping forward from their stands, in death-like silence; their features fixed in amazement and awe; all their senses riveted and intent upon the speaker, as if to catch the last strain of some heavenly visitant. The mockery of the clergy was soon turned into alarm; their triumph into confusion and despair; and at one burst of his rapid and overwhelming invective, they fled from the bench in precipitation and terror. As for his father, such was his surprise, such his amazement, such his rapture, that, forgetting where he was and the character he was filling, tears of ecstasy streamed down his cheeks, without the power or inclination to suppress them.

"The jury seemed to have been so completely bewildered that they lost sight not only of the act of 1748, but that of 1758 also; for thoughtless even of the admitted right of the plaintiff, they had scarcely left the bar when they returned with a verdict of *one penny damages.* A motion was made for a new trial: but the Court, too, had now lost the equipoise of their judgment, and overruled the action by a unanimous vote. The verdict and judgment overruling the motion were followed by redoubled acclamations from within and without the house. The people, who had with difficulty kept their hands off the champion from the moment of closing his harangue, no sooner saw the fate of the cause finally sealed, than they seized him at the bar, and in spite of his own exertions, and the continued cry of 'Order' from the Sheriff and Court, they bore him out of the Court House and raising him on their shoulders, carried him about the yard, in a kind of electioneering triumph."

There have recently been placed upon the walls of this historic old court house tablets to the memory of the citizens of Hanover County who were killed during the War between the States.

HANOVER COURT HOUSE TAVERN

The guest-house as well as the "hall of justice" of the historic little village of Hanover Court House has an interesting connection with Virginia's most famous orator. This quaint house was at one time kept by Patrick Henry's father-in-law, John Shelton, and when Mr. Shelton was away from home, Mr. Henry would obligingly take his place as "host."

The Marquis de Chastellux in his *Travels in North America, 1780 to 1782,* gives a piquant account of a visit to

Hanover Tavern. He says, " We arrived before sunset and alighted before a tolerably handsome Inn; a very large saloon and a covered portico are destined to receive the Company who assemble every three months at the Court House either on private or public affairs.

" The County of Hanover as well as that of New Kent have still reason to remember the passage of the English. Mr. Tilghman, our landlord, though he lamented his misfortune in having lodged and boarded Lord Cornwallis and his retinue without his Lordship's having made him the

TAVERN AT HANOVER COURT HOUSE

least recompense, could not yet help laughing at the fright which the unexpected arrival of Tarleton spread amongst a considerable number of gentlemen who had come to hear the news and were assembled in the Court House. A negro on horseback came full gallop to let them know that Tarleton was not above three miles off. The resolution of retreating was soon taken, but the alarm was so sudden and the confusion so great that every one mounted the first horse that he could find, so that few of those curious gentlemen returned upon their own horses."

HICKORY HILL

The plantation known as "Hickory Hill," home of the late Williams Carter Wickham, Brigadier-General of Cavalry, C. S. A., was originally an appanage to Shirley on the James, inherited by the General's mother (Anne) from her father, Robert Carter. John Carter, son of Robert ("King") Carter of Corotoman, purchased five hundred acres from John Littlepage by deed dated 2nd of March, 1734, since which date the property has passed by descent

HICKORY HILL, HANOVER COUNTY

or deeds of family settlement. The consideration as named in the deed of lease and release was the sum of five shillings lawful British money, yielding also yearly one ear of Indian corn at the feast of St. Michael the Archangel. The holding was greatly increased in 1768 by John Carter's son Charles Carter, of Shirley.

As narrated by the late Charles Carter Lee in his Virginia Georgics:

> Many remote estates supplied his purses,
> And Shirley food for his and his guests' horses.

Upon the marriage of Miss Anne Carter to Williams Fanning Wickham (son of the famous John Wickham of Richmond) she removed from Shirley to Richmond, and, the young couple wishing a summer home, her husband purchased from the heirs of Governor George W. Smith (lost in the burning of the Richmond Theatre) a tract of hill land, entirely surrounded by Mrs. Wickham's property. The dwelling was built and the plantation establishment moved from the lowlands of the Pamunkey River to the more salubrious elevation of "Hickory Hill" in 1820. This mansion passed through the vicissitudes of war, was destroyed by fire in 1875, but was immediately rebuilt.

The feature of the old home on which the eye loves to dwell is the old garden, "with its roses so fair and its tall stately trees," its violets—its arbors, avenues and terraces—the emerald of its broad stretches of grass, and its matchless box trees, now approaching their centenary and still growing with youthful riot.

The old home is peaceful now; but twice each year during the latter part of the Civil War both armies swept over it, and while it was spared horrors such as Belgium has experienced, yet, at the best, war is aptly described by General Sherman, and the fate of the family was the common lot of all during that fearful period. Historic incidents occurred from time to time, as when J. E. B. Stuart left his column for a moment on his famous raid around McClellan to cheer a sorely stricken soldier at this home. General William Henry Fitzhugh Lee, desperately wounded and a prisoner, here bade farewell forever to his sweet wife and children, who succumbed from the shock of separation, and the old pleasaunce with its luxurious shrubbery afforded safe concealment for his brother, Captain Robert E. Lee, Jr., as narrated in his charming book of recollections of his father. Later on in the war the tide of actual conflict surged back and forth across the old garden, and the great box walk echoed to the shots of fighting men; but through it all it still survives with its matchless charm of beauty and romance.

Hickory Hill is now the home of Mr. Henry T. Wickham.

OLD FORK CHURCH

Old Fork Church, St. Martin's Parish, Hanover County, came by its present name from its situation at the forks of the Pamunkey River, as the two little streams, the North Anna and South Anna, were popularly called. Its massive walls of checkered brick work are built upon severely simple lines, but their plainness is relieved by the pillared porches, of harmonious proportions, which shade both the main door and the minister's door.

FORK CHURCH, HANOVER COUNTY

This church dates from 1735, and during its long life has been conspicuous for its pious influences and for the number of young men it has sent into the ministry. Many notables have bowed the knee within its walls, among them Patrick Henry and the fair Dolly Madison, each of whom attended " Old Fork " in their youth. The noted author Thomas Nelson Page, whose family have been among its staunchest pillars for generations, was a regular member of this old church during his boyhood and early manhood.

The parish owns a beautiful communion service bearing upon both paten and chalice this inscription:

" For the use of the Church in St. Martins parish, in Hanover and Louisa Counties, Virginia, 1759."

In the churchyard are many interesting tombs.

OAKLAND

Oakland, the home of the Nelsons and Pages in the " upper end " of Hanover County, Virginia, is located on land originally granted to Thomas Nelson, the first settler of that name in Eastern Virginia. He was the grandfather

OAKLAND, HANOVER COUNTY

of General Thomas Nelson, junior, Signer of the Declaration of Independence, Governor of Virginia, and Commander of her forces in the campaign which resulted in the surrender at Yorktown.

The Nelsons owned a tract of land of about ten thousand acres between the Little and New Found Rivers, in that portion of New Kent County which by legislative enactment in the year 1721 became Hanover, and it was to this tract that the Honorable William Nelson, who succeeded Lord Botetourt at the latter's death in 1770 in the chief magistracy of the Colony, sent "my Lord Botetourt's" horses to be grazed. The Marquis de Chastellux has left in his *Memoirs* a charming account of the "post-Revolutionary" home of General Thomas Nelson which was located on a portion of this estate just a few miles from "Oakland" and where that interesting Frenchman visited in 1782. General Nelson died in 1789 at "Mont Air" (the home of his son Francis Nelson), which adjoined the "Oakland estate."

The "Oakland house" was not built until 1812, becoming the home of Judith, the youngest of General Nelson's daughters, who married her cousin, Captain Thomas Nelson. The choice of "the site" is attributed to the near presence of a noble spring which is still—these hundred years later—the delight of those whose privilege it is to claim Oakland as "home." "Oakland" and "hospitality" are synonymous.

From this "roof-tree" have gone into the world men and women celebrated in varied professions: the church, both at home and abroad, has doubtless been the greatest benefactor of this "blood"; statesmanship and diplomacy are not absent from the roll of achievements; while the pen and sword have been wielded by its scions with equal ability.

In 1847 "the youngest of the daughters of the house" —Frances Nelson—married her kinsman John Page, who in later years became a gallant officer in the Confederate Army, where he ranked as major.

In 1899 the original "Oakland house" was destroyed by fire, but was shortly afterwards replaced by a dwelling built on the same plan.

Oakland is now the joint possession of Thomas Nelson Page, Rosewell Page, Second Auditor of the State of Virginia, and Rev. Francis Page, the three sons of Major

John and Frances (Nelson) Page. Thomas Nelson Page, widely known as a man of letters and now American Ambassador to Italy, was born at Oakland and his "Two Little Confederates" were children of that house, while "Marse Chan" himself was not unfamiliar with the loved surroundings. In *Balla, and other Virginia Stories*—the work of the graceful pen of James Poyntz Nelson—another "child of the Oakland house," one also finds much of local color.

SCOTCHTOWN

The huge and interesting old house with the curious name of Scotchtown was for a time the home of Patrick Henry, who bought it in 1771 and was living in it when he was first elected governor of Virginia. He sold it six or

SCOTCHTOWN, HANOVER COUNTY before 1771

seven years later to Wilson Miles Cary. Afterward Scotchtown passed to the possession of John Payne, and was the girlhood home of Dolly Payne, who became the wife of President James Madison. It is said that during the Revolution, Tarleton and his raiders rode their horses up the stone steps of Scotchtown and clattered through the wide hall.

EDGEWOOD AND AIRWELL

Edgewood, a sturdy old mansion of the Berkeleys, of Hanover County, was built by Doctor Carter Berkeley[22] upon a part of Airwell, the estate of his father, Nelson Berkeley.

A sketch of the builder of Edgewood, by a brother "M.D.," which appeared in the *Southern Clinic,* says: "After completing his classical studies Dr. Berkeley was

EDGEWOOD, HANOVER COUNTY

sent to Edinburgh, Scotland, for several years, taking his degree about 1793. His thesis, in Latin, comprising 52 pages (*De Corpore Humano*), now lies before me."

Upon his return to Virginia Doctor Berkeley began the practice of his profession from his father's home, but built Edgewood and took up his abode there at the time of his marriage to Catherine Spotswood Carter—a daughter of Charles Carter, of Shirley, by his second wife, Anne Butler Moore. The house is, therefore, probably over a century old.

[22] Berkeley family: *The Critic* (Richmond, Va.), December 6, 1890, *etc.*

PARLOR AT EDGEWOOD

DINING-ROOM AT EDGEWOOD

By his marriage with "Kitty" Carter (as she was familiarly called) Doctor Berkeley had five children, whose descendants are scattered throughout the United States. Doctor Berkeley married a second time, Fanny, daughter of Governor John Page, and widow of Thomas Nelson, Jr., son of General Thomas Nelson, of Yorktown. Thomasia (one of the three children of Thomas and Fanny Nelson) was married at Edgewood to Bishop William Meade, as his second wife. Doctor Berkeley and his second wife, Fanny (Page) Nelson, were the parents of two children: Kitty (who became the wife of Lucius, son of General John Minor, of Hazel Hill, near Fredericksburg), who inherited Edgewood, and Carter Nelson Berkeley. Mr. and Mrs. Minor continued to live at Edgewood until the end of both their lives. After a time Edgewood was sold to strangers, from whom it came again into possession of descendants of the Berkeley family by purchase.

About 1886 Mrs. Mary E. Noland (a granddaughter of Nelson Berkeley II, of "Airwell," and great niece of Doctor Carter Berkeley) bought Edgewood, which upon her death became the property of Mr. Nelson Berkeley Noland. It is now owned by Mr. William C. Noland, of Richmond.

NEW MARKET, HANOVER COUNTY

" Airwell " was built some time before the Revolutionary War by Nelson Berkeley (born 1733, died 1794), who moved hither from Middlesex County.

Tradition has it that Tarleton, with some of his troopers, visited the house during that war, and Tarleton's own report shows that he passed through this neighborhood.

Mrs. Berkeley, of " Airwell," the widow of the founder, was the " lady of dignity, firmness, and authority " mentioned by Bishop Meade, who declined to deliver the communion silver in her keeping to the embassy that came to get it for the coffers of the county. By the stand she took, the church silver was preserved to the parish (St. Martin's).

It is still kept at Airwell by descendants of the spirited old lady, and still serves its sacred purpose in old " Fork Church."

Airwell was gutted by fire in 1836; but the walls were re-roofed and the house restored for occupancy about 1845.

During the War between the States it was visited by both Northern and Southern soldiers, and it contributed its full share toward the support of the latter, one of whom died and is buried there.

The present owner is Mr. Fenton Noland, to whom it has come by direct descent.

NEW MARKET AND BULLFIELD

New Market was an old home of the Doswell family, long resident in Hanover.

Better known was Bullfield, in the same county, the home of Major Thomas Doswell, who was for many years one of the most noted and successful turfmen of the State at a time when the leading supporters of " the sport of kings " were gentlemen. On the old race track at Bullfield many of Virginia's most noted race horses were trained.

PART V

THE RAPPAHANNOCK AND POTOMAC

THE counties along the Rappahannock and Potomac Rivers, from Chesapeake Bay to the head of tidewater, are closely connected historically and socially. In treating of houses and homes of note in this section those upon the south side of the Rappahannock will be taken up first.

ROSEGILL

Picturesque in the extreme is this old estate—and not only in its outward and visible form but as well in the inward and spiritual things. For generations the home of " Wormeley of Virginia "—scions of the house of " Hatfield," Yorkshire, England—ancient and honorable—Rosegill is perhaps the least popularly known of Virginia's colonial estates. In the third decade of the seventeenth century Christopher and Ralph Wormeley " came out " to Virginia and founded their first home in York County, each becoming a member of that " Virginia House of Lords "—the governor's Council of State. In 1649, Ralph Wormeley patented a tract of land wonderfully situated on the Rappahannock River—in what is now Middlesex County, at that date Lancaster—removing thither, establishing " Rosegill," "passing" in the year of our Lord 1651 from this truly " earthly paradise "—we trust, to that one " not made with hands." Agatha (of the name and family of " Eltonhead of Eltonhead "), widow of the first Ralph Wormeley (who was her second husband), took unto herself a third mate—the distinguished Sir Henry Chicheley, Knight, a cavalier officer, member of the Governor's Council in Virginia and deputy governor of the Colony—who made Rosegill his home throughout the remainder of his days.

Ralph Wormeley (1650-1700), second of the name, son of Ralph and Agatha (Eltonhead) Wormeley, matriculated at Oriel College, Oxford, in 1665, and, completing his education, returned to Virginia, where the succeeding years of his life proved a veritable multiplication table of honors: burgess, member of the Council, secretary of State, trustee of William and Mary College, naval officer of the Rappahannock, president of the Council; "the most powerful man in Virginia," according to a contemporaneous report. From him descended a line—all Ralphs, with one exception, all masters of Rosegill and in economic, social and political "estate" among the foremost men in Virginia.

The beginning of the Revolutionary struggle found two of the family resident at Rosegill—Ralph Wormeley (1715-1790), fourth of the name, for twenty-two years a member of the House of Burgesses, and his son Ralph Wormeley (1744-1806), the fifth, educated at Eton and Cambridge, one of the greatest book-collectors in Virginia and one of the last appointees to the Council under the Royal government. These honorable gentlemen both sympathized with the mother country in the revolt of her children, but, wise in their generation, they did not offer active opposition to the "new order" forming around them. Their passive attitude did not, however, save them from great annoyance during the war.

Ralph, the younger, in a letter to John Randolph Grymes, dated 4 April, 1776, expressed himself quite freely in "loyal terms"; the letter was intercepted, and Wormeley was ordered by resolution of the Virginia Convention to be confined to the county of Berkeley and that part of his father's estate which was in the county of Frederick, and not to depart the limits thereof, and to give bond for £20,000. For two years his movements were thus restricted. After his release he returned to Rosegill, where, in 1781, oh, irony of fate! his estate was pillaged and he robbed, by the crew

FOLLOWING THE HOUNDS

ROSEGILL, MIDDLESEX COUNTY

of a tory privateer, of thirty-six valuable slaves, silver plate, jewelry, watches and wearing apparel, some of the property, however, being later returned on application to General Leslie, the English officer then commanding at Portsmouth.

The two Wormeleys, however, survived the war and lived to enjoy the friendship of the citizens of the new State, the younger Ralph serving several times as a member of the House of Delegates and in the Virginia Convention of 1788. Not long after his death, in 1806, Rosegill was sold and in the course of years, passing through various ownerships, was some time since purchased by the late Senator Cochran of Pennsylvania, who restored the old mansion with the utmost care and good taste.[1]

The distant view of Rosegill given in the illustration (the only available one) hardly does justice.

Encircled with wild roses and honeysuckle, this wonderful old Virginia homestead deserves its pretty romantic name.

To wind up the long hill from the little village of Urbanna, along a shady road, and to behold the fine old mansion away off from its double outer gates is to realize delightfully how well some Virginians planned and builded.

Rosegill house sits square and imposing in thirty acres of lawn. On the left, as one enters the land gate, is the great kitchen, still glorying in its fireplace, crane, spiders and pot hooks.

The "mansion house" is unique. From the land porch a square hall opens; to the left of this are a sitting-room and a dining-room, both immense, to the right are the library and drawing-rooms, equally spacious. The dining-room is panelled in mahogany, the sitting-room as well as the library in oak, while the drawing-room is in

[1] For Wormeley Genealogy, see Hayden, *Virginia Genealogies*, and *Virginia Magazine of History and Biography*, viii, p. 179 *et seq.*; xvi, p. 16 *et seq.*, and xviii, p. 373 *et seq.*

white. Parallel to these large apartments runs one splendid hall, with a large door, and eight large windows with seat, opening to the square river porch. At either end of this very large hall are winding stairs.

Above are five great chambers and another sweep of hall with windows overlooking the Rappahannock.

In the attic is one great chamber with fourteen beds for bachelors. The lawn from the back hall runs to the Rappahannock, which is at this point five miles wide. The green walk from the house to the river is bordered with roses its whole length.

BLANDFIELD

For two generations before the founding of Blandfield, a commodious brick mansion situated on a large estate which stretched to the Rappahannock River, the Beverleys [2] had been conspicuous in Virginia. Robert Beverley, the emigrant (who died in 1686), clerk of the House of Burgesses, and his sons Harry (surveyor, and commander of a sloop fitted out by Governor Spotswood to go in quest of pirates), Peter (speaker of the House of Burgesses, treasurer of the Colony and member of the Council), and Robert (the first native historian of Virginia), had given the name distinction. Colonel William Beverley (*circa* 1698–1756), only child of Robert, the historian, and his wife Ursula, daughter of the first William Byrd, married Elizabeth, daughter of the Honorable Richard Bland (1665–1720), of Jordan's Point, on James River, and building for her a home in Essex County, named it Blandfield in her honor.

Colonel Beverley was a man of note in his day. He was a member of his Majesty's Council, and as a patentee of the great "Beverley Manor Estate" in Augusta County was one of the principal agents in the settlement of the valley of Virginia. Dying soon after the middle of the

[2] Beverley family: *Virginia Magazine of History and Biography*, ii, 405–413; iii, 47–52, 169–176, 261–271, 383–392.

BLANDFIELD, ESSEX COUNTY

eighteenth century, he was succeeded as master of Blandfield by his son Robert, who, sympathizing with England during the Revolution, was disarmed by the Virginia authorities. He, in turn, was succeeded at Blandfield by a second Robert, from whom the estate passed to still a third of the name, Colonel Robert Beverley, of Avenel, Fauquier County.

Blandfield is still in possession of the Beverley family and is now the home of one of the sons of Colonel Robert Beverley, of Avenel.

VAUTER'S CHURCH

Vauter's Church, St. Anne's Parish, Essex County, takes its name from the family on or near whose land it was built. A brick in its south wall bearing the date 1731 had

VAUTER'S CHURCH, ESSEX COUNTY

led to a belief that it was erected during that year, but it is likely the figures have reference to the year of some addition or repair, as there are abundant evidences of greater age. In an article published in the *Southern*

Churchman, February 2, 1907, P. S. Hunter, a member of the parish, gives the following interesting word-picture of this old church:

"Of all the magnificent river views in Tidewater Virginia, few excel that from the summit of Chimborazo Hill, in upper Essex County. Commanding on one side the long beautiful stretches of the beautiful Rappahannock, flowing through its fertile plains, it displays on the other, thickly-wooded uplands in ascending terraces of richly blended verdure. But the most prominent object in the foreground is old Vauter's Church, standing in its ancient grove of oak and walnut. It is approached by the 'Church Lane,' considerably elevated above the fields on either side, from the accumulation of soil washing down from the hills, and is bordered by dense hedges of growth so characteristic of the country, and in Spring so exquisitely fragrant with the bloom of the wild grape and eglantine.

"The church is a brick building of cruciform shape, with its three high, sharp gables supporting a shingle roof, cut close to the edge of the wall. Its high and narrow windows are guarded by heavy, solid wooden shutters.

"The present chancel raised one step from the stone-paved aisles is furnished now with two modern stands or lecterns, for the service and sermon, but back against the wall there still stands the old reading desk and pulpit above it. . . . The pews are the same old box stalls with benches of uncompromising rigidity, and furnished with clanging doors which announce the retirement of the occupants; but they have been cut down to nearly half of their former height. Formerly pews and pulpit were so high that both minister and congregation could enjoy deep seclusion. . . . To complete the description of the venerable building, there is only to be added that its walls are covered by the most luxuriant mantle of English ivy."

GAYMONT

Gaymont was the beautiful home of John H. Bernard, who was a State Senator, and who married, in 1816, Jane Gay Robertson. The house, which is noted for its handsome interior, received its name as a compliment to his wife. It is still owned by the family.

THE HALL AT GAYMONT

ORMESBY

Ormesby, an estate not far from Guiney's Depot on the Richmond, Fredericksburg and Potomac Railroad, was once the property of Anthony Thornton, of Stafford County, who married Winifred, daughter of Colonel Peter Presley, of Northumberland House, Northumberland County, and died in 1757. The Ormesby homestead is one of those interesting-looking, rambling frame houses which in the old Virginia fashion grew with the needs of the family that lived in it. It is said that Anthony Thornton I built the oldest part of the house in about 1715, and gave the plantation to his younger son, Anthony II, who was in turn succeeded by his son Colonel Anthony Thornton III, who as county lieutenant of Caroline commanded the militia of that county at the siege of Yorktown. Later Colonel Thornton sold Ormesby to his brother Thomas Griffin Thornton, and removed to Kentucky.

Thomas Griffin Thornton was in his day one of the

most famous fox-hunters in Virginia, and the old sporting magazines contain anecdotes illustrative of the great ex-

ORMESBY, CAROLINE COUNTY

HOUSE WHERE STONEWALL JACKSON DIED, FAIRFIELD, CAROLINE COUNTY

cellence of his hounds. He finally sold Ormesby to his brother John, whose heirs still own it.

Before removing to Ormesby, John Thornton had

owned and lived at Fairfield near Guiney's. It was in an outbuilding known as "the office" at Fairfield that Stonewall Jackson died.

NORTH GARDEN

North Garden was built not long after the Revolution by Captain Harry Thornton, son of Anthony Thornton, of Ormesby. Captain Thornton was a gentleman devoted to racing and other sports, in consequence of which his estate became seriously involved. The line between Caroline and Spottsylvania Counties runs through the North

NORTH GARDEN, CAROLINE AND SPOTTSYLVANIA COUNTIES

Garden yard, and the story goes that when the sheriff of either county would come to arrest him for debt, he would simply step over the line into the other county. One day the sheriffs of both counties came at the same time and the gay captain's life of freedom seemed doomed to be brought to a close. Appearing to give up all hope of escape he ordered his horse (which unknown to the sheriffs was a racing mare famous for speed) and rode quietly off between his captors. After riding for a mile or so, he stopped, pretending to arrange a stirrup leather, while the sheriffs went ahead for a few yards; when wheeling his horse about, the captain raised his hat and with a polite " Gentlemen, I have the honor to wish you a very good day," galloped off at a speed which the sheriffs knew they could not equal, and so escaped.

An old gentleman declares that he has often heard his father say that he had seen the wide hall of North Garden covered with blood and feathers, the result of a cock fight—a kind of sport then in favor with men of the highest social standing.

Captain Thornton, who soon after his escapade removed to Kentucky, married Anne, daughter of John Fitzhugh, of Belair, Stafford County, and left several children, one of whom was the mother of the late Judge E. H. Fitzhugh, of Richmond.

North Garden was afterward bought by Mr. Thomas Catlett, after the death of whose son Edward Catlett the estate was sold.

MARYE HOUSE, FREDERICKSBURG

OLD HOUSES IN FREDERICKSBURG

Fredericksburg contains many interesting old houses, among them the frame cottage in which Mary, the mother of Washington, spent so many years of her life, and where

MARY WASHINGTON HOUSE, FREDERICKSBURG

RISING SUN TAVERN, FREDERICKSBURG

she died. It is now owned by the Association for the Preservation of Virginia Antiquities, which organization has also lately purchased in the same town the Rising Sun Tavern, a famous old Colonial hostelry.

A house believed to be the one in which William Paul, the brother of John Paul Jones, lived and the home of John Paul Jones himself during his residence in Fredericksburg is pointed out.

On the heights above the town stands the well-known Marye House which figured conspicuously in the Battle of Fredericksburg.

KENMORE, FREDERICKSBURG c 1760

KENMORE

In the suburbs of Fredericksburg is Kenmore, built by Colonel Fielding Lewis (1725–1781),[3] who married Elizabeth (familiarly known as "Betty"), sister of George Washington.

[3] For the descendants of John and Frances (Fielding) Lewis, see *William and Mary Quarterly*, ix, 261 *et seq.*

Colonel Lewis, who was the son of Honorable John Lewis III (1702–1754) of Warner Hall, Gloucester County, and Frances Fielding, was a man of prominence in his day and during the Revolution conducted for the State a manufactory of arms, at Fredericksburg. His son Lawrence married the beautiful " Nelly " Custis.

THE PARLOR AT KENMORE

Later, Kenmore was owned for many years by the well-known family of Gordon. It was, until her death, the property and home of Mrs. William Key Howard.

Kenmore is especially noted for the beautiful ornamental plaster work on the ceilings of some of its rooms, said to have been the work of Hessian prisoners during the Revolution.

MANNSFIELD

A short distance below Fredericksburg, on the south side of the Rappahannock, may be seen some ruined walls which are all that remains of Mannsfield, originally the home of Mann Page (a member of the Continental Congress) and afterward the property of the Bernard family.[4] This fine old house was destroyed by the fire of Federal guns during the great battle.

THE FALLS AND FALL HILL

Francis Thornton (1681–post 1738), grandson of William Thornton of Gloucester County, first of the family in Virginia, settled in 1702, at Snow Creek, then in Essex,

THE FALLS, NEAR FREDERICKSBURG

now Caroline County, to the east of the present Fredericksburg, and at that date the very " outpost " on the Rappahannock River. Thornton was a large land owner, a representative for Caroline, in the House of Burgesses, in 1723 and 1736, and an early explorer of the Piedmont section. Thornton River is named for him. He built the quaint old home known as " The Falls," about a mile west of Fredericksburg. The house at " Fall Hill," which commands one of the most magnificent views in the Rappa-

[4] Bernard family: *William and Mary Quarterly*, v, 62–64, 181–187.

hannock Valley, was erected some years later. The extensive estate, which included both " The Falls " and " Fall Hill," was inherited by Francis Thornton (1714–1749), son of the old settler, who represented Spottsylvania County in the House of Burgesses 1744–1754, and married Frances, daughter of Roger and Mildred (Washington) Gregory. Another Francis Thornton (who died in 1795), son of Francis and Frances (Gregory) Thornton, succeeded to the estate, on the death of his father, and

FALL HILL

marrying Anne, daughter of the Rev. John Thompson and his wife, Butler Brayne (widow of Governor Alexander Spotswood), became the father of Francis Thornton (born 1760), who married Sally, daughter of the celebrated Judge Harry Innes, of Virginia and Kentucky. To Francis and Sally (Innes) Thornton were born four daughters, three of whom in after-years became—Mrs. J. H. Fitzgerald, Mrs. Murray Forbes, Mrs. Thomas Marshall; the fourth, Miss Butler Brayne, dying unmarried; and four sons: Francis Thornton, a minister; Harry Innes Thornton, of the Supreme Court of Alabama, and the Court of Claims of San Francisco; James Innes Thornton, Secretary of State for Alabama, and Robert Calloway Thornton, who died unmarried.

At "The Falls," which has long since passed out of the Thornton family, are the tombs of many generations of the house. "Fall Hill" is still a family possession and is now owned by Mrs. Frederick Robinson, of Transvaal, South Africa.

At "Fall Hill" is an interesting old grave: that of Katrina, an Indian, who was the nurse of Francis Thornton, the fourth of the name mentioned above. This Francis Thornton frequently told his little grandchildren of how the Indian maid covered him with leaves and hid herself among them and called the partridges around and sometimes caught them in this way. The Indians came to see him when passing through the country and he always spoke of them as his friends.

General Lee was a frequent visitor at "Fall Hill," and at one time, in the thick of the firing which he was watching from this place, he is said to have turned his glasses from the battlefield to Chatham, across the river, to see if the apple tree, under which he courted his wife, was still standing. Shortly after the war, General Lee, while on a visit to "Fall Hill," advised Mrs. Taylor (whose mother was Sally Innes Thornton, wife of Murray Forbes) to obliterate every trace of the war, she having preserved, as an historic landmark, the trunk of a large tree, on the lawn (then covered with ivy), the top of which had been torn away by a cannon ball from the enemy on the Stafford side.

ROXBURY

The Roxbury estate in Spottsylvania County, between the Ta and Po Rivers, originally consisted of 1500 acres, but was reduced after the War between the States to 1100. It is believed to have been patented by Captain Harry Beverley, son of Major Robert Beverley, clerk of the House of Burgesses, and to have been inherited by his grandson, Beverley Stanard (1721–1765), who was appointed a justice of Middlesex County in 1742, removed to Spottsylvania County and built the present house at Roxbury about 1745.[5] His tomb may still be seen in the graveyard there. He left Roxbury and Stanardsville (an estate of 5200 acres in what was then Orange but is now Greene County) to his eldest son William Stanard, who was an officer of minute men at the beginning of the Revolution, and was sheriff of Spottsylvania, 1802–1804.

ROXBURY, SPOTTSYLVANIA COUNTY

William Stanard married Elizabeth, daughter of Colonel Edward Carter, of Blenheim, Albemarle, and had many children.

After William Stanard's death, in October, 1809, his heirs sold Roxbury to his nephew, Robert Stanard, who was speaker of the House of Delegates and judge of the Court of Appeals. Judge Stanard's father was Larkin Stanard, of Stanfield, Spottsylvania (a cadet in the Revolution and a member of the House of Delegates, 1798–1803), and one of his brothers was Captain Beverley Chew Stanard (captain in the War of 1812 and member of the

[5] Stanard family: Hayden, *Virginia Genealogies*, p. 279.

House of Delegates for Chesterfield, 1805–1811), whose son John Champe Stanard, of Richmond, occupied Roxbury for many years.

After Judge Stanard's death, May 14, 1846, Roxbury was inherited by his son Robert C. Stanard, long a prominent lawyer of Richmond, and a member of the State Senate, and of the Convention of 1851. From him it descended to his only son Hugh Mercer Stanard, Captain in the Confederate Army on General Magruder's staff. After Captain Stanard's death it became the property of his mother, Mrs. Martha Stanard, who some years later sold it to her brother, Mr. Pierce. It has since again been sold. The estate was the property of the Stanard family for about one hundred and fifty years.

The house, which is believed to be the oldest residence in Spottsylvania County, is a well-preserved frame building, and the parlor, wainscoted to the ceiling, is a handsome example of the work of that early day.

Having ascended the south bank of the Rappahannock to Spottsylvania County, we now return to the Chesapeake Bay, in Northumberland County.

DITCHLEY

Ditchley looks upon the Chesapeake Bay. About the year 1647 Colonel Richard Lee, the first of the famous Lee family in Virginia, settled on a plantation at Dividing Creek, Northumberland County, which he named Ditchley. He was succeeded there by his seventh son Hancock Lee (1653–1709), a prominent man in his day, whose first wife was Mary, daughter of the Honorable William Kendall, of "the Eastern Shore," and his second, Elizabeth, daughter of the "converted" Puritan, Isaac Allerton II, and granddaughter of those stern New England worthies the first Isaac Allerton and "Elder" William Brewster. Hancock Lee was buried at Ditchley, where his tomb may still be seen.

The original Ditchley house is said to have dated from about 1687, but the present homestead, situated about two hundred yards from the site of its predecessor, was built by Kendall Lee, grandson of Hancock Lee, about the year 1765.

Ditchley remained in the Lee family until 1789, when William Lee sold it to James Ball, Jr. (1718–1789), who had married said Lee's aunt, Lettice Lee (1731–1811), and

DITCHLEY, NORTHUMBERLAND COUNTY

it has ever since been the property of the well-known family of Ball. A recent owner was Captain James F. Ball, a gallant officer in the Confederate Army.

There is still in use at Wycomoco Church, Northumberland Parish, a communion cup bearing the inscription, " Ex Dono Hancock Lee to Ye Parish of Lee, 1711."

MANTUA

Probably no house in Tidewater, Virginia, has such a site as Mantua, Northumberland County. Standing on a commanding hill, with the Coan River and the broad Coan Inlet almost beneath it, the view includes this beautiful sheet of water on one side and beyond the wide Potomac, here nearly at its mouth. To the right of the Coan, fertile fields and fruitful orchards, interspersed with woodlands, stretch to the great river. To one who has seen this view in early summer, its memory comes back as a thing of unusual beauty.

James Smith, who was born in the County of Derry,

MANTUA, NORTHUMBERLAND COUNTY

Ireland, emigrated to America and acquired a large fortune, in business, in Baltimore. Later, he bought several thousand acres in Northumberland County, Virginia (including the old Northumberland House estate, which was for a large part of two centuries the home of the notable family of Presley, now extinct), and built the present handsome house. At his death, in 1832, the estate was inherited by his son, Col. James M. Smith, who married Sarah, daughter of Willoughby Newton, of Lee Hall, Westmoreland County. At Col. Smith's death, the property was divided among his children, whose heirs are represented in the names of Brockenbrough, Hall, Barron, Lamb, and Howard.

Mantua with several hundred acres has for a number of

years been the property of Hon. Wm. A. Jones, of Warsaw, Va., who for so many years has been member of Congress for the " Northern Neck district."

BEWDLEY

Bewdley, in Lancaster County, is one of the most unusual looking houses in Virginia. It is a frame building with four great chimneys, two at each end, towering above it, and from its high, shingled roof two rows of dormer windows, like so many heavily-lidded eyes, look out. The exact date when the house was built is not known, but the estate has been owned by a branch of the Ball family for two hundred years, and perhaps longer. It is first mentioned as the home of Major James Ball (1678–1754), a grandson of the first of the Ball family in Virginia,[6] and a first cousin of Mary Ball, the mother of Washington.

Major Ball was succeeded at Bewdley by his son Colonel James Ball (1718–1789), who was many years a member of the Virginia House of Delegates and also a member of the Convention of 1788. His son and heir, Colonel James Ball (1755–1825), of Bewdley, was likewise frequently in the House of Delegates. Among the sons of this last named Colonel Ball was William Lee Ball, for several terms a member of Congress.

A recent owner of Bewdley was Captain James Kendall Ball, of the 9th Virginia Cavalry, Confederate States Army.

EPPING FOREST

Epping Forest is historic as the birthplace of Mary Ball (1707/8–1789), the mother of Washington. Her father, Colonel Joseph Ball (who was born in England, May 24, 1649), died at Epping Forest in 1711. As he left the plantation to his wife for life it is probable that after her death it became the property of his only son, Joseph Ball, who removed to England, where he was a bachelor of Grey's Inn, and died in London, 1762.

---

[6] Ball family: Hayden, *Virginia Genealogies*, p. 45 *et seq.*

BEWDLEY, LANCASTER COUNTY

EPPING FOREST, LANCASTER COUNTY

TOWLES POINT

Towles Point, in Lancaster County, is not only one of the oldest houses in Virginia, but is remarkable for having continued for more than two hundred years in the possession of one family. Henry Towles, Jr., removed from the Eastern Shore of Virginia in 1711, and built the house at Towles Point. He married Anne Therett and, dying in 1734, was succeeded by his son Stokeley Towles, who married Catherine Martin and had (besides Colonel Thomas Towles and Major Stokeley Towles, each of whom was a

TOWLES POINT, LANCASTER COUNTY

militia officer during the Revolution) a son, Colonel Henry Towles (1738–1799), who succeeded his father at Towles Point. Henry Towles, who was a colonel of militia during the Revolution, and County Lieutenant of Lancaster, in 1794, married, in 1760, Judith Haynes. Colonel Towles had eight children and at his death the estate was sold for division, but was bought by his daughter, Frances, who had married her cousin Porteus Towles (1777–1821). Porteus and Frances Towles were succeeded at Towles Point by their son, William Henry Towles (1808–1836), who married Keturah, widow of Thomas Towles. At the death of W. H. Towles the old home again passed by inheritance to his son James Towles (1829–1896), who married Josephine Isabella Whittington, and left a number of children, one of whom, Howard McJelton Towles, a prominent lawyer of Baltimore, is the present owner of Towles Point.[7]

CHRIST CHURCH, LANCASTER

One of the best examples of Colonial church architecture in Virginia is Christ Church, Lancaster County, built in 1732, to replace an earlier structure. The parish is an old one, dating, under various names, from about 1652.

Robert Carter, of Corotoman, generally known, on account of his estate and wealth, as "King Carter," offered to build the church at his own expense, provided it should be placed upon the site of the older sanctuary and, to quote his will, "Provided always the chancel be preserved as a burial place for my family, as the present chancel is, and that there be preserved for my family a commodious pew in the chancel."

The vestry book shows that Colonel Carter did bear the whole expense of this handsome building, reserving one-fourth of its seating capacity for his servants and tenants, besides a very large pew near the chancel-rail for his own family.

Three miles away on the broad Rappahannock, near its mouth, stood the Carter home, Corotoman, in the midst of its great plantation of 8000 acres. From his home to his church "King Carter" built a splendid road drained by deep ditches and walled on each side by a hedge of goodly cedars. Along this avenue the Corotoman coach rolled on Sundays, and tradition says that the rest of the congregation waited in the churchyard until its arrival,

[7] Towles Family, *Virginia Magazine of History and Biography*, viii, 320–321, 428–429, and ix, 198–200, 324–326, 433–435.

CHRIST CHURCH, LANCASTER COUNTY

INTERIOR CHRIST CHURCH

when they followed the bewigged and beruffled "King" into church.

Christ Church is the only Colonial house of worship in Virginia that has never been altered, and it stands to-day as characteristic of its time, as strong and as impressive as when the Carters enjoyed the seclusion of its high-backed pews that screened them from all eyes except those of the preacher in a pulpit so lofty that it seemed to Bishop Meade when standing in it to be "hung in the air." The church is in the form of a cross. Its walls of checkered brick-work are three feet thick, and into them are deeply set large windows with many little square panes. The ceiling, with its beautiful groined arches, is thirty-three feet from the floor at the highest point above the intersection of its stone-paved aisles. The walls are panelled with black walnut as high as the tops of the pew-backs, above which they are covered with white plaster, which still looks as smooth and as solid as rock. The great square pews, with seats running all around them (some of them capable of holding twenty persons, and all as many as twelve), the pulpit, with its pretty winding stair and quaint sounding-board, the clerk's desk, the carved chancel-rail and massive communion table, are also of walnut.

"King" Carter's father, Colonel John Carter, the founder of the Virginia family, had been buried in the chancel of the earlier church; but the rest of the Carters sleep outside beneath splendid, but dilapidated marbles, bearing fragments of elaborate coats-of-arms and long inscriptions.

Bishop Meade, writing of a service held by him in Christ Church in 1838, says, "Peculiarly delightful it was to raise the voice in a house whose sacred form and beautiful arches seemed to give force and music to the feeblest tongue beyond any other building in which I ever performed or heard the hallowed services of the sanctuary."

Through the assistance of the Association for the Preservation of Virginia Antiquities, and other friends of this most interesting old church, it has of late years been reshingled, broken panes of glass in the windows have been replaced and other repairs made.

On account of its inaccessibility to most members of the parish at the present day, it has only been used for occasional services for a long time past.

ST. MARY'S WHITE CHAPEL

Just when St. Mary's White Chapel, in Lancaster County, was built is not known, but dates on the communion plate and tombstones suggest that it was about

ST. MARY'S WHITE CHAPEL, LANCASTER COUNTY

the middle of the seventeenth century. It is a glazed brick building and was originally in the form of a cross, with three galleries, one of them owned by Major James Ball and Mr. Joseph Ball, one by the Downman family, while the third was reserved for colored servants whose masters were members of the parish.

In 1739 the church was badly out of repair and the congregation pulled down the arms of the cross and repaired and restored the rest of the building. This left a structure, sixty feet long and thirty broad, with an arched ceiling. Later still the high pews and pulpit were cut down.

St. Mary's White Chapel still possesses a silver chalice inscribed, "The gift of David Fox, 1669," and a silver paten believed to have been given by George Spencer, in 1691. David Fox also gave the church, in 1702, two tablets bearing the Ten Commandments, and the will of his son, Captain William Fox, under date 1717, contained the following direction, "My wife shall send for the Lord's Prayer and Creed, well drawn in gold letters, and my name under each of them, set in decent black frames, as a gift to St. Mary's White Chapel." All four of the tablets are of massive black walnut with hand carved letters heavily gilded with gold-leaf. The marble font is also a bequest of William Fox. Another interesting possession is a Bible given by Raleigh Downman.

St. Mary's White Chapel was the church of the Balls, Washington's ancestors on his mother's side, and in the churchyard most of the oldest tombs bear the name of Ball. The old communion table in the chancel once had a cover of green velvet with gold fringe and in the centre the Ball coat-of-arms heavily embossed in gold.

NOMINI HALL

All that now remains of Nomini Hall, the once noted seat of the Carters in Westmoreland County, is an avenue of poplars.

The estate, which contains several thousand acres, was the home of Robert Carter, called, from his membership in the Council of State, "Councillor Carter." He was a grandson of Robert ("King") Carter (1663–1732).

The spacious brick mansion which once graced the Nomini Hall plantation, and the family that lived in it, have been made widely known by the publication of the sprightly diary of Philip Vickers Fithian, a tutor in the Carter family during the years just preceding the Revolution.

Part of the original estate, with a modern house, is now owned and occupied by some of Councillor Carter's descendants, the Arnest family.

BLADENSFIELD

The farm near Warsaw, Richmond County, on which this quaint old house stands was once part of the great estate of Robert ("King") Carter. In 1733, on the division of part of his property, it was assigned to his grandson, Robert Carter of Nomini. This gentleman, or his wife, most probably (who was Frances, daughter of Benjamin

BLADENSFIELD, RICHMOND COUNTY

Tasker, President of the Council of Maryland, and his wife Anne Bladen), gave to the place the present name. In January, 1790, Mr. Carter conveyed Bladensfield to his son-in-law, John Peck, whose heirs, in 1842, sold it to Reverend William Norvell Ward, whose family has since owned it. Well founded tradition states that the home was once occupied by Nathaniel Rochester, a native of Westmoreland County, Virginia, who was a colonel in the Continental Army and for whom the city of Rochester, N. Y., was named. Bladensfield is believed to have been built early in the eighteenth century.

KIRNAN

Kirnan, in the upper part of Westmoreland County, was originally known as " China Hall." The Reverend Archibald Campbell, an uncle of the English poet Thomas Campbell, bought it before the Revolution and changed its name to Kirnan in honor of his ancestral home in Scot-

KIRNAN, WESTMORELAND COUNTY

land. Mr. Campbell was the rector of Washington Parish, Westmoreland, for years before the Revolution and also taught a school at Kirnan which tradition says was attended by Presidents Washington and Monroe.

Several of Parson Campbell's sons were prominent lawyers, one of them being the first United States district attorney. One of his grandsons, Ferdinand Stuart Campbell, a distinguished professor at William and Mary College, took the name of Stuart upon inheriting a Scottish estate.

In later days Kirnan became the home of the Bowie family.

STRATFORD

In an out of the way corner of Westmoreland County, in the midst of a vast and wooded estate, on a high bluff of the Potomac River, and approached from the landward by a narrow, lonely, and densely shaded road, stands Stratford, the sturdy castle of the sturdy race of Lee of Virginia.

From the landing of their first ancestor upon American shores, about 1640, until the present day, these Lees have never lacked sons to render service to their country and to make their name illustrious. Founded in Virginia by a gentleman of worth and estate who held some of the highest offices in the Colonial government, this family has given to Virginia one governor, four members of the Council of State, and twelve members of the House of Burgesses; to the colony of Maryland two councillors and three members of the Assembly; to the American Revolution four members of the Convention of 1776 which organized the State of Virginia, two signers of the Declaration of Independence, and their three other eminent brothers, Thomas Ludwell, William and Arthur Lee; and the foremost cavalry officer of the Revolutionary War, "Light Horse Harry" Lee. To the civil service of the United States the family has furnished one attorney general and several members of Congress, and to the State of Virginia, two governors; to the State of Maryland, a governor, and to the Confederate States, the great commander of its armies, three major generals and one brigadier general. Later, during the troubles which culminated in the war with Spain, General Fitzhugh Lee gained added distinction as consul general to Cuba and as a major general of the United States Army.

Part of the Stratford estate was patented by Richard Lee, the emigrant, and was inherited by his son John, who took his "bachelor's" degree in 1662 at Oxford, where his memory is perpetuated by a silver cup bearing the Lee arms and an inscription, given by him to Queen's College. This John Lee seems to have been a merry bachelor, as there is on record in Westmoreland County an agreement made in 1670, between him and his neighbors, Thomas Gerrard and Isaac Allerton, to build a banqueting hall at a point where their estates met, where annually each in turn should "make an honorable treatment." After John Lee's death, in 1673, Stratford passed to his brother, Colonel Richard Lee (1647–1714), of the Council, who, however, made his abode at Mt. Pleasant, also in Westmoreland County. The first mansion at Stratford was built by Thomas Lee (1690–1750), a younger son of this Richard, but it was soon afterward burned by convict servants, whom Mr. Lee, sitting as magistrate, had sentenced to be punished for some offence. A contemporaneous issue of *The Maryland Gazette* says, "Last Wednesday night Colonel Thomas Lee's fine house in Virginia was burnt, his office, barns and outhouses, his plate, cash (to the sum of £10,000), papers and everything entirely lost. His lady and child were forced to be thrown out of a window, and he himself hardly escaped the flames, being much scorched. A white girl about twelve years old, a servant, perished in the fire. It is said that Colonel Lee's loss is not less than £50,000." The fire occurred in 1729.

Public records in the Virginia State Capitol show that the English government gave Colonel Lee £300 sterling as a reward for loss incurred from faithfulness to duty. Soon after the fire Colonel Lee built the present Stratford house.

The builder of Stratford was a man of great prominence in his day and as president of the Council was acting governor of the colony from September 5, 1749, until his death, on November 14, 1750. He, like his famous son Richard Henry, was buried in the old family burying-ground at Mt. Pleasant. Perhaps no Virginian parents have had a greater number of distinguished sons than Colonel Thomas Lee and his wife Hannah, daughter of

Honorable Philip Ludwell II. Two of them, Richard Henry (1732–1794) and Francis Lightfoot (1734–1797), were signers of the Declaration of Independence; two others, William (1739–1795) and Arthur (1740–1792), rendered distinguished service for their country abroad during the Revolution; the fourth son, Thomas Ludwell Lee (1730–1778), held a conspicuous place as a patriot and lawyer, but died in 1778, and Philip Ludwell Lee (1726/7–1775), the eldest son, was a member of the Council of State of Virginia.

Honorable Philip Ludwell Lee at his death, in 1775, left two daughters, who eventually became his co-heiresses. The elder, Matilda, became the wife of her cousin Henry (1756–1818), the dashing "Light Horse Harry" Lee of Revolutionary fame. She died in 1790, but as she left several children, her husband continued to make his home at Stratford. Upon June 18, 1793, he married, as his second wife, Anne Hill Carter, of Shirley, and upon January 19, 1807, their immortal son, Robert Edward Lee, in whom the ancient dream of a spotless as well as valorous knight came true, was born at Stratford, and in the same room in which his famous kinsmen, Richard Henry and Francis Lightfoot Lee, had first seen the light. The room is that to the right of the entrance, as one looks at the picture.

After the death of "Light Horse Harry" Lee, Stratford passed to his son by his first marriage, Major Henry Lee, a man of brilliant talent, who died in Paris in 1837. After his death the estate passed from the family and is now the home and property of Dr. Stuart.

Stratford house consists of two wings thirty feet wide by sixty deep, connected by a "great hall" of twenty-five by thirty feet, which gives the mansion the form of the letter H. The ceiling of this hall is lofty and dome-shaped, and its walls are panelled in oak, with built-in bookcases of the same wood between the doors which lead into the wings. At the ends are doors, flanked on either side by large windows, leading into the grounds and garden. It is

Lee House - STRATFORD, WESTMORELAND COUNTY after 1730

SABINE HALL, RICHMOND COUNTY

thus well lighted and airy and in the old days was used as library and living-room.

Topping the pointed roof of each wing is a cluster of four tall, square chimneys, joined by arches, each cluster having much the effect of a square turret. This unique arrangement of the chimneys makes possible an interesting feature of one of the wings, which is known as the secret chamber. A small room is hidden in the stack of chimneys, the four of which form its walls. For many years it was so secret, indeed, that its existence was not so much as suspected, and it was only discovered when a carpenter in taking some lumber from the garret accidentally disturbed a plank which concealed its entrance. The room is entered from above, by means of this plank, which is made to slide backward and forward under the floor, fastening on the inner side by a spring, thus forming a sort of trap-door. It is about eight feet square and ten deep, and bears evident marks of use, the walls being disfigured in several places by smoke of a lamp or candle and the floor spotted with grease or ink.

In the grounds at a distance of some fifty or sixty feet from the four corners of the mansion were four outhouses, storehouses, office and kitchen. A fair-sized ox could be roasted in the kitchen's great fireplace, which is twelve feet wide, six high and five deep.

In the year 1790, Thomas Lee Shippen, of Philadelphia, a grandson of Colonel Thomas Lee, the builder of Stratford, visited the place and wrote the following description of it to his father: " Stratford, the seat of my forefathers, is a place of which too much cannot be said: whether you consider the venerable magnificence of its buildings, the happy disposition of its grounds or the extent and variety of its prospects. Stratford, whose delightful shades formed the comfort and retirement of my wise and philosophical grandfather, with what mixture of awe and pious gratification did I explore and admire your beauties. What a delightful occupation did it afford me sitting on one of the sofas of the great hall to trace the family resemblance in the portraits of all of my dear mother's forefathers, her father and mother, her grandfather and grandmother, and so on upward for four generations. Their pictures, drawn by the most eminent artists of England and in large gilt frames, adorn one of the most spacious and beautiful halls I have ever seen. There is something truly noble in my grandfather's picture. He is dressed in a large wig, flowing from his shoulders (probably his official wig as President of the Council), and a loose gown of crimson satin, richly ornamented. I mention the dress as it may serve to convey to you some idea of the style of the picture. But it is his physiognomy that strikes you with emotion. A blend of goodness and greatness; a sweet yet penetrating eye, a finely marked set of features and a heavenly countenance. Such I have almost never seen. Do not think me extravagant. My feelings were certainly so as I dwelt with rapture on the portraits of Stratford, and felt so strong an inclination to kneel to that of my grandfather. It was with difficulty that my uncle who accompanied me could persuade me to leave the hall to look at the gardens, vineyards, orangeries and lawns which surround the house." [8]

YEOCOMICO CHURCH

One of the most picturesque of Virginia's old churches is in Cople Parish, Westmoreland County. This is Yeocomico, which bears the Indian name of a little river not far away. Cople Parish originally contained two Colonial churches some distance apart, Yeocomico and Nomini, also named for the river, or creek, near which it stands. Nomini was destroyed by fire some years after the Revolution, but was later rebuilt.

Yeocomico, cloistered in a grove of ancient oaks, stands somewhat back from a quiet country road. It is a cross-shaped building, rudely, but strongly, constructed of

---

[8] A most complete and interesting account of the Lee family was written by Doctor Edmund Jennings Lee and published as *Lee of Virginia*.

Colonial brick, with steep, shingled roof and large square windows, filled with many little panes of glass and protected by heavy wooden outside shutters. Over the door appears the date, 1706, in which year the church was built. Outside, near the porch, stands an old sun-dial with the name Philip Smith and the date 1717 inscribed upon its face, and down the hill is a clear, sparkling spring with an ancient iron dipper, bearing the initials P. C. (Presley Cox) upon its bowl, chained to its brink. A brick wall

YEOCOMICO CHURCH, WESTMORELAND COUNTY

around the church and its full graveyard completes the picture and adds to the effect of seclusion and peacefulness.

After the Revolution, when everything English was unpopular in America, the Episcopal Church languished in this section. Cople Parish was without a rector for over fifty years, and Yeocomico fell into decay. During the War of 1812 a detachment of United States soldiers, sent to the neighborhood to watch the movements of the British fleet on the Potomac, quartered in the church, and later on in the same year a company of militia camped there.

These last shamefully desecrated the old sanctuary. The Communion table was taken into the yard and made to serve as a butcher's block, the beautiful marble font was carried off and used as a punch-bowl, and the tablets upon which the Ten Commandments, the Lord's Prayer and the Creed were inscribed were ruthlessly mutilated.

With the regular soldiers that had quartered in the church was Mr. William L. Rogers, of Princeton, New Jersey, to whom the building and its surroundings made a strong appeal. He returned to Westmoreland in 1820, and finding the church still in its dismantled state proposed to Mr. Murphy, a Scotch gentleman of culture and piety, and a Presbyterian, whose estate surrounded the church property, to aid him in an attempt at its restoration. Others joined in the movement and the good work was soon accomplished. The sacred table was polished and it and the font returned to their places, where they may still be seen, and the church regained its former dignity of appearance. The Communion plate and damask cloths and napkins marked with the name of the church had been kept safe and carefully guarded from violation by Mrs. Willoughby Newton, of Lee Hall.

In 1834 the Reverend George Washington Nelson became rector of Yeocomico and the churches in Richmond County, and the Episcopalians and Methodists of the neighborhood used Yeocomico jointly, " in Christian harmony and good will," says Bishop Meade. But during the rectorship of Mr. Nelson's successor, Mr. Ward, who took charge in 1842, the question of the right of possession was raised, and not until the matter was taken before the Legislature was it settled by a decision giving to the vestry and wardens of the Episcopal Church exclusive right to use and control the building.

Several of the Lee homes were in Cople Parish, and Wakefield, the Washington home, was not far away, and in the few lists of vestrymen of Yeocomico that remain both the Washingtons and Lees are well represented, with other names which have become historic to a less degree.

Notwithstanding its many vicissitudes the influence of the old church has been widespread. Among its sons, who by entering the ministry have handed on its teachings, may be mentioned the Right Reverend John Brockenbrough Newton, Right Reverend John Poyntz Tyler, and Reverend Willoughby Newton Claybrook.

The old glebe of Cople Parish is still standing.

FARNHAM CHURCH

Farnham Church, Richmond County, was originally a large cruciform building and was one of the best parish churches in the colony. Fire has destroyed all but the solid

FARNHAM CHURCH, RICHMOND COUNTY

walls, but a movement for its restoration has been for some time under way, and it is expected that before many years it will be again in use.

SABINE HALL *

Sabine Hall,* built in 1730 for Landon Carter (1710–1778), a younger son of Robert ("King") Carter by his second wife, Betty Landon, and still the home of his descendants, crowns a commanding site overlooking the

* See illustration at head of List of Illustrations and on page 327.

Rappahannock, in Richmond County, adjoining Westmoreland. It possesses a unique feature among Virginia homes, in the lodge at the gate occupied by a negro retainer and his family. The visitor is apt to receive his first welcome from a smiling pickaninny who runs out of the lodge, and with polite salutation swings wide the gate admitting him to a driveway that winds through a wide green park, to the noble mansion shining out from the grove that immediately surrounds it. The Greek portico gives entrance to a spacious hall, panelled to the ceiling, which is homelike and cosy with charming old furniture, and is used, after the familiar Virginia fashion in such homes, as reception and living room. Doors on either side of the hall open into drawing-rooms, library and dining-room, filled with Colonial furniture, and rich in family portraits and other heirlooms. Especially interesting is the dining-room, with its array of massive silver of unique pattern and workmanship—many pieces bearing the Carter arms—gleaming from its background of polished mahogany.

Among the most striking of the portraits are those of "King Carter" in the gorgeous costume in which fashion permitted a gentleman of his time to adorn himself, and his first wife, Judith, daughter of Honorable John Armistead, of Hesse, Gloucester County; Colonel Landon Carter himself, and the three stately dames, who in his time successively carried the keys of Sabine Hall. These ladies before they became, by turn, Madam Carter, of Sabine Hall, were Elizabeth Wormeley, of "Rosegill," Maria Byrd, of "Westover," and Elizabeth Beale.

A handsome stairway in the cross-hall leads to the second story, where the great central hall, panelled like the one below, is used as a billiard-room.

A second pillared portico extends across the rear of the house, and from this, looking beyond the terraced garden with its old-fashioned flowers and herbs, the master of Sabine Hall may enjoy an unobstructed view of his lands, for most of the wide sweep of fertile country that stretches away to the river still belongs to this estate of 4000 acres.

The builder of Sabine Hall and his family were conspicuous figures in the distinguished society for which Westmoreland and Richmond Counties were famous. As a burgess and vestryman he was influential both in Church and State. A recent writer says of him, "A high-minded public servant and a finished scholar, indulging a taste for science and a love for letters, Landon Carter's reputation has come down to us making him one of the most notable of the pre-Revolutionary statesmen in the colony. He was living in 1776, at Sabine Hall, retired from public praise . . . and looked up to by the younger generation as a Nestor among his compatriots. Some of his correspondence at this period with Washington and the Lees has been preserved; these letters attesting the estimation in which he was held for his wisdom, talents, and integrity, while his own epistles prove him worthy of the regard and veneration which were given him."

An interesting contribution to the "sources" of Virginia history has been made in the publication, in the *William and Mary College Quarterly Historical Magazine* (beginning with an instalment in the July, 1909, number: volume xiii, No. 1), of an abstract of a voluminous diary kept by Landon Carter. The first entry in the diary was dated January 14, 1770.

Sabine Hall descended from Colonel Landon Carter to his son by his third marriage, Robert Wormeley Carter, who was for a number of years a prominent member of the Virginia Assembly. He married Winifred Beale, was the father of a goodly number of children, among them a second Colonel Landon Carter, who inherited the "Hall" and by his first marriage with Catherine Tayloe, of "Mt. Airy," was the father of the "next heir"—a second Robert Wormeley Carter. Upon the death of this Robert Wormeley Carter, in 1861, the estate passed to his sister Elizabeth, the wife of Doctor Armistead Nelson Wellford, and thence to their son, Carter Wellford, Esquire, who with his wife (who was Elizabeth Harrison, of the James River family) and their children makes his abode in the beautiful old home of his forefathers.

MT. AIRY

Within walking distance of Sabine Hall, Mt. Airy stands in gracious dignity upon the top of a high hill, about three miles back from the Rappahannock. From the rear, the house looks upon miles of broad, gleaming river, with the houses of the little town of Tappahannock nestling among the green trees of Essex, on its farther shore, while on the nearer, spreads out like a map from the foot of the abrupt "Mount" an unbroken landscape, beautifully diversified with field and forest. Much of this stretch of level country is a part of the great Mt. Airy estate.

The house, containing with its wings about twenty-five rooms, was built in 1758, by Colonel John Tayloe,[9] who first lived on the part of the plantation nearer the river, where brick foundations are yet to be traced and which is still known as the "Old place field." Native brown sandstone was the material chosen, with facings of white stone brought from England. It is designed after the style of an Italian villa, and is unlike any other Colonial Virginia building. There is a centre building flanked by wings, which stand some distance from, and in advance of, the main structure, and are joined to it by curved glazed covered ways, formerly used as conservatories. The mansion is thus given a semi-circular form, half enclosing a grass plot reached from the main entrance by heavy, brownstone steps ornamented with bronze dogs. From the grass plot a terrace, descended by another massive stairway of brownstone, with balustrades bearing stone urns, slopes to the level of the park. Below the terrace and just in front of the stairway is an ancient sun-dial, and beyond this lies to the northward a great grove of old oaks and cedars, once the home of a goodly herd of deer.

The back windows of the house look southward upon the gardens, which encompass the sides as well as the rear of the building. The series of terraces here at the back

---

[9] Tayloe family: *Virginia Magazine of History and Biography*, xvii, p. 369 *et seq.*

MT. AIRY, RICHMOND COUNTY 1758

slope to a level piece of greensward in their midst, known as the "Bowling Green." In the garden, on the right, covered by ivy and shaded by willows, are some brick arches which call to mind monastic remains in the ancient English parks, but are really the ruins of an old conservatory.

Mt. Airy, like most of the old Virginia homes, was celebrated for hospitality. Many a pretty romance might be woven of the beauty and chivalry which met within its spacious walls; of good will and good cheer; of stately

MT. AIRY, REAR VIEW

compliment and sparkling jest; of tap of high-heeled slipper to the irresistible tune furnished by some ebon-hued master of the fiddle and bow; of dashing hunt and glowing race. The "Old Bowl at Mt. Airy" was often taxed to the limit of its ample proportions to furnish good healths for the numerous company that gathered about it. This festive piece of pottery with its jolly sides decorated with processions of comical Chinamen was the inspiration of a poet who sung its praise in some thirty lively stanzas published in the *Southern Literary Messenger*.

A graphic picture of life at Mt. Airy in the early part

of the last century has been preserved in a rare, privately printed book, by Nicholas St. John Baker, an English diplomatist who was in this country in May, 1827. He arrived at Mt. Airy at about six o'clock of a May afternoon, and "met with a very kind reception from Mrs. William Tayloe and the ladies." Mr. Tayloe was "absent at a race," but joined his guests and the ladies while they were "strolling over the garden before tea." Next morning the writer "joined a large party at breakfast." That meal over, the presence of the gentlemen was "required at the club on the course," so the entertainment of the stranger was again left to the ladies; but at half-past twelve, after partaking of a luncheon, all repaired to the race-course in a field on the Mt. Airy estate.

Mr. Baker was evidently much impressed with the Virginia ladies. He remarks upon the beauty of those he saw at the race, and tells how that evening he "took a walk with the ladies in the park," where "he saw many fine deer." He jots down notes concerning details of the house and grounds that interest him. Among them, "Upstairs a long gallery with family portraits—the Corbins, Platers, etc. The conservatory large, with orange and lemon trees put out in the grass. An extensive garden, in squares and terraces."

The collection of old portraits mentioned by the visitor is interesting. Among the personages to be found in this company of "courtly ladies of brocade" who have "long since ceased to be," and gentlemen "with powdered wigs and waistcoats long," are the three Colonels John Tayloe, of Mt. Airy, and their wives; Governors Samuel and Benjamin Ogle, of Maryland, and their wives; Governor George Plater; Colonel Richard Corbin and his wife (Betty Tayloe); William Tayloe II, and Benjamin Ogle Tayloe; Mrs. William H. Tayloe; Mrs. Gwynne and Cornelius Lyde.

The house abounds in heirlooms. In the library may be seen (among other objects characteristic of the early history of Mt. Airy) portraits of fine race-horses, including one of "Grey Diomede," and colored racing and sporting prints which hung in the rooms of the John Tayloes, second and third of the name, when they were students at an English university. In the collection of beautiful silver at Mt. Airy are some racing cups won by horses of the old-time Tayloes.

No old Virginia mansion is quite complete without a ghost. Among the gay gentlemen, who in the good old days always found the latch string on the outside of the door at the home of the Tayloes was a famous huntsman, Sir Jenings Beckwith, a descendant of a noble English family, who (though he was born in Virginia) inherited the family rank and title of baronet. For Sir Jenings the fine hunting, fair ladies and good cheer of this beautiful roof-tree proved such never-failing attractions that he spent much of his life there, and, when his days had run out, it was there that death found him. It is said that even to this day he oftentimes comes back and makes a round of his favorite haunts at Mt. Airy.

Colonel John Tayloe, the builder of Mt. Airy, belonged to the third generation of his family in Virginia. His grandfather, William Tayloe, of London, came to Virginia in the latter part of the seventeenth century, and was a burgess in 1710. He married Anne, daughter of Honorable Henry Corbin (*circa* 1629–1676), of Middlesex County, and had one son, John Tayloe I (1687–1747), who was a member of the Colonial Council in 1732. John I married Elizabeth, daughter of Maj. David Gwynne, and widow of Stephen Lyde, and left two daughters, Betty, who married Colonel Richard Corbin, of "Laneville," receiver-general of Virginia, and Anne Corbin, the second wife of Mann Page, of Rosewell, afterwards of Mannsfield, Spottsylvania County, and one son, Colonel John Tayloe II (1721–1779), the builder of Mt. Airy, in 1758, who was also a member of the Colonial Council and was noted as a turfman before the Revolution. He married Mary, sister of Governor George Plater (1736–1792), of Maryland, and was the father of eight daughters who married into the most distinguished families of the day, the Lees, the Washingtons, the Carters, the Berkeleys, the Pages, the Wormeleys, the Lomaxes and the Corbins, of Virginia, and the Lloyds of Maryland, and one son, Colonel John Tayloe III (1771–1828), who, of course, was the next heir and master of Mt. Airy. He was educated at Eton and Oxford, and was a member of the Senate and House of Delegates of the State of Virginia. Like his father, he was a successful turfman and owned such celebrated race-horses as Belair, Grey Diomede, and others. He married Anne, daughter of Governor Benjamin Ogle, of Maryland, and was survived by six sons and five daughters. His eldest son, John IV, entered the navy and was distinguished in the battles of the *Constitution* and the *Guerriere* and with the *Cyano* and *Levant*. After the first action the State of Virginia presented him with a sword. He was captured in the *Levant* by a British squadron, while lying at Port Praya, Cape de Verde Islands. He died in 1824, at Mt. Airy. His brother, William H. Tayloe, of Mt. Airy, was the father of Mr. Henry Tayloe, who married Miss Henrietta Chinn, and inherited this fair and storied villa, which in its hundred and fifty years has not been owned by any one not of the name and blood of Tayloe. Mt. Airy is now owned by the family of the late Henry Tayloe.

Another brother of John Tayloe, of the navy, was Mr. Benjamin Ogle Tayloe, who lived at the interesting " Octagon house " in Washington City.

MENOKIN

Francis Lightfoot Lee (1734–1797), sixth son of Thomas Lee (1690–1750), of Stratford, and Hannah Ludwell, his wife, was born at Stratford and was educated there by a private tutor, who made of him a good scholar, with a love for the classics and general literature. Upon coming of age he settled first in Loudoun County, where he was one of the founders of the town of Leesburg, and in 1765 represented Loudoun in the House of Burgesses. It was upon his marriage with Rebecca, daughter of John

Tayloe II, of Mt. Airy, that he removed to Richmond County, where he was chosen a burgess, and where he built the house that bears the Indian name of Menokin.

In 1775, 1776, 1777 and 1778 he was a member of the Continental Congress, and he was one of the signers of the Declaration of Independence. A recent writer upon the "signers" says, "In the spring of 1779 Mr. Lee retired from Congress and returned to his home, to which both his temper and inclination led him, with delight." This home was Menokin.

MENOKIN, RICHMOND COUNTY

After the Revolution Mr. Lee was an influential member of the Virginia Senate.

The master of Menokin was social and domestic in his tastes, and reading, farming and intercourse with his neighbors and kindred filled his latter days and made his home a centre of pleasant country life. He died there in 1797. He left no children and bequeathed Menokin to his wife for life, and afterward to his nephew, Ludwell Lee, second son of his distinguished brother, Richard Henry Lee. His wife survived him but a short while, and Ludwell Lee became the owner of Menokin, which after his time passed from the family.

CLEVE

A sturdy and handsome old mansion is Cleve, beautifully situated on the Rappahannock, in King George County. The original house, built by Colonel Charles Carter in 1729, was later burned, but it was restored upon its old walls in 1800.

The house is noticeable from the river by its large number of windows set in wide, white stone frames.

Colonel Charles Carter, of Cleve, a son of "King" Carter, by his second wife, Betty Landon, was long a bur-

CLEVE, KING GEORGE COUNTY

gess for his county, and was one of the three commissioners appointed by Lord Fairfax to look after his interests. His first wife was Mary Walker, whom he married in 1728. In July, 1743, Colonel John Lewis wrote Lawrence Washington, among other bits of news: "Mr. Wormeley and Colonel Charles Carter have lost their Ladys." Just a year later, William Beverley, in a letter to Lord Fairfax, then in England, announced the recent weddings of "Colonel Charles Carter and Colonel Landon Carter to the two Miss Byrds." The brides of these widower brothers were Anne and Maria, daughters of Colonel William Byrd II, of Westover. Interesting portraits of them at the ages of nine and eleven were painted by Bridges, and (after she became mistress of Cleve) Anne's portrait, with that of her husband and two of her children, was painted by Hesselius.

Colonel Charles Carter's third wife was Lucy Taliaferro.

Besides being a large land-holder, Colonel Carter was a scientific planter, and, in his will, directed that his estate should be managed according to a manuscript book he had prepared. He was succeeded at Cleve by a younger son, Landon, and he, in turn, by his bachelor sons, Edward and Colonel St. Leger Landon Carter. Colonel St. Leger Landon Carter was one of the early contributors to the *Southern Literary Messenger,* writing over the signature "Nugator." He also published a small volume entitled *Nugae.* One who saw Cleve during the ownership of the last Carters described the large hall hung with a double row of family portraits and a great quantity of family silver engraved with arms, but much tarnished, as bachelor possessions are apt to be. After their death Cleve passed, by sale, to the Lewis family (descendants of Fielding Lewis and his second wife, Betty Washington), and they still own it. Among its many interesting contents is a portrait of Mrs. Betty Washington Lewis.

Charming, also, is the portrait of Colonel Charles Carter, in wig and scarlet coat embellished with many gilt buttons, which still hangs at Cleve, though the estate has been so long out of the Carter famliy.

BARNSFIELD

Before the day of railroads, one of the most noted places on the route, North and South, was Hooe's Ferry over the Potomac. In King George County, close to the ferry and close to the broad river, is Barnsfield, where, since

1715, the Hooes have had a home. But few families in Virginia, and, indeed, but few in America, can trace so long a line in male descent in this country, for since Rice Hooe came to Virginia, in 1621, his descendants have been large land owners and prominent socially and in military and civil affairs.[10]

During the War between the States, the old house was the residence of Dr. A. B. Hooe. Hooe's Ferry was a favorite place for blockade-runners from Maryland to Virginia, and the Federal troops burned Barnsfield on the

BARNSFIELD, KING GEORGE COUNTY

ground, as they charged, that the blockade-runners were guided by signal lights from its windows.

The quaint picture, made many years ago, shows a typical Virginia farm-house, a part probably built as early as 1715, which was extended by rambling wings and additions

[10] Hayden, *Virginia Genealogies*, pp. 716–719, and *Virginia Magazine of History and Biography*, iv, pp. 427–429.

as the needs of the family increased. The row of Lombardy poplars close to the edge of the bluff, the weeping willows, the negroes working on boats or cutting driftwood unite to form a picture which could be duplicated many times along our rivers. The house was not a stately " mansion " but a roomy old farm-house which was of much more familiar type.

CHATHAM

Upon a green hill in Stafford County, just across the Rappahannock from Fredericksburg, stands Chatham, looking upon the old town and a long way up and down the river valley.

CHATHAM, STAFFORD COUNTY

This noble mansion with its ample central building and commodious wings, its stout brick walls and lofty columns, was built some time before the Revolution, by William Fitzhugh (1742–after 1787), whose earlier residence was Eagle's Nest, in King George County.

Mr. Fitzhugh was the son of Henry Fitzhugh (1706–1742), of Eagle's Nest (who matriculated at Christ Church College, Oxford, in 1722), and his wife, Lucy, daughter of Honorable Robert (" King ") Carter, of Corotoman.

Henry Fitzhugh was a grandson of Colonel William Fitzhugh (1651–1701), first of the family in Virginia.[11]

William Fitzhugh, of Chatham, who is said to have been educated in England, was long in public life and was a man of high character and wide influence. He was a member of the House of Burgesses, of all the Revolutionary Conventions and the Continental Congress. He was an ardent devotee of the turf, owning many noted race horses both before and after the Revolution. Among his several large estates was Ravensworth, in Fairfax County, to which he moved toward the close of his life. He married Anne, daughter of Peter Randolph, of Chatsworth, and their daughter Mary Randolph Fitzhugh married George Washington Parke Custis, of Arlington, and was the mother of the wife of General Robert E. Lee. Mr. Fitzhugh was a great-uncle of the distinguished divine, Bishop Meade, of Virginia.

In Mr. Fitzhugh's time and afterward, Chatham was famous for its hospitality. General Washington was a frequent guest there and it is said that he once wrote Mr. Fitzhugh that among the most interesting memories of his life were those of his visits to Chatham, adding, " I have put my legs oftener under your mahogany at Chatham than anywhere else in the world, and have enjoyed your good dinners, good wine and good company more than any other."

Mr. Fitzhugh finally sold Chatham to Major Churchill Jones, an officer in the Continental Army, who, having no children, bequeathed it to his only brother, William Jones. Hannah, the daughter of William Jones, became the second wife of Judge John Coalter, of the Court of Appeals of Virginia. William Jones conveyed Chatham to his son-in-law, Judge Coalter, upon condition that he should pay to the widow of Major Churchill Jones the annuity of

[11] Fitzhugh family: *Virginia Magazine of History and Biography*, vii, 196–199, 317–322, 425–427; viii, 41–45, 209–211, 314–317, 430–432; ix, 99–104.

$15,000.00 with which the estate was charged. Judge Coalter at his death gave a life interest to his widow, bequeathing the property, at her death, to his two children (by an earlier marriage with a daughter of Judge St. George Tucker), St. George Coalter and Elizabeth, the wife of Mr. John Randolph Bryan and mother of the late Mr. Joseph Bryan, of Richmond.

Chatham was later bought by Major J. Horace Lacy, was long his home, and during the War between the States was known as " The Lacy House." It was sold by Major Lacy to Oliver Watson, and by him to Mr. William Mays. From Mays the house and thirty acres of the original tract passed, by purchase, to Fleming Bailey, who later sold it to A. Randolph Howard.

General Robert E. Lee, as well as General Washington, was a frequent guest at Chatham, and it is said that under the beautiful old trees that stood on the lawn General Lee addressed his wife. These trees were felled by Northern soldiers when General Burnside made his headquarters at Chatham.

President Lincoln spent several days at Chatham, on a visit to the army under Burnside, and from the river bank before Chatham pontoon bridges were built, upon which the Federal Army crossed to the occupation of Fredericksburg, and the great battle.

BOSCOBEL

Boscobel, an estate now containing six hundred and twenty acres, is situated in Stafford County, four miles from Fredericksburg. The charming old dwelling house which stands on the highest point between the Potomac and Rappahannock Rivers was erected some one hundred and fifty years ago by Thomas Fitzhugh (1725–1768), a son of Henry Fitzhugh, of " Bedford," and grandson of that worthy William Fitzhugh, emigrant ancestor of the family in Virginia, lawyer, merchant, landed proprietor, member of the House of Burgesses and militia officer. From Thomas Fitzhugh (who inherited the estate from his father) Boscobel passed to Thomas Fitzhugh, the younger, who in turn devised the seat to his two daughters, Sarah Stuart and Henrietta, both maiden ladies, who sold it in 1847 to William Henry Fitzhugh (1788–1859), their brother, and William A. Little (whose wife was a Miss Fitzhugh).[12] After the War between the States a division of the estate was made by these two gentlemen, the " mansion house " and surrounding acreage falling to Mr. Little's lot, and thus Boscobel's title remained in the Fitzhugh family from

BOSCOBEL, NEAR FREDERICKSBURG

the time of the original grant until comparatively recently, when Mr. Charles H. Hurkamp (the present owner) purchased the place from Mr. Little.

The old homestead has been well preserved, and the lawn, grove and old-fashioned garden are kept to-day as originally laid off. The house is after the order of a roomy cottage and buried in a cluster of wonderful trees. In

[12] For an account of the Fitzhughs see *Virginia Magazine of History and Biography*, volumes vii, viii, and ix.

what was the old " parlor," now the living-room of the house, is an old-fashioned open fireplace of generous dimensions, in whose back is set a massive cast-iron plate, bearing the legend: "T. F. 1752," somewhat scarred by the flames of many a winter, 'tis true, but still clearly legible. Six or more other rooms of the house are endowed with these ample fireplaces.

From two moderately sized porches—one at the front and the other at the rear of the house—magnificent views

OLD-TIME METHOD OF COOKING AS USED AT BOSCOBEL UP TO 1905

to the north and south are to be had from this quaint " manor " which nestles on the very backbone of the ridge dividing the Northern Neck.

Until comparatively recently the old "outdoor" kitchen was in service at Boscobel, and many are the stories of accomplished cooks and temptingly prepared spreads which issued thence to the " great house." The old kitchen stands on one side of the yard and near the circular driveway leading to the entrance steps, while a building of similar size and shape stands opposite—a bit, as it were, " to balance the landscape "—and used doubtless as a quarter for house servants.

The Boscobel dwelling was destroyed by fire in March, 1915.

ACQUIA CHURCH

Over the south door of the old Acquia Church, in Overwharton Parish, Stafford County, is this inscription: "Built A. D. 1751. Destroyed by fire 1751 and rebuilt A. D. 1757 by Mourning Richards, Undertaker. William

ACQUIA CHURCH, STAFFORD COUNTY 1757

Copein, Mason." It may be well to remind the reader, especially in view of the Christian name of Mr. Richards, that undertaker in those days meant contractor.

Overwharton Parish goes back to a much earlier date than that upon the church, but earlier houses of worship in it were probably of wood, and all traces of them have passed away. Acquia still has in possession and in regular use a Communion service of massive, beaten silver, of three pieces—chalice, cup and paten—each piece bearing the inscription: " The gift of the Rev. Alex. Scott, A.M., late minister of this parish, Anno 1739." Mr. Scott served the parish nearly twenty-eight years, and the date upon the silver is that of the year of his death.[13] The service was buried in the ground for safe keeping during the Revolutionary War, the War of 1812 and the War between the States.

Acquia Church was built during the rectorship of the Reverend John Moncure (1709/10–1764),[14] who was

INTERIOR OF ACQUIA CHURCH

buried in the chancel, and whose descendants are still among the staunchest supporters of the parish. Under the Communion table is a marble slab upon which are the words " In memory of the Race of the House of Moncure."

Acquia is one of the most beautiful and best preserved

[13] A full sketch of the life of Reverend Alexander Scott (1686–1738) is given in Hayden, *Virginia Genealogies*, p. 591 *et seq.*

[14] For an account of Reverend John Moncure and his descendants see Hayden, *Virginia Genealogies*, p. 424 *et seq.*

examples of Colonial church architecture in America. It is cross-shaped, with thick walls of checkered brickwork, sloping roof and square tower for clock and bell. Though the existence of this impressive old sanctuary has been threatened by three wars, and during the last it was a camping place for soldiers, it stands to-day in perfect repair and unchanged by fancy or fashion. The stone-paved aisles, the lofty, " three decker " pulpit, with its overhanging sounding board, and the square pews are all there. In the chancel are four tablets upon which are inscribed the Lord's Prayer, the Creed and the Ten Commandments.

MT. VERNON

The most notable of Virginia mansions and plantations will always be Mt. Vernon, the home during life, in death the resting place of all that was mortal of George Washington.

The Mt. Vernon estate was part of a tract of 5000 acres granted by Lord Culpeper in 1644 to Colonel John Washington and Nicholas Spencer. Half of it descended in time to Colonel John Washington's great-grandson, Lawrence Washington, who built the mansion and named it Mt. Vernon after the British admiral under whom he served. At the death of Lawrence Washington it passed to his half-brother George, who enlarged both house and plantation. After General Washington's death Mrs. Washington made her home at Mt. Vernon until her own death, when the place passed to her husband's nephew, Bushrod Washington, and from him to John Augustine Washington, and from him to John Augustine Washington, Jr., who in 1858 sold 200 acres, including the mansion and tombs, to the Mt. Vernon Ladies' Association, a national organization formed for the purpose of restoring and preserving the home of George Washington.

The situation of Mt. Vernon is peculiarly happy, for the waters of the same broad Potomac upon whose banks lies Wakefield, the birth-place of Washington, lap its shores, while but a short way up the river the white dome

MT VERNON, POTOMAC RIVER

of the Capitol that his deeds made possible shines out against blue heaven. Mt. Vernon, the Mecca of all true Americans, thus stands upon what might well be called Washington's River, between the place where he first saw the light of day and the crowning monument to his genius.

The most interesting approach to Mt. Vernon is by water, for the river-landing by which "the many-sided Washington" kept in touch with the world and sent the produce of his beautiful plantation to market teems with memories of him as the thrifty husbandman and man of business.

MT. VERNON, REAR VIEW

Not far from the wharf is the family graveyard where above the doorway of a massive but severely plain brick vault the visitor reads: "Within this enclosure rest the remains of General Washington," and between the bars of heavy iron gates he gazes with reverent eyes upon two white marble sarcophagi in which lie, side by side, the bodies of George Washington and Martha, his wife. How calmly, how simply can true greatness, when the day is done, lie down to pleasant dreams! For pleasant indeed they must be within the embrace of his own home, in the region of his own achievements. So says the pilgrim to himself, then goes on his way with softened vision, and a spirit in tune for the view of the homestead and its environs.

Charming are the ample grounds with their many varieties of goodly trees, some of which are historic, their wooded deer-park with its shy, soft-eyed and fleet-footed inhabitants, their long bowling green and expanse of velvet turf stretching down to the river. Full of suggestion are the quaint outbuildings—the dormer-windowed servants' quarters; the kitchen, with its great crane and bake oven, planned for preparation of the abundant feasts upon which the guests that flocked to Mt. Vernon by coach and by boat were regaled; the smoke-house, where bacon of the true old Virginia flavor was cured; the coach-house, with its antiquated chariot; the spinning-house, where clothing for the slaves and rag-carpets and other fabrics for the house were woven, and where may still be seen the ancient loom wheels, reels and brake. But the most appealing of all the outside features, most redolent of memories of George in his queue and Martha in her cap, is the fascinating old flower garden which they planned, where the prim hedges of dwarf-box which they planted still define innumerable tidy beds of old-fashioned flowers. In Washington's time distinguished visitors were invited to plant trees, shrubs or flowers in the garden and many of these memorials still flourish—among them a tree planted by Lafayette and one by Jefferson. A musk-cluster rose named by Washington for his mother, and other roses named for himself and Nelly Custis are also pointed out.

Mt. Vernon house stands three stories high, including the dormer-windowed attic, with a cellar under the whole. It is built upon a foundation of stone and brick and its framework is of oak sheathed with North Carolina pine, cut, painted and sanded to resemble stone. The sloping roof is covered with cypress shingles. From the east front the mansion is entered through a long and wide square-pillared portico, paved with tiles imported from England by Washington. The driveway and the brass knocker upon the central door of the severely plain west front, show that it was the entrance for visitors. The windows upon this side look upon a wide green court bounded on either side by outbuildings joined to the mansion by colonnades. In the centre of the court a sun-dial marks the spot where one stood in Washington's time.

House and grounds are exquisitely kept by the Mt. Vernon Association. Within, the house is still a completely equipped home, and many pieces of the beautiful old furniture actually used by the Washingtons have been brought back and restored to their original places, while all of the furnishings and decorations are of the period. From the panelled hall one may look through open doors into four of the principal rooms of the first floor. They are the west parlor, with its sundry mementos of the great master of Mt. Vernon, its ornate wainscoting, its mantel with the Washington coat-of-arms carved above it; Nelly Custis's music room, where the pretty old harpsichord stands open, and where Washington's flute is preserved; the family dining-room, with its charming old sideboard; and Mrs. Washington's sitting-room, where the mantel-mirror, spindle-legged centre-table and some of the old furnishings are original. The library is also on this floor and in addition to the built-in book-shelves contains an old mahogany bookcase and some other pieces of its original furniture, but unfortunately few of Washington's own books are among those now on its shelves. The banquet-hall, at the east end of the house, contains many articles of beauty and interest.

Ascending by the graceful stair to the second floor, we find six bedrooms possessed of that picturesqueness which stately " four posters " dressed in canopy and valance of snowy dimity or beflowered chintz, quaint chests of drawers, spindle-legged dressing tables and candle-stands give. These chambers are known as " Lafayette's room," the " river room," the " guest room," " Nelly Custis's room," the " green room," and " Washington's room." The bed in Washington's room is the one upon which he died,

December 14, 1799, and some of the other articles in the room were used by him. In the dormer-windowed attic are six bedrooms used for guest-chambers when the house was crowded. One of them is known as " Mrs. Washington's room." After General Washington's death his bedchamber was (after the manner of the time) closed, and the wife chose for her own use the little room in the end of the attic, through whose only window she could look upon her husband's tomb. It was in this attic room that " Lady Washington " died on the twenty-second day of May, 1802.

Young Thomas Lee Shippen, of Philadelphia, a grandson of Thomas Lee, the founder of Stratford, made, in 1790, a round of visits to the friends and relatives of his family in Virginia. In a letter to his father he thus describes his impressions of the home of Washington:

Mount Vernon, 16 Sept., 1790.

My dear Father and Friend.

This is to be sure a delightful place. Nothing seems wanting to render it a fit residence of its owner, worthy to employ and amuse the leisure of so great a man as our President.

I have been here two days and have seen most of the improvements which do honor at once to the taste and industry of our Washington. I have been treated, as usual, with every most distinguished mark of kindness and attention. Hospitality indeed seems to have spread over the whole place its happiest, kindest influence. The President exercises it in a superlative degree, from the greatest of its duties to the most trifling minutiæ, and Mrs. Washington is the very essence of kindness. Her soul seems to overflow with it like the most abundant fountain, and her happiness is in exact proportion to the number of objects upon which she can dispense her benefits.

POHICK CHURCH

But a short distance from Mt. Vernon stands old Pohick, the parish church of both Mt. Vernon and Gunston Hall—the Mason home. This church was built in 1769 to replace an earlier frame structure, and the Washingtons and Masons were worshippers in the first sanctuary, as well as the second.

In 1735 Augustine Washington was elected a vestryman of Pohick and in 1762 George Washington and George William Fairfax were appointed church wardens. It is said that the plans of the present massive and commodious building of brick, with stone trimmings, were drawn by General Washington himself. The building committee consisted of George Washington, George

POHICK CHURCH, FAIRFAX COUNTY

William Fairfax, George Mason, Daniel McCarthy and Edward Payne.

Pohick Church was badly damaged by Federal troops during the War between the States, and when it was later repaired, through the generosity of a gentleman from New York, the interior was unfortunately modernized. More recently, however, its quaint and interesting appearance has been restored.

It is the custom of the regents of the Mt. Vernon Association to attend service once a year in old Pohick.

GUNSTON HALL

About one mile distant from Pohick Church stands Gunston Hall, the famous home of George Mason (1725–1792), author of the Bill of Rights and the Constitution of Virginia.[15]

The Gunston estate of 7000 acres was long since divided into small farms, most of which are now the property of

GUNSTON HALL, FAIRFAX COUNTY 1758

northern settlers, but the mansion is as well preserved as Mt. Vernon, and more pretentious. It is eighty feet long by forty feet wide, with thick brick walls, tall chimneys and a long sloping roof. Standing somewhat back from the Potomac, upon a bold bluff, it makes a striking picture

[15] Mason family: Rowland, *The Life and Letters of George Mason, 1725–1792*, vol. i, chap. i.

and commands a splendid view of the river. It possesses the spacious rooms and hall of Colonial mansions of its type, finished with handsomely carved wainscoting, much of which is said to have been brought from England.

George Mason (fifth in descent from George Mason the Cavalier, who took refuge in Virginia in 1657) built Gunston Hall in 1758 and lived in it many years, during which it was a favorite resort of some of the most historic characters of those history-making days. Mt. Vernon is only four miles away, by river, and Washington, who kept a four-oared gig, rowed by a uniformed negro crew, often chose this way of visiting his friend and neighbor, Mason. Sometimes, too, on Sundays, after going to service at Pohick, in his coach and four, the master of Mt. Vernon would drive home to dinner with the master of Gunston Hall. The dining-room at Gunston Hall in which the Father of his Country and other patriots were entertained is still pointed out. There are also "Jefferson's room," occupied by Thomas Jefferson, during his frequent visits to Gunston, and "Lafayette's room," in which the Marquis of Lafayette slept when he was a guest there during his visit to America after the Revolution. But the most notable apartment in the house is the great library, for though George Mason's greatest claim to fame is as the father of the Bill of Rights, his name is also intimately associated with the Declaration of Independence, and it is said that it was in this library that Jefferson and Mason together made the first draft of that immortal paper.

After George Mason's death, Gunston Hall remained for some years in possession of his descendants, but was finally sold and has several times since changed hands.

CHRIST CHURCH, ALEXANDRIA

The pride of the old town of Alexandria is historic Christ Church, an impressive and well-kept building, standing in a spacious brick-walled churchyard, in the heart of the town. The architecture is much like that of Pohick

Church, and like Pohick its chief claim to distinction is the fact that Washington was at one time a vestryman. The Washington pew is still pointed out, and many are the

CHRIST CHURCH, ALEXANDRIA 1773

tourists who come from Washington City by train and ferry for the privilege of sitting in it, if only for a few moments. It was in 1773 that the finished church was handed over to the vestry by the contractor and upon the same day General Washington purchased a pew for £26, 10, 8.

General Lee also attended Christ Church during his boyhood, when he lived in Alexandria, and was in the habit of joining with the other young folk of the parish in dressing the church with evergreens at Christmas. In 1853, when he was a colonel in the United States Army, he was confirmed by Bishop Johns, in this church. His pew, like Washington's, is marked with a silver plate, and is one of the chief objects of interest in the building where these two great generals are further memorialized by mural tablets.

In the early days of its history, Christ Church had women as sextons; first, one Susannah Edwards, "who preceded the members of the congregation up the aisles, locating each family in their respective pews according to dignity," and later "Mistress Cook," who we are told was "peculiar in dress and physiognomy." She had "a stately manner of ushering people into their pews, and locking the door upon them, and with almost military air she patrolled the aisles, alert to detect and prompt to suppress any violation of order."

THE CARLYLE HOUSE

The Carlyle House, now a portion of the Braddock Hotel, on Fairfax Street, Alexandria, was built by John Carlyle (1720–1780), a wealthy merchant, in 1745.[16] In architecture it is a fine example of an old Virginia mansion, with its spacious rooms, finished with beautiful woodwork, and, besides, it has a history. In 1755 it was occupied by Major General Edward Braddock, who here held a council, composed of himself and Governors Shirley, of Massachusetts, Delancy, of New York, Morris, of Pennsylvania, Sharpe, of Maryland, Dinwiddie, of Virginia, Dobbs, of North Carolina, General St. Clair and Benjamin Franklin, for the purpose of planning the campaign against Fort

[16] Carlyle family: *William and Mary Quarterly*, xviii. pp. 201–212, 278–289.

[illegible]

[illegible] The [illegible] [illegible] pointed out.

[illegible] Braddock [illegible] at the Carlyle House [illegible] Washington became a member of his staff.

CARLYLE HOUSE, ALEXANDRIA [illegible]

Efforts are being made by zealous antiquarians of Alexandria to secure the Carlyle House and preserve it as a museum.

ARLINGTON, ALEXANDRIA COUNTY after 1802

ARLINGTON

Thought of Arlington brings before the mind's eye two pictures, one the white-columned mansion standing out from the crest of a high hill whose slopes are wooded with ancient oaks, the other (seen from the portico of the mansion itself) Washington City lying in clear view, but touched with the softened beauty that distance gives, seven miles away. The walk, or rather the climb, up hill under the oaks, and the view when the mansion in its plat of greensward at the top has been reached, must be a thing of actual experience to be appreciated.

After the death of Mrs. Martha Washington, in 1802, George Washington Parke Custis, her grandson (who was also General Washington's adopted son), removed from Mt. Vernon to Arlington, which was built by him and named after the older Custis mansion in Northampton County, long since destroyed by fire.

Mr. Custis married, in 1806, Mary Lee, daughter of William Fitzhugh, of Chatham, and he and his wife made Arlington a veritable seat of hospitality, where the most distinguished Europeans and Americans of the time were entertained. At least one notable wedding took place there when, upon June 30, 1831, Mary Ann Randolph Custis, the only child of Mr. and Mrs. Custis to survive infancy, gave her hand to Lieutenant Robert Edward Lee, then of the United States Corps of Engineers, afterward to become the great general and hero of the War between the States. Mr. Custis died October 10, 1857, and was buried by the side of his wife in the beautiful grove near Arlington house, where their tombs may still be seen. Their daughter, Mrs. Lee, inherited Arlington, and General Lee became deeply attached to the place and made his home there whenever his military duties would permit. Writing, in 1861, of Arlington and its possible destruction by the Northern Army he said, " They cannot take away the remembrance of the spot, and the memories of those that to us rendered it sacred. That will remain to us as long as life will last, and that we can preserve. In the absence of a home I wish I could purchase Stratford."

The house was stored with the most precious relics of "the Father of his Country," many of which were stolen in the early days of the War between the States. The place itself was taken possession of by the United States Government and a military cemetery established there. This made it impossible to restore the estate to Mrs. Lee's heirs, but such relics as were seized by the Government have been returned and the estate has been paid for.

Arlington is still used by the Government as a cemetery for army and naval officers, and the interest that gives it, added to the fact that it was the home of the Custises and Lees, draws thousands of tourists thither every year.

PART VI

PIEDMONT AND THE SOUTH SIDE

PIEDMONT

ONE of the most attractive parts of Virginia is the Piedmont section lying, as its name indicates, at the foot of the mountains—that is, just east of the Blue Ridge—and embracing the counties of Loudoun, Fauquier, Culpeper, Orange and others. It is a country of fertile, well watered, beautifully undulating lands, whose many bold hills looking across wood and stream and meadow upon the blue mountains afford ideal sites for homes. The counties of this group were the last to be formed east of the Blue Ridge before the Revolution, and for this reason, together with their remote situation at the time, there do not remain many noted houses of the Colonial period. There are, however, some handsome and interesting ones of more recent date.

OAK HILL

Oak Hill, in Loudoun County, was the home of a president of the United States and looks the part. Standing out from among century-old trees, upon a hill clothed with the deep-toned, deep-piled velvet of blue-grass, this noble brick mansion with its tall chimneys, and its Greek portico whose white columns are thirty feet high, dominates the country for miles around. Its windows look across rolling farm-lands, upon the Blue Ridge in one direction and the Catoctin Hills in another, while against the south-eastern sky stands lofty " Sugar-loaf."

The house was built by James Monroe, during his presidency, to replace a dormer-windowed cottage which had long been the home of the Monroe family. It takes its name from a group of fine oaks on the wide-spreading lawn on which President Monroe planted a tree from each State in the Union, presented to him for the purpose by the congressmen from the respective States.

General Lafayette was a guest at Oak Hill during his visit to Virginia in 1824, and mementos of his stay may

OAK HILL (FRONT), LOUDOUN COUNTY before 1830

still be seen in the beautiful mantel-pieces in the drawing-room, which were presents from him to the house.

Upon Monroe's death, in 1831, at the home of his daughter, Mrs. Gouverneur, of New York, Oak Hill passed to the Gouverneurs, who, in 1852, sold it to Colonel John M. Fairfax. Among Monroe relics that went with the place was a handsome backgammon table with ivory playing pieces, presented to Mr. Monroe by the American Minister at Paris. Between the wood and marble tops of this table Mrs. Fairfax found a safe hiding-place for her jewels when the house was searched by Northern soldiers, who frequently occupied it during the War between the States, but treated the home of Monroe with unusual respect.

Many of the famous raids of the redoubtable Mosby were directed from the Oak Hill house, the front porch serving as a position of vantage. Colonel Fairfax was himself an officer on General Longstreet's staff, and was distinguished for bravery. A few years after the war he sold Oak Hill to Dr. Quinby, of New York, but in 1885

OAK HILL (REAR)

it was bought back by his son, Mr. Henry Fairfax, who now makes his home there. Mr. Fairfax devotes himself to the care of the estate and the breeding of fine horses, and old Oak Hill, with its 1200 acres of grass-land and its stables providing winter quarters for over two hundred horses, is famous throughout Virginia and beyond.

OATLANDS

Oatlands, near the old town of Leesburg, in beautiful Loudoun County, was built in the year 1800 by George Carter, son of Robert (commonly called " Councillor ") Carter, of Nomini Hall, Westmoreland, and great-grandson of " King " Carter.

The plantation of 5000 acres was part of the great

Fairfax estate, and was bought from Lord Fairfax by Councillor Carter and given to his son George upon his coming of age.

The master of Oatlands was, like his father, the councillor, a man of liberal education, devoted to books and music, and his home bears witness to his cultivated taste. The building of Oatlands and laying out of its grounds was a labor of love with him. He was his own architect and most of the work was done under his direction, by his

OATLANDS, LOUDOUN COUNTY 1800

slaves. He died in 1846, leaving Oatlands house with 3000 acres of land and 75 slaves to his eldest son, George Carter, who occupied it until 1894, when it was sold, with sixty acres, to Mr. Stilson Hutchins, of Washington, who in turn sold it to its present owner, Mr. William Corcoran Eustis.

Oatlands has always played a prominent part in the social life of its neighborhood. Its present master is an enthusiastic hunter and lover of horses and is making the old place famous as a stock farm.

OLD METHODIST CHURCH, LEESBURG

MORVEN PARK

Morven Park * with its 1000 acres of fertile land, its spacious and distinguished looking mansion, its wide stretches of greensward and its stately trees is one of the finest estates in all Virginia. It was built by Governor Swan, of Maryland, who made its name a synonym for hospitality. Its present master is Mr. Westmoreland Davis, M. F. H., of Loudoun County, who is, like so many country gentlemen of that section, an enthusiastic hunter and stock-raiser.

RASPBERRY PLAIN

Raspberry Plain, Loudoun County, was built about 1771 by Thomson Mason (1733–1785), a brother of George Mason, of Gunston Hall. Mr. Mason, who was a man of note in his day, was long a member of the House of Burgesses, and was a judge of the General Court during the Revolution.

At Mr. Mason's death, in 1785, Raspberry Plain passed to his distinguished son, Stevens Thomson Mason (1760–

---

* See illustration, p. 379.

1803), United States senator from Virginia, who married Mary, daughter of Robert Armistead, of Louisa County, and was the father of Honorable Armistead Thomson Mason, of Selma (killed in the famous Mason-McCarty duel), General John Thomson Mason, Stevens Thomson Mason, who died young, and a bevy of daughters celebrated for their beauty and charm. These Mason girls were belles in Washington society when they were guests of the Virginia presidents at the White House, and drove in a coach

RASPBERRY PLAIN, LOUDOUN COUNTY

and four with out-riders in livery. They drew many of the most eligible beaux of the day to Raspberry Plain, and it is said that the round window in the upper hall was a favorite place for the girls to " station themselves to watch for their cavaliers as they would be descried on their prancing horses a long distance up the road." All three of them married distinguished men. Mary was the wife of Governor Benjamin Howard, of Missouri; Emily, of Honorable William McCarty; and Catherine, the wife of Post-

MORVEN PARK, LOUDOUN COUNTY

master General William T. Barry, of President Jackson's cabinet.

Beautiful colored crayon portraits of the Honorable and Mrs. Stevens Thomson Mason, by Sharpless, are preserved by their descendants.

After the Masons' time, Raspberry Plain was closed for years, during which it was said to be haunted.

SELMA

Selma was built by Honorable Armistead Thomson Mason (1787–1819), early in the nineteenth century. It has had a grim history.

Colonel Mason was a man of fine talent and wide popularity. He served in the War of 1812 as a colonel of the cavalry, and, like his father, Stevens Thomson Mason, of Raspberry Plain, was United States senator from Virginia. On account of a political quarrel he engaged in a duel with his near cousin, Colonel John Mason McCarty, so tragic that the whole country rang with it. It was fought at Bladensburg, Maryland, on February 6, 1819, with muskets at ten paces. Mason dropped dead at the first fire, while McCarty was only saved by an accident.

Mason had a young and devoted wife, with one child, a pretty little boy but a few months old. McCarty was a brilliant young lawyer of the same county, and he was soon to be married to the lovely Lucinda Lee.

After the duel McCarty wrote to her, relating what he had done, giving her a week for reflection, and asking her to tell him at the end of that time whether she would marry him after what had happened. She related long afterward the agony of that week, how she knelt in despair at her mother's feet and asked her to decide; how the old lady could only advise her to follow her own heart; how at last she sent a note to her lover, inviting him to call.

After their marriage they settled near Selma, where the young widow of Mason lived with her little boy, and to them also was born an only son, very promising, in whom they took great pride.

Though living but a few miles apart, however, the two families, the Masons and McCartys, never renewed their acquaintance or spoke to each other. There was a natural avoidance, nothing more. Young McCarty was a frequent sportsman, but in all his gunning was never known to set his foot on part of the Mason estate, whatever the luck it might promise. One fatal day, however, in following the flight of game, he mounted a fence, which formed the boundary of the Mason property, and attempted to load in this position. His attention diverted by the movements of the birds or the dogs, he let slip his gun, which exploded and sent the ramrod through his head. He fell on the Mason side, which he had avoided all his life, upon the ground which he was to press only in death. And to make the dramatic situation complete Stevens Mason at that moment came riding by, and the dying youth was carried to Raspberry Plain, the birthplace of his father's victim, and laid dead in the hall. This was almost the death-blow to the parents of young McCarty. His bereaved father, the slayer of Senator Mason, became erratic and for much of the time a wanderer. He would leave his home without a word, and be gone for years, his own wife not knowing where; and then would as suddenly reappear, unkempt and haggard, with long hair on his shoulders and beard descending to his waist.

Selma was inherited by Stevens Thomson Mason, Jr., whose infancy was surrounded with so much that was tragic. At twenty-one he was a rich, attractive and dashing young fellow, often seen driving a handsome pair of horses tandem through the streets of Leesburg, but he seemed to have been born for disaster. A too generous expenditure of his fortunes brought reverses which forced him to sell Selma, after which he joined the army, and while serving as a captain in the Mexican War was mortally wounded.

OAK HILL

Oak Hill, in Fauquier County, is interesting as the home in which Chief Justice John Marshall (1755–1835) grew to manhood. A house of seven rooms, which is a part of the present homestead, was built here, in 1773, by Judge Marshall's father, Colonel Thomas Marshall (1730–1802), a gallant officer in the Revolution, and was given by him to his son John. The great Chief Justice owned Oak Hill the rest of his life and frequently occupied it. At his death it passed to his eldest son, Thomas Marshall, who married Margaret, daughter of Fielding Lewis, of Weyanoke, on James River.

OAK HILL, FAUQUIER COUNTY

Thomas Marshall was a master of arts of Princeton University and member of the Virginia Convention of 1829. He added to the Oak Hill house five large rooms and two halls, besides basement rooms. The estate descended to his eldest son, John Marshall, many years a member of the Virginia Legislature, who sold it to his brother Thomas Marshall, colonel in the Confederate Army, who was killed at the Battle of Winchester, November 12, 1864. After his death the old homestead was sold and since it passed from the Marshall family has had several owners. It is now the property of Mr. T. M. Maddox.

GORDONSDALE *

Reverend John Scott (1747–1785) led an adventurous life for a clergyman.[1] He went to Scotland on account of having been one of the participants, though not a principal, in a fatal duel. There he took the degree of master of arts in King's College, Aberdeen, and soon after his graduation married Elizabeth, daughter of Professor Thomas Gordon of that institution. At the beginning of the Revolution he was minister in charge of a church in Maryland, but was arrested and tried for remaining loyal to the Mother Country. After that he retired to his plantation in Fauquier County, Virginia, which he named Gordonsdale, in honor of his wife.

One of Mr. Scott's sons, Robert Eden Scott (1769–1811), was a professor at Aberdeen, another, Judge John Scott (1781–1850), was a distinguished lawyer in Virginia. After her husband's death Mrs. Scott sold her home to her son-in-law, Dr. Chandler Peyton, who died in 1827, leaving Gordonsdale to his son Dr. Robert E. Peyton, who sold it, in 1868, to General Benjamin Huger, of the Confederate Army.

FARLEY

One of the oldest homesteads in the Piedmont section is Farley, in Culpeper County, which was built more than a century ago by Carter Beverley but was soon after bought by William Champe Carter, son of Colonel Edward Carter, of Blenheim, Albemarle County, who was a grandson of Robert ("King") Carter. Mr. Carter gave the place the name of Farley in honor of his wife, who was his

---

* See illustration at head of Preface.

[1] An interesting account of the Reverend John Scott and his descendants is given in Hayden, *Virginia Genealogies*, p. 603 *et seq.*

cousin, Maria Champe Farley, daughter of James Parke Farley and his wife, Elizabeth Hill Byrd, daughter of Honorable William Byrd III, of Westover, and also descended, in the fifth generation, from Robert (" King ") Carter.

Elizabeth Hill Farley Carter, the only daughter of the Carters of Farley, married Colonel Samuel Storrow, of the United States Army, and she and her husband made their home at Farley during her father's lifetime, and afterward. In 1836 her husband died and she and her children continued to live at Farley until about 1842, when it was sold, and was long the home of Dr. W. A. Wellford and his wife, who was Miss Corbin. The Wellfords finally sold it to Mr. Franklin Stearns.

The Farley estate consists of a goodly number of fertile acres and a commodious mansion situated among fine old trees, and commanding an extensive view. The rooms are spacious and there is a great central hall where in the olden days (says one who knew the place well) " many danced joyfully to the music of old Uncle Jim's fiddle."

MONTPELIER

James Madison, like other Virginians who were presidents of the United States, was fortunate in his home. Montpelier with its ample, and at the same time harmonious, proportions, its lovely grounds and horseshoe-shaped terraced garden, and, beyond, its superb view of the Blue Ridge, is in both architecture and situation the rival of Oak Hill, President Monroe's home in Loudoun. The estate was originally a large one, President Madison's father owning at the close of the Revolution 7000 to 8000 acres of land. The house at first consisted of only the central portion, built about 1760, by James Madison, Sr., but was afterward brought to its present imposing size and appearance. The principal improvements were made in 1809, after designs by William Thornton, architect of the Capitol at Washington, while Latrobe had a hand in still later improvements, which include the wings.

President Madison was born while his mother was on a visit to her parents, at Port Conway, King George County, but grew up and spent his life (except when called away by official duties) at Montpelier. In 1794 he married, in Philadelphia, a beautiful Quakeress—a widow—Mistress Dorothea Payne Todd. Though during her girlhood and earlier married life she had known only the habits and customs of the prim society with which her family was identified, it was in Virginia, as mistress of the heart and home of one of the most distinguished men of the day, that Dolly Madison, the sprightly, the lovable, found her true sphere. She had, added to gifts of mind and character, remarkable social talent. In the words of one who knew her: " She never forgot a name she had once heard nor a face she had once seen, nor the personal circumstances connected with every individual of her acquaintance. Her quick recognition of persons; her recurrence to their peculiar interests produced the gratifying impression in each and all of those who conversed with her that they were especial objects of regard." Says the same writer: " Her snuffbox had a magic influence—for who could partake of its contents offered in a manner so gracious and retain a feeling inimical to its owner." As Madison himself was a genial host and delightful talker it is easy to imagine how charming must have been the life at fair Montpelier, which, like so many Virginia homes, was a " seat of hospitality."

One wing of the house was occupied by the mother of the president, and there the venerable dame, attended by her old family servants, constantly visited by her children and grandchildren and tenderly ministered to by her daughter-in-law, the engaging " Dolly," preserved the customs and habits of an earlier generation. One who visited her there draws a striking picture of her at the age of

MONTPELIER, ORANGE COUNTY

1760 -- 1809

ninety-seven, placidly enjoying the evening of her long life and " always busy," either knitting or reading from her favorite books—" large, dark and worn quartos and folios of most venerable appearance," which were kept upon a table by her side.

Much has been said and written about the mother of Washington; truly does it seem that this mother of Madison must have been a woman worth knowing in her time and keeping in remembrance after.

When he was about sixty-six years old, Madison retired from public life and spent his last nineteen years in the enjoyment of his country home, happy in his agricultural interests, his books, his friends, and his correspondence. He and Jefferson were intimate friends, and Monticello and Montpelier were not too far apart for their masters to exchange frequent visits.

Madison died at Montpelier on June 28, 1836, aged eighty-five, and he and his wife are buried there, side by side. A handsome shaft, erected by his admirers, marks the spot.

Montpelier is now the home of Mr. William Dupont, formerly of Delaware, who has added another story to the wings and adorned the terraced gardens with statuary and a variety of rare and beautiful shrubs and flowers.

ROCKLANDS

The tract of land on which Rocklands is located was purchased about the year 1845, by Edmund Henshaw, who during his ownership erected a dwelling which was later enlarged by Barton H. Haxall, who acquired the estate by purchase, in 1851. At Mr. Haxall's death, in 1882, an Englishman by the name of Moorwood bought the property and made his residence there for several years, finally disposing of Rocklands to Thomas Atkinson, the present owner.

A year or two after Mr. Atkinson purchased the estate, the original dwelling was totally destroyed by fire, and the present handsome house was built by him on the site of the old one. The picture shown here is of the original dwelling.

ROCKLANDS, ORANGE COUNTY

FRASCATI

Frascati, the beautiful home of Judge Philip Pendleton Barbour (1783–1841), speaker of the United States House of Representatives and justice of the United States Supreme Court, was built some time before 1830 by the same workmen who had been employed in erecting the buildings for the University of Virginia.

After Judge Barbour's death Frascati changed owners

many times. For years before the War between the States it was the home of Colonel James Magruder, whose sons, bred at Frascati, were famous for bravery in the Confed-

FRASCATI, ORANGE COUNTY

erate Army. Three of these five gallant Magruder boys were killed in battle, while the other two were desperately wounded. The husband of their sister was also killed in battle.[2]

In more recent times Frascati was long the home of Mrs. William H. Lyne. Its present master is Mr. A. D. Irving, a kinsman of Washington Irving.

BARBOURSVILLE

In a picturesque state of ruin, its walls and its columns draped with ivy, stands Barboursville,[3] once the handsomest home in Orange County. Jefferson is said to have helped to plan the house, which was built in 1822, by his friend James Barbour (1775–1842), governor of Virginia, and United States senator. In outward appearance it was much like Frascati, the home of Governor Barbour's

---

[2] Scott, *History of Orange County*, p. 156.

[3] See illustration, p. 393.

brother, Judge Philip Pendleton Barbour; but the interior was more ambitious. The stately central hall was six-sided and was capped above the second story by a dome. A door from the hall led to the drawing-room, a large and beautiful apartment, octagonal in shape, with windows opening upon a pillared portico.

The gardens at both Barboursville and Frascati were originally surrounded by serpentine walls like those at the University of Virginia and the one at Barboursville still remains.

After Governor Barbour's death his home passed to his son, Mr. Johnson Barbour, a gentleman famous for scholarship and wit, who kept up Barboursville's traditions for cultivation, refinement and hospitality. The destruction of such a home is tragedy. It burned down on Christmas Day, 1884.

KESWICK

Keswick on its green hill, with its shady trees, its box-walks and its charming old garden, was originally part of the Castle Hill estate in Albemarle County and was the inheritance of Jane Frances Walker, eldest child of Honorable Francis Walker (1764–1806), of Castle Hill. The plantation was first called Turkey Hill and could boast of thirty-seven hundred acres. Its mistress gave her hand in marriage at the age of sixteen years to Doctor Mann Page, who, after thirty-five years of married life, died at Keswick, in 1850—his wife surviving him until 1873. The Mann Pages were succeeded in their ownership of the estate by their son Doctor Thomas Walker Page, who died there in 1887, leaving children who still make their home at Keswick. Another son of Doctor Mann and Jane (Walker) Page was Doctor Richard Channing Moore Page, of New York, the historian of the Page family. Doctor Page has given an interesting account of the long series of tutors who taught at Keswick, which eventually became the site of a noted boarding school conducted by two of Thomas Walker Page's sons, James Morris and Thomas Walker Page, Jr.

BARBOURSVILLE, ORANGE COUNTY

EDGE HILL, ALBERMARLE COUNTY

EDGE HILL

In the year 1735, William Randolph, of Tuckahoe, patented twenty-four hundred acres of land in Albemarle County. Though he continued to live at Tuckahoe, in Goochland, his holdings in Albemarle had, as will be seen, an interesting effect upon the Randolph family history.

Over and over again in Virginia, adjoining lands have been responsible for the joining of hands. About 1770 Thomas Mann Randolph, Senior (1741–1793), of Tuckahoe, a wealthy widower, and his son Thomas Mann Randolph, Junior (1768–1828), were both numbered among the eligible beaux (or "catches," as the popular phrase would have expressed it) of Virginia. The Randolph estate in Albemarle lay between Belmont, the Harvie estate, and Monticello, the Jefferson estate; and at both Belmont and Monticello was a lovely young daughter. What more natural than that ere long dusky proficients in the dance music of the good old times were tuning their fiddles for two weddings: Thomas Mann Randolph, the father, and the witty Gabriella Harvie making one pair; and Thomas Mann Randolph, the son, and the gentle Martha Jefferson, the other. The elder bridegroom took his bride to Tuckahoe and gave the Albemarle plantation to his son, who named it Edge Hill, and built upon it a commodious frame homestead.

The young master of Edge Hill became one of the leading men of his time. He represented his district in Congress, and in 1818 became governor of Virginia. His own prominence, and his wife's, together with their personal charm, made Edge Hill a resort for distinguished visitors second only to Monticello.

Upon Governor Randolph's death the estate passed to his son, Thomas Jefferson Randolph, who, in 1828, removed the old house to the rear and built, upon the original site, the present brick mansion. After his death Edge Hill became famous as a boarding school which was opened by his widow, Mrs. Jane (Nicholas) Randolph, and carried on many years after her time by her daughters, Misses Mary and Sarah Randolph. It was interrupted by the War between the States, but was reopened in 1869 and continued until 1896, when Edge Hill passed from the Randolph family, and became once more a private residence.

The house is filled with relics of Thomas Jefferson. Its situation in view of the Blue Ridge, its lovely lawn and gardens, and its park of great forest trees, make the old home of Jefferson's daughter as beautiful as it is interesting.

CASTLE HILL AND BELVOIR

Doctor Thomas Walker (1715–1794), a descendant of Captain Thomas Walker, of Gloucester County, who came to Virginia, about 1650, from Staffordshire, England,[3] was a prominent physician in his day, interested in politics and exploration, an influential member of the House of Burgesses, the Revolutionary Conventions and the Committee of Safety, several times Virginia's commissioner to effect treaties with the Indians, commissary under Washington in the French and Indian War, and probably the first white man who ever entered the territory which is now the State of Kentucky. In 1750 Doctor Walker went to the " western country " and during this expedition named Cumberland gap and river in honor of the Duke of Cumberland. It is said that Doctor Walker introduced the celebrated apple, the Albemarle pippin, into Albemarle County from New York. He was the guardian of Thomas Jefferson and an intimate friend of both Washington and Jefferson.

A descendant of Doctor Walker writes in a sketch of the Walker family: " In 1765 Doctor Walker built the house at Castle Hill, which has become a well-known place to Virginians. The small panes of glass and the brass door-locks, which may still be seen in the venerable build-

[3] Walker family: Watson's, *Some Notable Families of America*, p. 86 *et seq.*

CASTLE HILL, ALBEMARLE COUNTY

STARTING THE HUNT

ing, were brought from London, and the quaint old hall, which is still the centre of a graceful hospitality, has echoed to the violin of Jefferson and the step of Madison in the merry dance.

"Here five men, either presidents or presidents-to-be, have been entertained as familiar friends or relatives, while many others, notable at home and abroad, have met here in charming companionship."

Doctor Walker married first, in 1741, Mildred, widow of Nicholas Meriwether, and daughter of Colonel Francis

BELVOIR, ALBEMARLE COUNTY

and Mary (Taliaferro) Thornton, of Snow Creek, Caroline County. His second wife was Elizabeth Thornton, a sister of his first wife. His children were all by the first wife.

Doctor Walker died November 19, 1794, leaving many descendants. His eldest son, Honorable John Walker (1744–1809), who was a member of General Washington's staff during the Revolutionary War and United States senator from Virginia, married Elizabeth, daughter of Bernard and Catherine (Spotswood) Moore, and

[illegible]

[illegible]

[illegible]

[illegible]

(The father of Elizabeth Moore to the father of John Walker:)

May 28th 1764.

Dear Sir:

Your son, Mr. John Walker applied to me for leave to make his addresses to my daughter Elizabeth. I gave him leave and told him at the same time that my affairs were in such a state that it was not in my power to pay him all the money this year that I intended to give my daughter provided he succeeded, but would give him five hundred pounds more as soon after as I could raise or get the money; which sums you may depend I will most punctually pay to him.

I am, sir, your obedient servant,

Bernard Moore.

To Thomas Walker,
Castle Hill, Albemarle County, Va.

Honorable Francis Walker (1764–1806), the youngest son of Doctor Thomas Walker, married Jane Byrd Nelson, of Yorktown. He was a member of Congress and inherited Castle Hill. Judith Page Walker (1802–1882), the daughter of Francis and Jane Byrd Walker, married Honorable William Cabell Rives (1793–1868), who held many high offices in the State. Mr. and Mrs. Rives made their home at Castle Hill and were succeeded there by their son Alfred Landon Rives, who married Miss Sadie McMurdo and were the parents of the author Amelie Rives (Princess Troubetzkoy), who has made the place famous in recent years.

An interesting story in connection with Castle Hill is that of a visit—for quite other than friendly purposes—paid there in 1781, by Colonel Tarleton. He was on his way to Charlottesville to make capture of the Assembly of Virginia and state officers who were gathered there. This attempt was frustrated by the famous ride of gallant Jack Jouett, but Tarleton, turning aside to make capture of some men of prominence at Castle Hill and Belvoir, found at the former Colonel John Syme—the half brother of Patrick Henry—and Judge Peter Lyons. "These gentlemen were surprised in their beds," says Mr. William Wirt Henry, in his ***Life of Patrick Henry,*** and it is related, as an instance of Tarleton's humor, that when Colonel Syme, who was remarkably homely, was brought from his bedroom undressed, and with dishevelled hair, the celebrated cavalryman threw himself into the attitude of Hamlet upon discovering his father's ghost, and exclaimed:

> Angels and ministers of grace, defend us!
> Be thou a spirit of health, or goblin damned?

MONTICELLO

Monticello was not only the home but the creation of Thomas Jefferson. That versatile genius, who seems to have excelled in everything he undertook, save playing the violin, was as great an architect of houses as of States, and Monticello and the University of Virginia (four miles away) are poems in brick and mortar. Standing upon a plain at the top of a high hill, from which it takes its name, Monticello, or " little mountain," looks upon a wide stretch of fertile country through which winds the Rivanna River, and beyond, an unbroken view of the Blue Ridge for one hundred and fifty miles.

The mansion is in Jefferson's favorite classic style of architecture, with Doric porticoes and a dome whose windows flood the great hall below with light. This hall is thirty feet square, with graceful winding stairways leading to the upper stories. In Jefferson's day it was a sort of museum. William Wirt tells us that along one side of it were specimens of sculpture set in such order as to show the progress of that art " from the first rude attempts of the aborigines of our country " to a bust of Jefferson himself, by Carracci. On the other was displayed a vast collection of specimens of the Indian art—their pottery, weapons, ornaments, etc.; on another, the fossil productions of our country. In other parts of the house, says Wirt, were hung valuable paintings from all countries and all ages, and portraits of distinguished men, both of Europe and America, and medallions and engravings in endless profusion.

The drawing-room in which Jefferson entertained the many guests that flocked to Monticello is finished with inlaid satin-wood and rose-wood, with richly-carved cornices, and the doors are of solid mahogany. It is said that Jefferson sometimes entertained as many as fifty guests at one time at Monticello.

The bed-chambers at Monticello are hexagonal in shape. Jefferson's arrangement of his and his wife's rooms was unique. The two apartments were connected by a wide arch in which stood, lengthwise, a luxurious bed six feet wide, half of which extended into his own room, the other half into Mrs. Jefferson's.

Jefferson was like Washington and Madison in losing his heart to a young, fascinating and wealthy widow. Mistress Martha Skelton was her name, and Jefferson won her from many rival suitors, in spite of the fact that his wretched performances on the violin played a conspicuous part in his wooing. Indeed, it is said that the lady's seeming enjoyment of these performances convinced Jefferson's rivals of the depth of her devotion to him and the hopelessness of their own and all other suits.

The story goes that the distinguished pair of lovers made their wedding journey to Monticello in a blinding snow-storm, arriving there at two o'clock in the morning. The servants were not expecting them and were sleeping so soundly that they could not be aroused; so the bridal pair had to make the best of spending the night in a one-room brick office, wherein the master of Monticello had kept bachelor's quarters while superintending the building of his mansion. As they had a blazing log-fire and a bottle of wine to cheer them after their drive through the storm, no doubt the statesman and his bride were enough like other young folk to enjoy their adventure.

The grounds at Monticello are as attractive in their own way as the house, with their stretches of greensward and their old Lombardy poplars. In the graveyard, which blooms like a garden, lie the mortal remains of Jefferson, who died at Monticello, July 4, 1826, and his wife and daughters. Over his grave stands a plain obelisk bearing the epitaph he wrote for himself: "Here lies buried Thomas Jefferson, Author of the Declaration of Independence, of the Statute of Virginia for Religious Freedom, and Father of the University of Virginia"—a simple statement of the three achievements for which he hoped to be, and always will be, remembered.

In the grave with Jefferson lies the body of a friend of his boyhood. When they were children he and this friend agreed to be buried together, the one who died last to see to it that the compact was fulfilled. The other boy died at the age of seventeen, and when Jefferson chose his own burial place, he had the body of his friend removed thither, and so the two friends sleep in one grave to-day.

Jefferson was a scientific farmer. Before his time the plow was an exceedingly primitive implement and he improved it for the benefit of his own lands. Monticello plantation was a busy place; wrought iron nails were made, and cloth woven there, and the ruins of a flour mill may still be seen.

Jefferson was a close observer of nature and the weather, and took pains to register the state of both thermometer and barometer every day throughout his life. Just above the main entrance at Monticello he constructed an ingenious clock with two faces, one inside and one outside of the hall. This clock marked the days of the week as well as the hours, and by means of an arrow connected with a weather-vane on the top of the house showed the direction of the wind.

During the Revolution Tarleton's cavalry raided Monticello in an attempt to take Jefferson captive. Jefferson had received a timely warning, however, and escaping through an underground passage, still to be seen at Monticello, rode off on horseback to Colonel Edward Carter's plantation, about sixty miles distant, to which he had already hurried his wife and children. Some of the members of the Assembly (which had been in session at Charlottesville) were less fortunate—seven of them falling into Tarleton's hands at Castle Hill, then the home of Doctor Thomas Walker.

Monticello is now the property and home of Mr. Jefferson Levy.

THE UNIVERSITY OF VIRGINIA

President Madison, writing of Thomas Jefferson, in 1826, said: "The University of Virginia, as a temple dedicated to science and liberty, was after his retirement from the political sphere the object nearest his heart, and so continued to the close of his life. His devotion to it was intense and his exertions unceasing. It bears the stamp of his genius and will be a noble monument to his fame."

Says Professor Herbert B. Adams, in a monograph upon this "noblest work of Jefferson's life": "The buildings of the University of Virginia are Jefferson's thoughts materialized in artistic form."

It would seem to one looking upon this "academical village" with its velvet lawns bordered by the white colonnades of the dormitories, the pillars and pediments of the professors' homes, and, dominating all, the dome and the lofty columns of the Rotunda, that these thoughts of Jefferson's so beautifully materialized here in the heart of Virginia, with her blue mountains for a background, were all of the "glory that was Greece and the grandeur that was Rome."

Jefferson's idea was to make the university an ever-present object-lesson to the students in correct principles of the builder's art. He chose the poetic, classic form and designed the porticoes and colonnades to illustrate the Doric, Ionic and Corinthian orders of architecture. The white-pillared village is built around a stretch of level green lawn 1000 feet long and 200 feet wide. Along the east and west sides stand at intervals the homes of the professors, shaded by ancient trees and connected by the long, low, colonnaded dormitories, while on the terrace across the north end gleams the Rotunda—the glory of the old university. Across the south end of the lawn now stands the new academic building.

Behind the buildings fronting upon the " East Lawn " and " West Lawn " lie the gardens, separated by narrow walks and enclosed by the famous serpentine walls, which were designed by Jefferson and are a unique feature of the university. These high, zigzag walls, one brick thick, are wonderfully picturesque, especially in summer when festooned with greenery. Beyond the gardens at either side, and parallel with the buildings on the lawn, stands a row of other dormitories, opening on brick arcades. These are known as " East Range " and " West Range."

The University of Virginia was the passion of the later years of Jefferson's life. He not only drew the plans for the buildings but personally superintended their construction, supervising the minutest details and even designing tools for the workmen and showing them how to use them. Two " Italian artists " were brought over to cut the capitals of the columns, and when it was found that Virginia stone was unsuitable for this purpose a number of beautifully chiselled white marble capitals were imported from Italy; but most of the work was done on the ground by Jefferson's own workmen, trained by him.

In August, 1820, he wrote to John Adams, from Monticello: " Our University, four miles distant, gives me frequent exercise, as I direct its architecture."

Professor Herbert B. Adams, in his sketch of the university, already quoted, writes as follows:

" A visitor pacing slowly through these monastic colonnades extending along two sides of the great quadrangle campus of the University of Virginia will receive a strange variety of impressions from the extraordinary architectural combinations which greet his wandering eyes. The arcades themselves from which open directly the single-chambered rooms of the students, remind one of cloistered walks in some ancient monastery. These student-rooms are like monkish-cells. But wonderful facades are those which

THE ROTUNDA—UNIVERSITY OF VIRGINIA

front the professors' houses, or pavilions. They reproduce classic styles of architecture. The shadows of remote antiquity are cast upon those beautiful grassy lawns, which form the campus.

"From Jefferson's drawings we learn what is well nigh forgotten, that these varying types of classical architecture were copied from well-known Roman buildings pictured by Palladio in his great work on architecture. There, in the theatre of Marcellus, dwells the household of Professor Minor. Yonder are reminders of the baths of Diocletian, the baths of Caracalla and the temple of Fortuna Virillis. And there at the upper or northern end of the quadrangle, stands the Roman Pantheon, the temple of all the gods, reduced to one-third of its original size, but still majestic and imposing. This building with its Rotunda, upon which Jefferson spent almost as much pains as Michael Angelo did upon the dome of St. Peter's, is used for the library and for various lecture halls. Young people dance merrily under the stately dome at the end of the academic year. The young monks then escape from their cells into the modern social world. How charmingly old Rome, mediæval Europe and modern America blend together before the very eyes of young Virginia!"

In 1895 news that the university was on fire filled the heart of every son and daughter of Virginia within the bounds of the old commonwealth, and beyond, with grief. A large building at the rear of the Rotunda, known as the Annex, was destroyed and the Rotunda itself burnt out, with the valuable collections of books and manuscripts in the library.

The loss was at first felt to be irreparable, but great compensation has been found in the love and loyalty to Virginia's greatest institute which it brought out. Gifts for the restoration poured in from every direction and soon the rebuilt Rotunda stood in all its wonted beauty at the head of the lawn, while in place of the Annex a group of fire-proof, well equipped, new buildings, architecturally harmonious with the old ones, provided a thoroughly up-to-date Physical Laboratory, Mechanical Laboratory, and Public Hall.

The room occupied by Edgar Allan Poe while a student at the university is preserved as a Poe museum and a meeting place of " The Raven Society."

FARMINGTON

A stately mansion, broad acres clothed with the green of blue grass, corn and wheat, and a splendid view of the Blue Ridge combine to make Farmington, some three miles from the University of Virginia, a most attractive home.

FARMINGTON, ALBEMARLE COUNTY

The house was designed by Thomas Jefferson for and at the request of his friend, Mr. George Divers, and is said to be a reproduction of a country house seen by Jefferson when abroad. It is probably over a hundred years old, as Mr. Divers bought the plantation in 1788.

Upon the death of Mr. Divers, Farmington passed by inheritance to Mrs. Isaac White, who sold it to Mr. John

C. Carter. In 1858 it was again sold to General Bernard Peyton, who, it is said, expended $30,000.00 in improvements upon the house and plantation. In 1860 Mr. Joseph Miller, a wealthy and accomplished English gentleman, on a visit to Virginia was so much pleased with Farmington that he bought it and presented it to his sister, Mrs. Mary Ann Harper, who bequeathed it to her son, Mr. Warner Wood.

REDLANDS

Redlands, just east of Carter's Bridge, Albemarle, was the home of Robert Carter, son of Edward Carter of Blen-

REDLANDS, ALBEMARLE COUNTY

heim. He died there, in 1810. His son Robert H. Carter, who inherited the place, married Margaret Smith, a granddaughter of Governor Nicholas.

PENN PARK

Penn Park is one of the oldest homesteads in Albemarle County. It was bought by Doctor George Gilmer and was, from 1777 to 1800, the home of the Gilmer family.

Doctor Gilmer died at Penn Park in 1796, and after the death of his wife, in 1800, the estate was sold and has since had various owners.

The Gilmers were people of marked refinement and culture. Francis W. Gilmer, Doctor Gilmer's son, was a protégé of Thomas Jefferson's. He was the first professor of Latin in the University of Virginia and was entrusted with the selection of the members of the first faculty of that institution.

A distinguished grandson of Doctor Gilmer was the Honorable Thomas Walker Gilmer, governor of Virginia and secretary of the navy, who was killed by an explosion on board the United States ship *Princeton* in 1844.

Doctor Gilmer's daughter Mildred became the first wife of Honorable William Wirt, and Kennedy in his life of Mr. Wirt charmingly describes the life at Penn Park in early days.

MONTICOLA

Monticola, the home of Miss Emily M. Nolting, is located near Howardsville, in Albemarle County. The dwelling, situated on the high land overlooking the broad and fertile valley of James River, commands an extended view over three counties—Albemarle, Nelson and Buckingham—with the hazy outline of the Blue Ridge Mountains in the background. It was built prior to the War between the States by Mr. D. J. Hartsook, who, in 1887, sold it to Mr. E. O. Nolting, of Richmond, Virginia, the father of its present owner.

In style of architecture the main house, built of brick, with columns in front of its wide porch, and with two "offices," one on either side to correspond, resembles many of the ante-bellum country homes in Piedmont, Virginia, showing in its design the impress of Jeffersonian influence.

During the devastating raids of General Sheridan, "Monticola" was occupied by him as headquarters. A large square cut in the flooring of an upper bedroom marks the place where valuables were hid at that time to save them from pillage.

The plantation itself dates back to Revolutionary times, as evidenced by a strip of road near the house said to have been surveyed by General Washington himself, and constituting a part of the Post Road connecting Lynchburg

MONTICOLA, ALBEMARLE COUNTY

with Richmond, other links of which appear in the intervening counties.

The original residence, still standing on this estate, was built by a Mr. Fowle in Colonial days, its hand-wrought nails, glazed bricks and hand-carved mantels testifying to this fact, and tradition has it that General Washington lodged there.

ENNISCORTHY

John Coles I came from Ireland to Virginia during the eighteenth century. He was an early settler in Richmond Town and, tradition has it, built one of the first houses there. He was senior warden of the parish, and dying in Richmond in 1747 was buried in the chancel of old St. John's Church. William Coles, a younger brother of John, and the grandfather of "Dolly Madison," followed his brother to Virginia and settled in Hanover County, where he built "Coles Hill."

John Coles I was a man of ample means and owning an estate in what is now Albemarle County (then Goochland), on the Green Mountain, built a residence there. This home he named Enniscorthy after the place of residence of his ancestors in Leinster, County Wexford, Ireland.

John Coles II (who was a colonel of militia during the Revolutionary War), son of the first John Coles, inherited Enniscorthy and greatly enlarged the original dwelling by the addition of wings, pinions, double pinions, and ample piazzas. This house was completely destroyed by fire in 1839.

The present house at Enniscorthy was built in 1850.

Mr. and Mrs. Charles S. Bennett, the present owners of this estate, are great-grandchildren of the second John Coles.

The first burial in the old family burying-ground at Enniscorthy was that of a child of John Coles II, in 1772, and in its soil also sleep the remains of Elizabeth Travis Tucker, born in Jamestown in 1727. She was the mother of Elizabeth, wife of John Coles II.

WOODVILLE

Woodville was built in 1796, as indicated by a date marked on a brick in the front hall fireplace. The house was erected by John Coles II, of Enniscorthy, for his eldest son Walter, on land which was part of one of the second grants from the Colonial authorities in the name of the Crown, to the Coles family. This estate has been occupied by a Walter Coles for four successive generations—Walter R. Coles, of St. Louis, being the fourth of that name.

WOODVILLE, ALBEMARLE COUNTY

ESTOUTEVILLE, ALBEMARLE COUNTY 1830

ESTOUTEVILLE

Estouteville, one of the most beautiful homes in Virginia, was built in 1830 by John Coles III. Its name is derived from the Count d'Estouteville, an ancestor of the

Skipwith family from whom Mr. Coles' wife, who was Salina, younger daughter of Sir Peyton Skipwith, of

THE HALL AT ESTOUTEVILLE

Prestwould, Mecklenburg County, descended. The present owner of this estate is Mr. Virgil P. Randolph.

TALLWOOD, ALBEMARLE COUNTY

TALLWOOD

Tallwood was built in 1804 by Tucker Coles, son of John Coles II, who married Helen, daughter of Sir Peyton Skipwith, of Prestwould. This couple lived to celebrate their golden wedding in this house.

Tallwood is now owned by William D. Waters, Esq., formerly of St. Louis.

PLAIN DEALING

Thomas Staples secured both by patent and purchase many hundreds of acres of land in Albemarle County on Hudson and Totier Creeks, and, in 1787, sold a tract of

PLAIN DEALING, ALBEMARLE COUNTY

five hundred acres of his holdings to Samuel Dyer. The lands thus disposed of extended from Hudson to Totier and included the site of " Plain Dealing."

Samuel Dyer [4] was born in Bristol, England, October 8, 1756, and emigrated to Virginia, in 1770, and served throughout the Revolutionary War. For some time he was assistant to the agent, or Quartermaster, of the Virginia line. Immediately following the war, Mr. Dyer became associated with David Ross and Company, of Richmond, a strong firm of merchants, later withdrawing and

---

[4] Woods, *Albemarle County in Virginia*, pp. 185-186.

forming a partnership with William Hay. About 1786, Mr. Dyer disposed of his Richmond interests and went to live on his Albemarle estate, which, in course of years, grew to be a tract of twenty-two hundred acres. He greatly enlarged the old Staples house.

Samuel Dyer's store at his Albemarle home was " a well-known place of business in those days, situated at the junction of the roads from Staunton and Charlottesville to Scott's landing," and served also the purposes of stage-coach office and post-office.

Dyer's old store is now the vicarage of Christ Church; the sign " Plain Dealing," nailed above the door, gave the store its name and the name has ever clung to the estate.

Mr. Dyer was very successful in his mercantile, milling and planting ventures and amassed a large fortune.

In 1786 Samuel Dyer married Celia Bickley, granddaughter of Joseph Bickley, gentleman, of Louisa County, whose son Sir William Bickley, Baronet, of Louisa County, succeeded as 6th Baronet of the family of Bickley of Attleborough Hall, County Norfolk, England.[5]

Samuel Dyer died in 1839, Mrs. Dyer surviving him but a year. Their children were (1) William Hay Dyer, lieutenant of the " Richmond Blues," 1812, and magistrate of Albemarle County; (2) Major Samuel Dyer, of the " Elite (Randolph's) Corps "; (3) Ann, wife of George Robertson; (4) Francis Bickley Dyer, attorney, captain of Albemarle company of field artillery, and magistrate; (5) Celia Bickley Dyer; (6) Robert Dyer; (7) Elizabeth, wife of George M. Payne; (8) John Dyer; (9) Thomas Dyer; (10) Mary Jane, wife of George A. Nicholson; (11) Martha, wife of Joseph A. Watkins; (12) Sarah Dyer.

During the decade of 1830 most of the children moved to Missouri.

Shortly after Mrs. Dyer's death, in 1840, Bishop

---

[5] Bickley Family: *William and Mary College Quarterly Historical Magazine*, v, 28–30 and 124–127.

J. P. B. Wilmer acquiring the mansion and some one thousand acres of Plain Dealing estate, and it was while he was in possession of the property that General Robert E. Lee paid him a visit and informed him of a decision to accept the presidency of "Washington College." This estate descended to Bishop Wilmer's son, from whom Theodore Roosevelt purchased "Pine Knot." "Pine Knot" was originally the "cottage" on the "Plain Dealing" estate.

MOUNTAIN TOP

Rock Fish Gap, which takes its name from the sparkling little Rock Fish River, was long one of the main passage-ways through the Blue Ridge between Albemarle and

MOUNTAIN TOP, ALBEMARLE COUNTY

Augusta Counties. In early days there stood in this gap a tavern for the accommodation of travellers across the mountains, and in the parlor of this primitive house of entertainment met the commission, of which Jefferson, Madison and Monroe were all members, which fixed Charlottesville as the site for the University of Virginia.

In later times additions were made to the old tavern, and cottages built upon the lawn, and under the name of Mountain Top it became a popular summer resort. A few years ago it was destroyed by fire and a private residence has been built upon its site.

THE SOUTHSIDE

The arrangement into chapters, or parts, followed in this work has been used partly for convenience, and partly on account of the geographical divisions, which have always been familiar to Virginians by the names here given them. We have now come to the last of these divisions east of the mountains. The designation " The Southside " is variously understood in Virginia but is perhaps most generally taken to mean the section including the counties of Prince Edward, Brunswick, Mecklenburg, Charlotte, Lunenburg, Halifax and Pittsylvania.

CLOVER FOREST

In Prince Edward County, which is separated by the Appomattox River from what we have called the " Upper James " section, is a unique homestead which was for many years the property of the Lancaster family, while across the Appomattox is Clover Forest, another quaint old home of the Lancasters. Both of these houses were built in the early time when the prevailing type of dwelling was the log-cabin and were doubtless then looked upon as considerable mansions.

Old Clover Forest was the home of John Lancaster, a native of Prince Edward County, and a brave Revolutionary soldier. He died on January 28, 1826, and was buried at Clover Forest, where sleeps also his wife, Drusilla, daughter of Alexander Le Grand, who died on December 14, 1825, and Lucy Walker, his wife.

John A. Lancaster (son of John and Drusilla Lancaster) moved to Richmond, in 1813, and later became the first president of the first railroad in Virginia—the *Rich-*

mond, Fredericksburgh & Potomac R. R. He was the father of Robert A. Lancaster, a prominent business man of Richmond. The latter was the father of Robert A. Lancaster, Jr., the author of this book.

Another interesting personage who was an ancestor of the present Lancaster family and who was buried at Clover

CLOVER FOREST, PRINCE EDWARD COUNTY

Forest in 1824 was Justin Pierre Plumard, Comte de Rieux, who was born in Nantes, France, on March 10, 1756, was a captain in the Blue Guards of Louis XVI, and came to America in 1784, with his wife, Maria Margueretta Martini, step-daughter of Philip Mazzei, the well-known friend of Thomas Jefferson.

GREEN HILL

"Green Hill" was built by Samuel Pannill, a native of Orange County, Virginia, born 1770, the 7th child of William and Ann (Morton) Pannill. On attaining his majority, Mr. Pannill was given by his father a large tract of land in the Blue Grass region of Kentucky, but becoming dissatisfied with life "in the back-woods" he sold these lands, returned to Virginia, purchased the "Green Hill" estate, in Campbell County, and there continued to reside throughout the remainder of his life.

"Green Hill" is wonderfully situated on an elevated plateau, overlooking Staunton River and commanding a view for miles of the surrounding country. The estate, containing some five thousand acres lying on both sides of the river, with its "quarters," barns, shops, store and mill, resembled more an industrial village than simply the seat of a country gentleman. "Good roads" seem to have

GREEN HILL, CAMPBELL COUNTY

been a marked characteristic of the estate for we are told by a contemporary that some of these, together with the many picturesque lanes intersecting them, were paved with stone. The large number of slaves owned by the master of Green Hill, and resident on the estate, included not only ordinary farmhands, but also many valuable mechanics: carpenters, stone-masons, shoemakers, blacksmiths, coopers, sawyers and millers, besides whom there were men to handle the boats in which the flour made at the large mill was sent down the river. Among the female contingent were seamstresses, weavers and house-servants.

Mr. Pannill was as careful in providing for the spiritual as for the material welfare of his servants and built for their specific use a commodious stone church which will ever remain as a proof of his solicitude for the religious life of his " black-folk."

At his death Mr. Pannill was survived by five daughters and two sons. Neither of the sons ever married.

RED HILL

Red Hill, the last home and the burial-place of Patrick Henry, is in Charlotte County, Virginia. He purchased it in 1794, and his will contains this clause: " I do give to my said wife Dorothea, all my lands at and adjoining my dwelling-place called Red Hill, purchased from Booker, Watkins and others, out of a tract called Watkins' order, to hold during her natural life."

The name is derived from the red-brown soil in front of the house, which is beautifully situated on an elevated ridge. Thirty-eight miles to the northwest is Lynchburg, the nearest city. To the south, the valley of the Staunton stretches its oval form as it winds through fertile low grounds; while, across the river, the far off hills of Halifax rise in bold relief. On the west, on any clear day can be seen the Peaks of Otter. The house was a simple wooden structure in the days of the patriot. It is said that the only addition made by him was the shed kitchen. This was said to have been added not on account of need of room, but that he might hear the patter of rain on the roof. It has had additions which make it a beautiful reproduction of Colonial architecture. It has belonged successively to his son John Henry, to his grandson, William Wirt Henry, and to his great-granddaughter, Mrs. Matthew Bland Harrison, its present owner. The estate originally contained 2920 acres, and was selected on account of its rich land and its many springs of pure water.

During the Revolutionary War, Red Hill was owned by Louis Tyler, an uncle of President Tyler. During its ownership by Mr. Booker, Powhatan Bouldin, in *The Old*

Trunk, tells of a Christmas frolic attended by his aunt Mary Bouldin, who rode on horseback twenty miles, jumped upon the ground as light as a feather, and was, soon on the floor dancing. At this time country life in Virginia was very primitive.

Patrick Henry's fame drew many visitors to his home, all of whom he welcomed with gracious hospitality; nor was he forgotten by the country he had loved so well. In 1794 he declined the appointment of United States senator offered him by Governor Henry Lee, as also the office of governor to which he was elected by the general assembly in 1795. Washington offered him the position of secretary of state in 1795, and again, that same year, he appointed him chief justice; John Adams, in 1799, offered to send him as minister to France, but he declined all these positions on account of failing health.

He occupied his last days in the education of his children, to whom he was deeply attached. He engaged for them, as tutor, the services of the poet Campbell, who, however, was prevented from fulfilling his engagement. During the lifetime of their father, two daughters were married at Red Hill; Dorothea married her cousin George D. Winston, and Martha Catherine, Edward W. Henry, another kinsman.

At the earnest request of Washington, Patrick Henry offered himself for the Legislature the last year of his life. He made his last great speech at Charlotte Court House, March, 1799, and, worn out by the effort, returned to Red Hill, never to leave it again.

On the sixth of June, 1799, surrounded by his devoted family and his beloved physician, his great soul took flight. No act of his life became him more than his manner of leaving it. When informed that the end was at hand, he prayed fervently for divine support, then spent his remaining moments comforting his family and praising the religion of Christ, which, never having failed him in life, did not fail him in his last need of it.

In the garden of Red Hill are two oblong slabs of

OLD NEGRO COUPLE AT CABIN AT RED HILL
(The man in his boyhood waited on Mrs. Patrick Henry)

RED HILL, CHARLOTTE COUNTY

marble; the inscription on one is "To the memory of Patrick Henry. Born May 29, 1736. Died June 6, 1799. His fame his best Epitaph"; the other reads, "To the memory of Dorothea Dandridge, wife of Patrick Henry. Born 1755. Died February 14, 1831."

OLD NEGRO COUPLE AT RED HILL

When Patrick Henry purchased Red Hill, a few Indians were still living on what had been their happy hunting grounds. One of them, Indian Jim, intermarried with a slave, and her grandson, Harrison, was living until a few years ago on the land of his fathers. He was born in 1815, and was sixteen years old when Patrick Henry's widow (then Mrs. Edmund Winston) died, February 14, 1831. Mrs. Winston had taken him in the house when he was ten years old, and he used to carry her key basket, slippers, and the yarn for her knitting. In 1831, at the time of the death of his mistress, Harrison was coachman for her son, John Henry, at whose death, in 1868, Red Hill fell by inheritance and purchase to his son, the late William Wirt Henry, who provided for the faithful old servant by giving him a cabin and a bit of land where he lived throughout the remainder of his days, very contented and honored alike by white and black. To the last, he took pride in carrying visitors to the grave of the orator, whom he called "Marse Patrick." His wife, Milly, was some years older than himself and he always lamented that she was of "common blood."

STAUNTON HILL

A considerable portion of the estate on which stands Staunton Hill came into the possession of the Bruce family, by whom it is still owned, when a tract of land six hundred and eighty-two acres in extent was, in 1801, conveyed to James Bruce and his wife, of Woodbourn, Halifax County, Virginia, by Isaac Coles and Paul Carrington, Jr., and Mildred, his wife.

Mr. Bruce had removed in early manhood from eastern

Virginia, where, as records show, his paternal ancestors had lived since the beginning of the latter half of the seventeenth century, and perhaps since an earlier date, to Southside Virginia. Here he spent the remainder of a long and useful life, acquiring one of the most commanding fortunes at that time in the possession of any citizen of the United States.

From 1801 to 1884 the original estate of Staunton Hill was gradually enlarged by purchase, first by James Bruce, and then by his son, Charles Bruce, until it attained its present extent of over 5000 acres. A beautiful view of the

STAUNTON HILL, CHARLOTTE COUNTY

Staunton River may be had from the front porch of the mansion.

Until 1848 no dwelling house of any size was built on the estate, the place being managed by an agent under the direction of James Bruce, and later by his son, James Coles Bruce of Berry Hill, Halifax County, Virginia, who was guardian to his younger brother, Charles Bruce, by whom it had been inherited.

The graduation of Charles Bruce from Harvard College and his engagement to Miss Sarah Seddon, of Fredericksburg (a sister of the Honorable James A. Seddon, afterward the Confederate States secretary of war), took place almost simultaneously. Leaving instructions with Mr. John E. Johnson, a Virginian architect, and a graduate of West Point, for the erection of a dwelling house on the Staunton Hill estate, Charles Bruce sailed for Europe. Returning in 1848, after some months of travel, he was married, and eighteen months afterward took possession of his new home.

The building of the house, which at that time was three days' journey by carriage from the capital of the State, and remote from any town, was attended with much difficulty. Trained workmen were brought from Philadelphia, and the woodwork, marble pillars of the porch and all but the rough materials composing the house were transported from that city to the North Carolina coast, and from thence by " batteaux " up the Roanoke and Staunton Rivers.

The system of agriculture prevailing on this farm was, until 1865, similar to that on all large plantations in Southside Virginia. Shipping tobacco, corn, wheat and oats were the staple crops and were worked by slaves, of whom a few still survive at Staunton Hill, living in the cabins where their fathers lived before them.

Staunton Hill, by its remoteness from the scene of the chief events of the War between the States, escaped almost entirely its minor calamities, such as vandalism and pillage. Not anticipating such good fortune or change in the route of the Federal Army, however, Mr. and Mrs. Bruce had all their silver and valuables secretly carried across the Staunton River into Halifax County, where they were buried in the midst of a deep wood. Later a part of the Federal Army camped in this wood, and finally burned it, but without injury, as later events proved, to the hidden articles.

The slaves, of whom there were several hundred on the Staunton Hill estate, remained absolutely quiet throughout the whole course of the war; one of them, remembered affectionately as "Old Israel," proving his faithfulness at the risk of his life on one or two occasions.

During this period Mrs. Bruce was left alone with her little children for months, her husband being absent in the army or State Senate, and no other white person save the overseer and his family being on the place. Yet she declared that with "Old Israel" and his wife Phoebe (her children's "mammy") within call she had no fear. At the close of the war few of the negroes left the place and most of those who did so afterward returned. During the life of Mr. Charles Bruce the Reverend Morgan Dix, of New York, while on a visit to Staunton Hill, asked a former slave whether any of the servants ever went away from the place and received for a reply, "None ever leaves ole Marster 'cept the dead."

During the trying days of reconstruction there was but one development of insubordination amongst them and that was quelled almost immediately by the mere sight of a Federal officer with a squad of men from Charlotte Court House. It was surmised that this state of discontent was produced by a failure amongst the negroes to agree as to which of them should own the mill on the estate when the general division of the property giving to each "40 acres and a mule" should take place; an idea which long deluded the freedmen throughout the South.

Under the new system of hired labor which was a consequence of the War between the States, agriculture was carried on at Staunton Hill on a larger scale than ever before. All crops brought high prices during the years succeeding the commencement of the new order of things, and the acres planted in tobacco and corn on this estate were enormous, the first amounting during several years to one million hills, and the latter producing at times as much as twenty-five thousand bushels.

Mr. Charles Bruce died in 1896. Those who understood the passionate love of the soil that was strong in him as in most of his day and class—a love that was inherited instinct—can hardly realize that the place which was in a manner his own creation, which attests his affection and care in innumerable visible forms, can go on without his watchful supervision. Yet there is no change in its aspect; the system that was inaugurated by him continues with but little variation and the Staunton Hill estate is to-day as productive, as amply and sedulously cultivated, and as fair to the eye as at any time in its history.

INGLESIDE

This dignified old mansion with its attractive setting of foliage and lawn was built in 1810, by Colonel Thomas Read, a prominent citizen of Charlotte County, who was a member of all of the Revolutionary Conventions, and of

INGLESIDE, CHARLOTTE COUNTY

the Convention of 1788, which ratified the Constitution of the United States. He was the first county clerk of Charlotte and a brick office in his yard was long the county clerk's office.

At Colonel Read's death, in 1817, Ingleside became the property of Henry Carrington, who lived there until his own death, in 1867. About 1870 it was sold to the late John W. Daniel, whose heirs still own it.

WOODFORK

The modest frame cottage at Woodfork was the home of Colonel Joel Watkins, a Revolutionary patriot, who died in 1820. John Randolph, of Roanoke, wrote that " He died beloved, honored and lamented by all who knew him " and that he had " accumulated an ample fortune in which there was not one dirty shilling." His son, Captain Henry A. Watkins, succeeded to the estate and in 1829 built the commodious brick house near his father's small dwelling.

Upon the death of Captain Watkins, in 1848, Woodfork passed to Doctor Joel Watkins and is now owned by the heirs of the late James W. Elliot.

THE OLD MILL AT GREENFIELD, CHARLOTTE COUNTY

GREENFIELD

" Greenfield," the home of the Reads, of Charlotte County, was built by Isaac Read, lieutenant colonel of the Fourth Regiment in the Revolutionary Army. The estate of Greenfield was carved out of a tract of 10,000 acres purchased by Colonel Clement Read, the father of Colonel

GREENFIELD, CHARLOTTE COUNTY

THE GARDEN AT GREENFIELD

Isaac Read, in 1730, in what was then known as the County of Brunswick, from which County Lunenburg was afterwards formed in 1745. In 1764 Charlotte County was cut off from Lunenburg.

Greenfield is now the oldest house in Charlotte County. Tradition says that when it was first built settlers came for miles to see so palatial a residence as it was then considered. The timbers of the house are very massive, many of them being hewn. The dressed lumber was sawn in old-fashioned saw pits, while the nails and iron fittings are all hand-made of wrought iron.

The original house has two stories, two rooms divided by a large hall on each floor. It has since been added to, to accommodate increasing families and for hospitable reasons, until the present house is about 150 feet in length. Greenfield has passed from father to child by descent, and has always been in possession of a Read.

The plantation mill with its old wheel is still grinding corn and wheat, as it has done for the last 175 years, and producing the same good, honest, water-ground meal that made the bone and sinew of our ancestors.

BERRY HILL

Berry Hill, in Halifax County, is one of the finest models of the so-called Colonial type in the South. The high pillared portico, extending entirely across the front of the house, and the double stairway, sweeping with wide and graceful curves from the great central hall to rooms above, give this home of the Bruces an air of unusual distinction. It was built by James Coles Bruce, son of James Bruce, of Woodbourne, Halifax County, and a half brother of Charles Bruce, of Staunton Hill. Mr. Bruce furnished his house in a style worthy of its imposing proportions and architecture, and the house was noted for its extraordinary amount of silver of the handsomest workmanship. Not only was the silver table service complete and massive, but several of the bedrooms were provided with washstand sets of the precious metal.

BERRY HILL, HALIFAX COUNTY

THE HALL AT BERRY HILL

The Berry Hill plantation was originally part of the estates of Colonel William Byrd, of Westover, and of Colonel Edward Carrington. It was acquired by the Bruces in the early part of the nineteenth century.

Here, on his great landed estate, in the midst of hundreds of slaves and adherents, lived the builder of Berry Hill, a gentleman distinguished for talent and cultivation, until his death, in 1865, just before the close of the War between the States. Though originally a Union man his contribution to the Confederacy had amounted to at least $150,000.00.

Mr. Bruce married Miss Eliza Wilkins, daughter of William Wilkins, Esquire, of North Carolina, and their son, Alexander Bruce, succeeded him as master of Berry Hill.

BELLEVUE

This property was the home of Mr. John B. Carrington, who, about 1825, erected the dwelling-house in a beautiful grove of trees, all of original growth. The property

BELLEVUE, HALIFAX COUNTY

remained in his family for about seventy-five years, since which time it has had several owners. The flower garden here was most attractive. On two sides were tall box trees.

At one end they were so planted and trimmed as to make a nice room with sides and top of box. On another side of the garden was a close hedge of fig trees and in the centre a large circle of box about four and one-half feet high. Within the circle were beautiful roses and around it beds of old-fashioned flowers of various kinds. Back of this hedge of fig trees was the vegetable garden. The box and fig trees still remain.

BANISTER LODGE

Frontage of a mile and a half along the Banister River gave the Clark plantation, in Halifax County, its name. The roomy mansion was built in 1830 by Mr. William H. Clark. The bricks in the thick walls, which still retain

BANISTER LODGE, HALIFAX COUNTY

their deep red hue, were made upon the place by the slaves, while the folding doors between the rooms were the first seen in that part of the country, and were regarded as an interesting novelty.

The beautiful grounds and gardens were the special care and pride of Mrs. Clark and were laid off under her direction. This lady, who was a granddaughter of Patrick

Henry, was admired for her unusual character and talents, " a Godly woman with a master mind " she is said to have been. She was a notable musician and not only played on a number of musical instruments but much manuscript of music composed by her is still in possession of her descendants at Banister Lodge. Her piano and harp are also still there, while a tapestry fire-screen embroidered by her speaks of her proficiency with the needle.

The planning of her home grounds gave Mrs. Clark's artistic tendencies full play. There is a grove of splendid oaks and a driveway around a circle set in arbor vitae and box and mimosa trees. The flower-garden is surrounded by box and laid off in beds, each of which is devoted to a different flower. There are also many shrubs; roses, of course, and calycanthus, syringas, snowballs, Japan apples, spiræas, pomegranates, altheas, crepe myrtles, and many others. In the vegetable garden Mrs. Clark obtained a beautiful and novel effect by hedging all of the squares with lilacs, purple and white. Upon each side of the garden gate a tree overgrown with ivy stands sentinel.

Among the interesting pieces of mahogany furniture made to order for Mr. Clark, and still in use at Banister Lodge, is the dining-table at which twenty-five persons can be comfortably seated. Many distinguished guests have sat at this hospitable table. John Randolph, of Roanoke, often sat there, for he was on most intimate terms with the family. He was in the habit of exchanging books with them and among the books in the library may still be seen some with his autograph upon the title page. General Lee was once a guest at Banister Lodge over night, and General Joseph E. Johnston was a frequent visitor there. During the war Bishop Johns, of the Episcopal Church, and Mrs. Johns refugeed at Banister Lodge for a whole year, during which Mr. Clark placed a small house in the grounds at their disposal and supplied them with all the comforts of life, including servants and a driving horse. Banister Lodge was, by the way, noted for its fine horses, twenty-five of which were carried off by Northern soldiers at one time.

Banister Lodge is now the home of Mr. John Clark, son of Mr. William H. Clark. The plantation still contains 1000 of its original 3000 acres.

ROANOKE

John Randolph, of Roanoke, inherited the estate, with whose name his own is always coupled, from his father. This brilliant and strange man made his dwelling in no lordly mansion, but in two plain frame cottages, one of which he called his winter and the other his summer house. Outside the door of one of them was the rough block of stone which he frequently used as a washstand, and which

ROANOKE, CHARLOTTE COUNTY

he directed should be placed over his grave. In spite of the modest appearance of these houses, they contained a fine library and much handsome furniture and old silver.

John Randolph was buried at Roanoke, but his remains were afterwards removed to Richmond, and interred in Hollywood Cemetery. After his death Roanoke was sold and became the property of the Bouldin family. It was the home of the distinguished lawyer, Judge Wood Bouldin (who died in 1876), and was destroyed by fire in 1878, but John Randolph's office is still standing.

Roanoke is now the property of Mr. Clarence G. Cheney, of Chicago, who has built a handsome new house upon the old site.

MULBERRY HILL

Mulberry Hill was the home of Paul Carrington, one of the most distinguished Virginians of the Revolutionary period. He was a member of the Conventions, and Com-

MULBERRY HILL, CHARLOTTE COUNTY

mittee of Safety, and for many years a judge of the Virginia Court of Appeals. He died at the age of eighty-five and was buried at Mulberry Hill. The estate is now the property of the family of his great-grandson, Paul Carrington McPhail.

MILDENDO

John Coles, of Richmond, Va., who has been noticed in the account of the Coles family and homes, owned large estates in the Southside. His son, Walter, settled in Halifax on a plantation which he named Mildendo, after the metropolis of the imaginary country of "Lilliput" in "Gulliver's Travels." Mr. Coles died in 1780, leaving several sons and daughters. All of the sons died unmarried. One of the daughters, Mildred Howell Coles, married Mr. Carrington and had a number of sons. To these Car-

MILDENDO, HALIFAX COUNTY

rington nephews, Isaac H. Coles, who died in 1814 and was the last surviving son of Walter Coles, left the bulk of his estate: "The Dan River tract" to Edward Carrington; "the Burch Skin" tract to Walter Carrington; The Cub Creek tract to Paul Carrington, and the Home House tract to William Carrington. Each of these plantations was fully provided with negroes and stock. The "Home House" tract, William Carrington's inheritance, was Mildendo. The original house was burned long ago, and some time afterward William Carrington built the present house, modelling it after a cottage which had caught his fancy during a visit to England. It is only one story high and the windows upon one side open directly upon a lovely old flower garden, which slopes down to the Staunton River. The splendid oaks which surround the house were the original forest trees.

Mr. Carrington married a Miss Scott, who was a noted beauty and belle in her youth, and who is recalled by persons still living, who remember her in the closing days of her life, as a very beautiful old lady. From this couple, Mildendo passed to their son, Charles S. Carrington, president of the James River and Kanawha Canal Company, and his wife, who was Miss Susan McDowell, daughter of Governor James McDowell. Mildendo, after their time, passed from the Carrington family. Many Indian relics have been found at Mildendo and some of them may be seen at the Valentine Museum, Richmond.

PRESTWOULD

Prestwould, in Mecklenburg County (which derives its name from the Skipwith estate in Leicestershire, England), home of the later generations of the Skipwith family, in Virginia, was probably acquired by Sir William Skipwith (1707–1764), Baronet, a grandson of Sir Gray Skipwith (who died in 1680), a loyal cavalier, who emigrated to Virginia during Cromwell's time and settled in Middlesex County. Sir William removed from Middlesex to Blandford, in Prince George County, and at his death, in 1764, was succeeded, in his Prestwould estate, by his son Sir Peyton Skipwith (1740–1805), Baronet, and he, in turn, by his son Humberston Skipwith, whose son Fulwar Skipwith was the last of the name to own Prestwould.

This home of the Skipwith family is one of the most interesting and imposing places in Virginia. Situated on a very high hill overlooking the river, it commands an extensive view of the valley of the Staunton. The "manor house" was erected in the eighteenth century by the mechanic-servants of the Master of Prestwould, from stone quarried on the plantation.

The "mansion" is square and large, with porticoes north, south and east. The drive to the house is between high stone walls, now rapidly going to decay; and the most conspicuous object on the lawn is a giant oak, which is said to have been a landmark for the Indians going north and south.

One enters the house through a portico which opens into a large hall; on the right of this hall (known as the

PRESTWOULD, MECKLENBURG COUNTY

"land hall") is the immense dining-room, whose wall decoration is paper covered by life-sized figures of huntsmen in red coats, mounted on gay chargers, with dogs a-plenty and trees and grass; the hall also is beautified with the same paper. On the left of this hall is the "Chamber" of the Master and Mistress, and parallel to it the children's nursery. From this "land hall" wide doors lead to the "river hall," more spacious and magnificent than the former. This latter is papered with English scenes, ladies on horses, dogs, bridges, verdure and trees; and to the left is the formal drawing-room, whose walls are hung with paper picturing Venetian scenes—gondolas, palaces, etc.

A beautiful stairway leads from this "river hall" to the upper hall, on which open six large bed-rooms. Each window in the house has a large seat.

In June, 1914, much of the Skipwith furniture (some of which had been built in early times by cabinet-makers on the place) was still in this ancient house, and probably there was not such a collection in existence elsewhere. In this collection were specimens of the finest seventeenth century craft, with wonderful pictures and other objects of vertu.

An interesting building on the estate is a dancing pavilion, octagonal in shape, which stands some distance from the "manor house." The graveyard contains handsome armorial tombs.

Mr. A. J. Goddard, the present owner of Prestwould, is restoring the dwelling house and grounds to their former beauty.

IVY CLIFF, BEDFORD COUNTY

IVY CLIFF

Henry Brown (1712–98) settled here in 1755 after massacre of his parents by Indians near Salem, Va. He built as his residence a stone block-house, which was the birthplace of his sons Henry (1760–1840), and Reverend Samuel (— -1818), who married Mary Moore, "Captive of Abb's Valley." Henry was captain in Green's army and wounded at Guilford Court House. He built the present house in 1829. His sons were John Thompson (1802–36), and Samuel, who lived here. After his death, in 1855, the property passed to his nephew, Henry Peronneau Brown, father of John Thompson Brown, the present owner.

PART VII

BEYOND THE MOUNTAINS

WEST of the Blue Ridge and somewhat cut off from the rest of the State by that noble mountain range lies a region extensive and varied and highly picturesque, with its views of mountain, river, field and forest.

The most notable part of this section is the valley known by the Indian name of "Shenandoah," and settled chiefly by the thrifty Germans and Scotch Irish. In one of its counties, however, Clarke, originally a part of Frederick, the Carters, Burwells, Pages, and other families of the old Colonial counties, chiefly Gloucester, patented great tracts of lands upon which their descendants, who had intermarried until they formed a sort of clan, built a number of homesteads—some of them ample and stately, others more modest.

OLD STONE CHURCH, AUGUSTA COUNTY

OLD STONE CHURCH

About eight miles from Staunton is the Old Stone Church, one of the earliest and perhaps the most interesting of the Presbyterian churches in Virginia. It was built in 1747, and was formerly surrounded by a ditch and palisade, making of it a fort for protection against the Indians. " The old house has seen generations pass; it has heard the sermons of the Virginia Synod in its youthful days. Here the famous Waddell was taken under care of Hanover Presbytery as a candidate for the ministry in 1760; here the venerated Hoge was licensed in 1781; here the Rev. Archibald Alexander passed some of his trials in preparation for the ministry."

GREENWAY COURT, CLARKE COUNTY

GREENWAY COURT, THE HOME OF LORD FAIRFAX

The greatest landed estate ever held in Virginia was the famous Northern Neck owned successively by the Lords Culpeper and Fairfax. How Thomas, Lord Fairfax, left his English home to come and live at Greenway Court in the midst of his princely estate, within the present Clarke County, is a familiar story. The Greenway Court mansion where Washington often visited during his youth has long since gone, but Lord Fairfax's land office where grants for land within his domain were made, and the "White Post," one of his landmarks, which has given its name to a village of the vicinity, still remain.

SPRINGDALE

Upon the Opequon River, in Frederick County, six miles south of Winchester, lies Springdale, one of the oldest plantations in the Shenandoah Valley. Upon it to-day stand the picturesque ruin of a plain, but sturdy old stone house and a more ambitious structure of the same material, with dormer windows and a Greek porch. They are the earlier and later homes of Joist Hite, the ancestor of all the Virginia Hites, who settled here in 1732, under grant from the governor of Virginia. The older dwelling was built over a bold spring to prevent risk of being cut off from water by the Indians. It was in

OLD SPRINGDALE HOUSE, FREDERICK COUNTY

this that General Washington was Mr. Hite's guest for a night, while surveying for Lord Fairfax. After the new mansion was built, in 1753, the old house was used as negro quarters. Upon the removal of Mr. Hite to a residence some twelve miles to the south, upon the banks of the Cedar Creek, Springdale passed into the possession

SPRINGDALE, FREDERICK COUNTY

of a family named Brown, from whom it was bought, about 1801, by Mr. Richard Peters Barton, son of a clergyman of the Church of England, and remained in the Barton family until after the Civil War.

ABRAHAM'S DELIGHT

Abraham's Delight is the quaint name of an old mansion, one mile from the town of Winchester, on Abraham's Creek. The homestead and a flour mill were built in 1754, by Isaac Hollinsworth, a Quaker, whose grandfather, Thomas Hollinsworth, came to America with William Penn and settled in New Castle County, Delaware.

Thomas Hollinsworth's oldest son, Abraham, who married, in 1737, Anna Robinson, bought of Alexander Ross, under his patent, from Governor Gooch, of Virginia, 582 acres of land near Winchester, upon which his son and heir, Isaac Hollinsworth, planted this sturdy rooftree, still owned by his descendants.

Upon the eastern gable of the house are the initials "I. H." with date 1754.

ABRAHAM'S DELIGHT, NEAR WINCHESTER

MOUNTAIN VIEW

When the war came to blight and blot out forever much of the charm of Southern life, no portion of Virginia, perhaps, was richer in old family seats than Clarke County in the Lower Valley. About the little village of Millwood in those days were dotted the homes of the Nelsons, Carters, Pages, Burwells, and others locally known as the "Millwood neighborhood."

Among all these delightful homes of that time, none, perhaps, would have evoked a keener interest than Mountain View, the residence of Bishop Meade.

Mountain View could claim no part in the interest that attaches to Colonial antiquity, nor did it possess any architectural beauty. Indeed, the first house that bore the name was a very modest, unpretentious structure, which was burnt about the middle of the last century, and the building which replaced it was nothing more than a simple, comfortable country residence, as far removed as possible from the traditional Episcopal palace. Devoid though the house was of architectural or other esthetic charm, the place was of rare beauty and distinction. The location was very fine, a high hill from which the terrace fell away towards the Shenandoah River, a few miles distant, in pleasing variety of hill, meadow and forest.

East and south the eye rested in the near distance upon the almost circular sweep of the Blue Ridge.

On the west and north fine old forest oaks arrested or mitigated the harshness of the windy storms. Immediately about the house clustered magnificent evergreens and other ornamental trees, but the chief pride of Mountain View and the apple of the bishop's eye was a plantation, a lawn of about 20 acres in front of the house of rare trees which he had gathered from many lands and fostered and cherished, with a love that ended only with his life.

To many dignitaries of the church, and others who from time to time visited Mountain View, it was the bishop's supreme delight to show these trees, which were so near his heart, dwelling with affectionate detail upon the history of each. Captain Robert E. Lee and his wife visited Mountain View shortly after the Mexican War. How little did anyone then suspect how great a part this modest, handsome gentleman was destined to play in the tremendous struggle of the coming years. Yet in little over a decade Bishop Meade lay dying in Richmond and General Lee was at the bedside of his aged friend to receive his blessing and encouragement to persevere in the great battle for freedom, the chief weight of which was to rest upon his shoulders.

Something of tragic interest attaches to another and later visitor to Mountain View. Bishop Polk came to consult his older brother in the Episcopate as to the propriety of his accepting the commission of lieutenant-general in the Confederate Army, which President Davis was urging upon him.

All know the tragic sequel of his brief, glorious career and his heroic death in the Georgia campaign.

The good bishop—the iron bishop of Virginia, some one has called him—has slept for nearly half a century on the slope of the hill, whose summit is crowned by the great theological seminary—the child of his lifelong prayers and devotion; the trees that he gathered and planted and loved are dead and the ploughshares pass where they once stood. For many a year Mountain View has been the home of strangers.

Pulvis et umbra sumus.

THE OLD STONE CHAPEL

One of the most venerable and interesting houses in Clarke County is the Old Stone Chapel, sometimes called Bishop Meade's chapel. It is but a tiny and plain sanctuary of rough stone in the midst of an old graveyard surrounded by a rustic stone fence, but it is most impressive. Before the Revolution the two acres of land, upon which church and churchyard stand, were offered to the vestry by their owner, Colonel Hugh Nelson.

The plan to build failed at that time, but after the war was over the matter was taken up again. Colonel Nathaniel Burwell, who had now acquired the land, gave the same two acres that Colonel Nelson had offered, and the chapel was built in 1790. In 1834 it was found that the congregation had outgrown the church, so a larger one was built in a more convenient location in the village of Millwood, upon land also given by a member of the Burwell family, Colonel George, of Carter Hall.

After the completion of the new church, regular services in the Old Chapel were suspended, but for many years past it has been customary, for good Episcopalians within the reach of this sacred relic, to make a pilgrimage there upon some bright Sunday during summer when again the old walls echo the ancient prayers and praises.

The burying ground at the old chapel is sometimes called the Burwell graveyard, not only because the Burwells gave the land upon which it lies, but because many

OLD STONE CHAPEL, CLARKE COUNTY

more of that family than of any other have found a resting place there. Yet, says Bishop Meade, "Ever since the appropriation to this purpose, it has been the graveyard of the rich and poor, bond and free, those who live near it and the stranger from afar, who died near it."

CARTER HALL

Colonel Nathaniel Burwell, of The Grove, near Williamsburg (of which a sketch has been given in the chapter entitled "The Lower James"), moved to Clarke soon after the Revolution, and built Carter Hall before 1790. Colonel Burwell was twice married. His first wife was Susan Grymes, to whom he was deeply devoted. After her death he was so bereaved that he found it impossible to bear his grief without a companion in misery, and cast about to find one who had been similarly afflicted, and could, therefore, sympathize with him. Finally he went to Rosewell and asked Governor John Page to send for his half-sister, Mrs. George Baylor, who was a young and beautiful widow, that he might marry her. She came, but promptly rejected the disconsolate widower's proposal. "Lucy," he remonstrated, "you do not know what is good for you; your brother John and I arranged it all before you came." That seemed to settle the matter, and the wedding soon took place. After the ceremony the bridegroom said, "Now, Lucy, you can weep for your dear George, and I will weep for my beloved Sucky."

In Carter Hall these companions in woe had a most alluring place in which to mourn their departed other halves; with the white columns of its Greek portico standing out against the background of the surrounding trees, it is now and must have been then one of the fairest rooftrees in Virginia. Samuel Kercheval, in his history of the valley of Virginia, describes it as it was during the lifetime of Colonel Nathaniel Burwell's son and heir, George H. Burwell, who was then its master. He says, "The residence of Mr. George Harrison Burwell is splendidly improved with stone buildings. The main building is sixty-six feet by thirty, three stories with a wing at each end, twenty-one feet long, two stories high. The whole building is finished in the most tasteful style of modern architecture. This was the former residence of Colonel Nathaniel Burwell, a gentleman of great wealth. The building stands on a beautiful eminence and commands a delightful view of the Blue Ridge and the adjacent neighborhood. The water is conveyed by force-pumps from a fine spring to the dwelling house, yards, and stable, at a distance of about three hundred yards. This fine farm may with truth be said to be among the most elegantly improved estates west of the Blue Ridge."

CARTER HALL, CLARKE COUNTY

LONG BRANCH, CLARKE COUNTY

A beautiful grove and the great spring mentioned by Kercheval, in its green, shady dell a little way to the rear of the house, are charming features of the grounds.

Mr. George Harrison Burwell, by his second marriage, with Miss Agnes Atkinson, was the father of three daughters: Eliza Page, who married Mr. Thomas Randolph, of Clarke; Isabelle, who married Mr. P. H. Mayo, of Richmond; Agnes, who married Mr. Powell Page, of Saratoga, Clarke County; and of one son, George Harrison Burwell, Jr., who inherited Carter Hall.

After the death of her husband, Mrs. Burwell made her home with her daughter, Mrs. Powell Page, at Saratoga, until her own death at a ripe age. She was " Cousin Agnes " to half of the county, and is lovingly remembered as one of the dear and saintly old ladies of *ancient régime,* in a dainty cap and soft shawl. She was charmingly old-fashioned, and until the end, went abroad to church or visiting in the ancient high swung coach, which was probably the last of its type, with whose dignified proportions and swaying motion she was pleasantly familiar; and happy was the child who was invited to a seat beside her in this imposing equipage.

Carter Hall, after having been owned and occupied by three successive generations of Burwells, passed from the family, but, happily, it has lately been bought back by Mr. Townsend Burwell, great-grandson of its founder, Colonel Nathaniel Burwell, and son of Mr. George H. Burwell, and his first wife, Laura Dunbar Lee.

LONG BRANCH

Turning our backs upon Carter Hall, a short drive brings us to Long Branch, the home of the Nelsons. The mansion fitly crowns a hill-top surrounded by groves of noble trees. It is built upon a most ample plan, of brick with thick walls, high ceilings, and spacious rooms, and opens both at front and rear, upon stately pillared porticoes. Very beautiful is the interior. The wide doors open from the front and back porticoes upon the great hall, which occupies the centre of the house. Midway of this hall two lofty columns rise to the ceiling which they help to support. There is much handsome hand-carved woodwork in the hall and rooms, and the most striking feature of the house is the beautiful stair, with hand-carved balustrade, which winds upward from the hall to the observatory upon the roof. Two of the big square rooms are given an exceedingly interesting air by the quaint old wall papers, still in a state of perfect preservation, with which they are hung. One of these represents scenes in Paris, the other the Bay of Naples.

Long Branch is over a century old. It was built in 1805 or 1806, by Captain Robert Carter Burwell, who commanded a company of militia in the War of 1812 and died in the service at Norfolk. Before going to the war he made his will leaving Long Branch to Mr. Philip Nelson, son of Governor Nelson, of Yorktown, who had in 1789 married his sister Sarah Nelson Burwell. In about 1836 Mr. Nelson sold the estate to his nephew Hugh Nelson, who had in that year married Miss Adelaide Holker, of Boston, and who left it to his only son, Hugh Nelson, Jr., who married his cousin Miss Sally Page Nelson, and is its present owner.

Long Branch has always been a seat of hospitality and never more so than during the time of its present genial master and mistress.

SARATOGA

Upon the other side of the village of Millwood from Long Branch and Carter Hall, and somewhat retired from the celebrated " Valley turnpike," is one of the most interesting homesteads in the county; this is Saratoga, built by General Daniel Morgan, who took up his abode in Clarke after the Revolution, and named his home after the great battle, which made him famous. Its massive and rugged walls were built of gray stone found in the neighborhood, and it is said that the laborers employed by General Morgan in its construction were Hessian prisoners, taken during the Revolution.

In course of time Saratoga passed, by purchase, to the Page family and has long been the residence of Mr. Robert

SARATOGA, CLARKE COUNTY

Powell Page, Jr., who inherited it from his father, Dr. Robert Powell Page, of "The Briars," a few miles away, and who married, about 1870, Miss Agnes Burwell, of Carter Hall.

CLIFTON, CLARKE COUNTY

This house was built about 1800 by David Hume Allen, and after his death was owned for fifteen years by his widow, who before her marriage had been Miss Sarah Griffen Taylor. After Mrs. Allen's death the estate was inherited by their youngest son Edgar Allen, who held it until his death, in 1903. Edgar Allen never married and the property was left to his nephews and nieces. It was purchased by Robert Owen Allen (eldest son of Algernon Sidney Allen, who was eldest son of David Hume Allen), who owned it until 1914, when it passed into the possession of his son, Dr. L. M. Allen, of Winchester, Va., who is the present owner.

CLIFTON, CLARKE COUNTY

PAGEBROOK

Pagebrook, one of the oldest homes in Clarke County, stands a short distance back from the " valley pike," upon the brow of a hill commanding a view of extensive, but rustic grounds, and the Blue Ridge beyond. The plantation, like many others in the neighborhood, is enclosed from the road by the grey, rugged stone fences, which the Virginia creeper and trumpet flower love, and which, bewreathed with these and other gray-hued climbers, add a charming feature to the already picturesque landscape. A little way down the hill from one side of the mansion, a group of fine old weeping-willows hang their long fringes over the spring-house, with its suggestions of cool buttermilk and other palatable things. The overflow from the spring makes a little brook which runs on down the hill and into the glen beyond it, which with its great shade trees and its mossy gray boulders makes a natural park. The house is simple, but substantial and commodious. It was built soon after the Revolution by John Page, son of Robert

PAGEBROOK, CLARKE COUNTY

Page, of Broadneck, Hanover County—"that holy man, John Page," a writer of the time calls him. He married Maria, daughter of Colonel William Byrd III, of Westover, and died in 1838. He was succeeded at Pagebrook by his son, Judge John Evelyn Page, of the Virginia Circuit Court, who occupied it until his own death, in 1881. Judge Page married Miss Emily McGuire, of Loudoun County, and had many children, but upon his death, in 1881, Pagebrook passed, by purchase, to his nephew, Mr. Herbert H. Page, of Edenton, N. C., who used it as a summer home.

After the death of Mr. Herbert Page the estate passed from the family that had always owned it and has since changed hands several times. It is now the property of Mr. Mulliken.

NATURAL BRIDGE

So interesting an object could not escape the curiosity and observation of Mr. Jefferson. His account of it is as follows:

"The Natural Bridge, the most sublime of nature's work, is on the ascent of a hill, which seems to have been cloven through its length by some great convulsion. The fissure, just at the bridge, is by some admeasurements 270 feet deep, by others only 205. It is about 45 feet wide at the bottom, and 90 feet at the top; this of course deter-

NATURAL BRIDGE

mines the length of the bridge, and its height from the water. Its breadth in the middle is about 60 feet, but more at the ends, and the thickness of the mass at the summit of the arch, about 40 feet. A part of this thickness is constituted by a coat of earth, which gives growth to many large trees. The residue, with the hill on both sides, is one solid rock of limestone. The arch approaches the semi-elliptical form; but the larger axis of the ellipses, which would be the chord of the arch, is many times longer than the transverse. Though the sides of the bridge are provided in some parts with a parapet of fixed rocks, yet few men have resolution to walk to them, and look over into the abyss. You involuntarily fall on your hands and feet, creep to the parapet, and look over it. Looking down from this height about a minute, gave me a violent head-

ON THE ROAD TO NATURAL BRIDGE (1889).

ache. If the view from the top be painful and intolerable, that from below is delightful in the extreme. It is impossible for the emotions arising from the sublime to be felt beyond what they are here: on the sight of so beautiful an arch, so elevated, so light, and springing as it were up to heaven, the rapture of the spectator is really indescribable! The fissure continuing narrow, deep and straight for a considerable distance above and below the bridge, opens a short but very pleasing view of the North Mountain on one side, and Blue Ridge on the other, at the distance each of them of about five miles. This bridge is in the county of Rockbridge, to which it has given name, and affords a public and commodious passage over a valley, which cannot be crossed elsewhere for a considerable distance. The stream passing under it is called Cedar Creek."

The Marquis de Chastellux in his *Travels in North-America in the years 1780–81–82* gives a description of Natural Bridge which was sent him by Baron de Turpin, who was sent to take dimensions of the bridge and make report thereof. The conclusion of the Baron's report is as follows:

" The excavation of eight or ten inches, formed in the *pied droit,* or supporter, on the left bank of the stream, under the spring of the arch, lengthens it into the form of a crow's beak. This decay and some other parts which are blown up, give reason to presume that this surprising edifice will one day become a victim of that time which has destroyed so many others."

Measurements of the Bridge at this time show that it is very much as it was when the Baron's account was written, about one hundred and thirty-five years ago.

WINDY COVE CHURCH AND WALLAWHATOOLA

In picturesque Bath County, across the Alleghany Mountains, from the Shenandoah Valley, is an interesting relic of pioneer days. This is Windy Cove Church, which, though not built until 1838, is the fourth sanctuary occupied by the congregation of devout Presbyterians, which was here organized nearly a hundred years before, in the year 1749, and had worshipped in a succession of log houses, each one larger and more comfortable than its predecessor. The families which formed the first congregation and built the first church were a band of those sturdy Scotch-Irish immigrants who brought to Virginia character many of its most sterling traits. The settlement was on the extreme frontier and constant danger of molestation from the Indians made it necessary there, as it had earlier been at Jamestown, for the men to take their firearms to church.

The first church was situated about a mile from the present building down the lovely little river called by the

Indians Wallawhatoola, and on the side of the hill, which the pioneers named "Betsy Bell." It was a small house of unhewn logs, with puncheons, or squared logs, for seats, and was heated by an open log fire at each end. Its pastor was the Reverend Alexander Craighead, a native of the north of Ireland. The little church took the name by which it is still known from a remarkable natural cave not far away.

The third church was larger than the first and second, and was built of hewn logs, with a "session house" adjoining, and stood upon the site of the present building.

WALLAWHATOOLA, BATH COUNTY

The "Betsy Bell" is a part of the Wallawhatoola property. The dwelling was built about one hundred and fifty years ago and was a typical frontiersman's log weatherboarded house of four rooms. This has been gradually added to until it has now more than twenty rooms. It was formerly owned by the Sitlingtons, a family prominent in the early history of Bath County.

The estate was purchased from this family by Mr. John L. Lee, now of Lynchburg, and sold by him in 1883, to the late Robert A. Lancaster, of Richmond, for a summer home and is still in the possession of his family.

THE MEADOWS

This property was bought from a man named Bradley by Captain Francis Smith, of Abingdon, in 1817. Captain Smith's first wife was a daughter of "Madam Russell" (successively the wife of General William Campbell and General William Russell), who was sister of Patrick Henry. There were no children by this first marriage. Captain Smith married, secondly, Mary Trigg, the widow of William King, the founder of the famous Salt Works in Smyth County. From this marriage there was one daughter, Mary, who married Governor Wyndham Robertson, of Richmond. She was a child five years old when her father bought this property and the name "Mary's Meadows" was given in her honor. When Mrs. Robertson succeeded to the estate on the death of her father,

THE MEADOWS, WASHINGTON COUNTY

the name was changed to "The Meadows." The property is now owned by her son, Captain Francis Smith Robertson, an ex-officer of Stuart's Staff.

BROOK HALL

Brook Hall in Washington County, a large brick house of some eighteen or twenty rooms situated on a beautiful hill, was erected in 1835, by Colonel William Byars, a wealthy and prosperous planter and merchant. Until comparatively recently the estate was occupied by Mrs. Ernest, the youngest daughter of Colonel Byars, and is now the property of a family of Robertsons.

At the foot of the hill on which the "mansion house" stands is an old mill situated on a lovely creek. Near the mill is an old log house, nearly a hundred years old, which was Colonel Byars' home before the erection of Brook Hall. This estate is just two miles from Emory and Henry College, of which Colonel Byars was one of the "founders."

OLD BYARS HOUSE, WASHINGTON COUNTY

Southern View—a place of great beauty—is three miles east of Brook Hall, and the present house was remodelled some fifty years ago by Colonel James M. Byars, son of Colonel William Byars of Brook Hall. Southern View was originally Fort Kilmekmanley, a massive structure of river stone with walls three feet thick, which had been erected in the days of the Indian terror as a protection to women and children of this section. When Colonel James

M. Byars inherited from his father some two thousand acres of this fertile estate, he desired to erect a handsome residence on the site of the old fort and employed many workmen for the purpose. Work was begun on demolishing the old building. The tightly cemented " gable ends " of the old house presented so formidable a resistance that it required two weeks to remove them and Colonel Byars determined to let the walls remain and cover them with a " modern " tin roof and terra-cotta chimneys. The discolored and dilapidated appearance of the walls was not, however, in keeping with the intended magnificence of the building and it was decided to " stucco " them. Workmen were brought from Louisville, Kentucky, for this purpose and the result of their efforts is the present house, seemingly a construction of gray granite blocks.

The wonderful Ebbing and Flowing Spring is on this estate, a mile from the house and just on the bank of the river (Middle Fork of Holston). When the river is " full " the spring is submerged, resuming its normal condition when the waters subside. At this spring, many, many years ago there was a church. On a Sunday, when there was a large congregation, and the preacher at his best, three Tories were seen passing, whereupon congregation, preacher and all, ran out of the church, pursued them up the river a mile, caught and hung them on a sycamore tree, on the banks of the river. Their bodies were buried there. Some years ago when there was a freshet, one of the skeletons was washed up. The old church at Ebbing and Flowing Spring has long since passed out of existence, a small chapel now occupying the site.

SMITHFIELD

Smithfield, the home of the Prestons, is situated in Montgomery County, in the southwestern part of Virginia. It was a grant of three thousand acres from the Colonial government to John Preston, whose son, William Preston, began the erection of the house. His building was interrupted by the outbreak of the Revolution, in which war he served as colonel. At the close of the war, Colonel Preston resumed work on his home and completed it. At his death the place passed to his son, James Patton Preston, Governor of Virginia, who, in turn, left it to his son, the Honorable William Ballard Preston.

Smithfield is now owned by the youngest daughter of William Ballard Preston, Mrs. Aubin Lee Boulware, of Richmond, Virginia.

Much of interest centres in this historic home. Situated at the top of the Allegheny Mountains, in a valley of

SMITHFIELD, MONTGOMERY COUNTY

waving blue grass, it presents a picture of rich beauty. The verdure of the meadowlands with their crystal stream stretching like a white ribbon through their entire length, the grandeur of the surrounding mountains, and the dense forest land, free from undergrowth, combine to make of Smithfield one of Nature's fairest scenes. The big walnut trees, shading the blue grass meadows, give cool resting places for horses and cattle which graze among the deep, luscious green.

The house is a large one, topped with dormer windows.

The interior woodwork is hand carved, and the elaborate mantel pieces reach nearly to the ceiling. All through the house handwork is noticeable, and the nails were wrought on the place.

In the early days of Smithfield, Mrs. John Preston's brother, Colonel James Patton, who was in "the upper country on business," was murdered by the Indians.

Smithfield was famed for its hospitality. It was the Mecca to which the Kentucky and South Carolina Prestons made yearly pilgrimages, travelling the long distances in their stately coaches, driving four horses, and followed by their retinues of servants. Especially during the summer and autumn months was the old house overflowing with guests, and dispensing entertainment with a generous, lavish hand.

The place is well kept up now. And in the old graveyard are many monuments to the illustrious men and women of past generations, who keep before us—in vivid, glowing and indelible colors—a picture of their brilliant past in this old mansion, "Smithfield."

PRESTON HOUSE

General Francis Preston, who was an able lawyer and member of Congress, who married Sarah Buchanan, daughter of General William Campbell of King's Mountain fame, removed to Abingdon in 1810, and built the house which is now one of the buildings of Martha Washington College. In few houses in Virginia has so distinguished a group of sons and daughters been raised as were the children of General Preston. Among them were his sons, William C. and John S. Preston of South Carolina and the wives of Governors John B. Floyd and James McDowell of Virginia and General Wade Hampton of South Carolina. In 1845, General Preston's son Thomas L. Preston, Professor at the University of Virginia, sold the place to the Trustees of Martha Washington College.

PRESTON HOUSE, ABINGDON

FORT LEWIS, BATH COUNTY

FORT LEWIS

Fort Lewis, in the present Bath County, was originally the home of the gallant Colonel Charles Lewis, who lost his life in the battle of Point Pleasant.

Charles Lewis was the youngest of the sons of John Lewis of Augusta County, who emigrated from Ireland, and his wife Margaret Lynn, said to have been a daughter of "The Laird of Loch Lynn," and most certainly the sister of Doctor Andrew Lynn, who emigrated and settled in Fredericksburg, Virginia, and who mentions in his will (among other kinsmen) "Sister Lewis and her four sons, Thomas, Andrew, William and Charles Lewis." Charles Lewis was born shortly after his parents reached Virginia. His brothers, Andrew, Thomas and William, were, like himself, distinguished soldiers and frontiersmen.

Colonel Charles Lewis' holdings in the present Bath County consisted of many thousands of acres of land, including both of the celebrated springs—"the Hot" and "the Warm." He moved to his "Fort Lewis" estate several years before his death, and, as its name indicates, this was one of the "out-post" strongholds for protection against the Indians, who called the old stockade "Lewis' Hog Pen."

The present dwelling, within the boundaries of the old fort, was erected by Benjamin Crawford about 1859, Mr. Crawford having purchased the site from Samuel Lewis, son of John Lewis, who was son of Colonel Charles Lewis. Later Mr. Crawford sold the estate to Frederick Fultz, who in turn sold it to Doctor Henkel of Staunton, Virginia.

"The fame of Charles Lewis," says Waddell, in his *Annals of Augusta County,* "has come down to us as that of a hero of romance. From all accounts he was an admirable man, and if his life had not ended prematurely would have achieved great distinction. At an early age he was reported to be the most skilful of all the frontier Indian fighters." Wills De Haas, in his *History of the*

Early Settlement and Indian Wars of Western Virginia, gives the following very interesting description of an incident in Lewis' career. "On one occasion," says De Haas, "he (Lewis) was captured by the Indians while on a hunting excursion, and after travelling over two hundred miles barefooted, his arms pinioned behind, and goaded by the knives of his remorseless captors, he effected his escape. While travelling along the bank of a precipice some twenty feet in height, he suddenly, by a strong muscular exertion, burst the cords which bound him, and plunged over the steep into the bed of a mountain torrent. His persecutors hesitated to follow. In a race of several hundred yards Lewis had gained some few yards upon his pursuers, when, upon leaping a fallen tree which lay across his course, his strength suddenly failed and he fell prostrate among the weeds which had grown up in great luxuriance around the body of the tree. Three of the Indians sprang over the tree within a few feet of where their prey lay concealed, but with feelings of the most devout thankfulness to a kind and superintending Providence, he saw them one by one disappear in the dark recess of the forest. He now bethought himself of rising from his uneasy bed, when lo! a new enemy appeared, in the shape of an enormous rattlesnake, who had thrown himself into a deadly coil so near his face that his fangs were within a few inches of his nose: and his enormous rattle, as it waved to and fro, once rested upon his ear. A single contraction of the eyelid—a convulsive shudder—the relaxation of a single muscle, and the deadly beast would have sprung upon him. In this situation he lay for several minutes, when the reptile, probably supposing him to be dead, crawled over his body and moved slowly away. 'I had eaten nothing,' said Lewis to his companions, after his return, 'for many days; I had no firearms and I ran the risk of dying with hunger ere I could reach the settlement; but rather would I have died than make a meal of the generous beast.'"

GREEN VALLEY

Green Valley in Bath County was also the site of an old fort used for protection from the Indians. The fort originally occupied a position near the present dwelling. In 1755 the Indians made a capture of this fort and among the prisoners then made was one Joe Mayse, who had been wounded. Neighbors went in pursuit of the Indians and rescued Mayse, whom they found riding and forced to carry some of the red man's plunder, among which was a coil of rope which was thrown over his head. The firing of the rescuing party frightened the horse which was

GREEN VALLEY, BATH COUNTY

carrying Mayse and he was thrown and dragged for a considerable distance, with great difficulty finally releasing himself.

The original house at Green Valley was merely a frontiersman's cabin, and was built by a Mr. McCallop, who later sold the place to James Frazer, who enlarged the house to its present proportions and kept it as a "stage-tavern." About 1854 Samuel Lewis purchased Green Valley from William Frazer. From Samuel Lewis the place descended to his son Jasper Lewis, the present owner.

MONT CALM

The historic old homestead, Mont Calm, now occupied as a residence by Mr. W. E. Mingea, was built by Governor David Campbell about the year 1830. It crowns a hilltop on the south side of Abingdon which overlooks the whole town, and to the south one of the finest mountain views to be seen anywhere in this section spreads out

MONT CALM, ABINGDON

before the eye of the observer. White Top and Mount Rogers, the two highest points in Virginia, are plainly visible, with miles and miles of fertile lands and an occasional range of smaller mountains lying between.

Upon the death of Governor Campbell, the property descended to Governor William B. Campbell of Tennessee, and his sister, Mrs. Shelton. It was then rented by various parties—Judge John A. Campbell among the number. After the deaths of Governor William Campbell and sister, the property was purchased from their estate by Colonel Arthur C. Cummings, who married Elizabeth Preston, daughter of Jno. M. Preston, 1st, of Seven Mile Ford. Colonel Cummings' family having passed away, he bequeathed the place to his wife's nieces and nephews, sixteen in number; they, in turn, sold it to Mr. W. E. Mingea, the present owner.

The trees on the lawn are giant white pines, planted out by Governor Campbell's own hands. Leading from this lawn to the macadam pike is a splendid avenue of maples, making the approach one of great attractiveness. Wonderful holly trees add greatly to the beauty of the spacious lawn, and the old-time garden, with the hedges of boxwood, beds of violets, lilies of the valley and pinks, is still there.

Presumably the name selected by its distinguished first owner was due to the fact that Governor Campbell was an officer in the War of 1812, and saw service in Canada under General Alexander Smyth, for whom Smyth County, Virginia, is named. In his military service he probably saw the historic Heights of Abraham at Quebec, where the French General, Montcalm, lost his life. At this particular epoch in our history we were at daggers drawn with Britain and bosom friends with France. This consideration also probably influenced Governor Campbell in the choice of the name for his home.

Through the various changes of ownership, the original plan, both in the interior and exterior of the house, has been wonderfully preserved. Two striking features are the long drawing room, possibly sixty feet in length, fifteen in height (public receptions were held here); and a beautiful spiral staircase, beginning in the front hall and extending to the attic. The steps of solid cedar, elaborately hand carved on the outside, are as sound as ever.

The bed-room of Mrs. Campbell is still to be seen; for years her bed remained there,—an elaborately carved affair, with tester, after the fashion of that day. So lofty was this couch that it was impossible for a lady to reach it unassisted. At bedtime her maid was dispatched to call a stately man-servant, her special attendant. He would come, carrying a quaint ladder, which, with great dignity, he would place for Mrs. Governor that she might make the ascent in safety.

A few words as to his favorite servant, David Bird by name. He belonged to a type now almost entirely extinct, loyal and faithful, indispensable to those whom he served. Not only was he thoroughly accomplished in all the craft of house life of the day, but his imposing stature, impressive dignity, and polished manners rendered him truly ornamental. He lived to ripe old age, and upon his death in recent years the funeral train was largely composed of the descendants of his white friends of earlier days.

Mrs. Campbell was the possessor of beautiful hands, of which she took great care. She was equally careful of *her gloves,* which she desired always to be immaculate; so much so, that when she had to undergo the many handshakes incidental to public receptions she always wore a larger second pair of gloves until the handshaking was over, when she would discard this covering and display her hands in all the glory of gloves, perfect in fit, immaculate in freshness.

The population of that section of Virginia beyond the mountains was one in which the Scotch-Irish element predominated. Physically hardy, mentally and spiritually vigorous, " liberty " was the very keynote to this people's being. From father to son and from mother to daughter was transmitted the spirit of protest against any abridgment of the divine principle of personal freedom, and accompanying this spirit in its transmission the will and the power to act both speedily and effectively to save themselves and their property from bonds.

It is doubtful if there may be found anywhere a document which better illustrates the liberty-loving character of the Scotch-Irish on the frontier of Virginia than the Fincastle Declaration of Independence which follows: *

FINCASTLE COUNTY (VIRGINIA) MEETING.

In obedience to the Resolves of the Continental Congress, a Meeting of the Freeholders of *Fincastle* County, in *Virginia*, was held on the 20th day of *January*, 1775, who, after approving of the Association framed by that august body in behalf of all the Colonies, and subscribing thereto, proceeded to the election of a Committee, to see the same carried punctually into execution, when the following gentlemen were nominated: the Reverend *Charles Cummings*, Colonel *William Preston*, Colonel *William Christian*, Captain *Stephen Trigg*, Major *Arthur Campbell*, Major *William Inglis*, Captain *Walter Crockett*, Captain *John Montgomery*, Captain *James M'Gavock*, Captain *William Campbell*, Captain *Thomas Madison*, Captain *Daniel Smith*, Captain *William Russell*, Captain *Evan Shelby*, and Lieutenant *William Edmondson*. After the election the Committee made choice of Colonel *William Christian* for their Chairman, and appointed Mr. *David Campbell* to be Clerk.

The following Address was then unanimously agreed to by the people of the County, and is as follows:

To the Honourable Peyton Randolph, Esquire, Richard Henry Lee, George Washington, Patrick Henry, Junior, Richard Bland, Benjamin Harrison and Edmund Pendleton, Esquires, the Delegates from this Colony who attended the Continental Congress held at Philadelphia:

Gentlemen: Had it not been for our remote situation, and the *Indian* War which we were lately engaged in, to chastise those cruel and savage people for the many murders and depredations they have committed amongst us, now happily terminated under the auspices of our present worthy Governour, his Excellency the Right Honourable the Earl of *Dunmore*, we should before this time have made known to you our thankfulness for the very important services you have rendered to your country, in conjunction with the worthy Delegates from the other Provinces. Your noble efforts for reconciling the mother country and the Colonies, on

* American Archives, 4th Series, vol. 1, pp. 1165–6.

rational and constitutional principles, and your pacifick, steady, and uniform conduct in that arduous work, entitle you to the esteem of all *British America*, and will immortalize you in the annals of your country. We heartily concur in your Resolutions, and shall, in every instance, strictly and invariably adhere thereto.

We assure you, gentlemen, and all our countrymen, that we are a people whose hearts overflow with love and duty to our lawful Sovereign *George* the Third, whose illustrious House for several successive reigns have been the guardians of the civil and religious rights and liberties of *British* subjects, as settled at the glorious Revolution; that we are willing to risk our lives in the service of his Majesty, for the support of the Protestant Religion, and the rights and liberties of his subjects, as they have been established by Compact, Law, and Ancient Charters. We are heartily grieved at the differences which now subsist between the parent state and the Colonies, and most ardently wish to see harmony restored on an equitable basis, and by the most lenient measures that can be devised by the heart of man. Many of us and our forefathers left our native land, considering it as a Kingdom subjected to inordinate power, and greatly abridged of its liberties; we crossed the *Atlantic*, and explored this then uncultivated wilderness, bordering on many nations of Savages, and surrounded by Mountains almost inaccessible to any but those very Savages, who have incessantly been committing barbarities and depredations on us since our first seating the country. These fatigues and dangers we patiently encountered, supported by the pleasing hope of enjoying those rights and liberties which had been granted to *Virginians*, and were denied us in our native country, and of transmitting them inviolate to our posterity; but even to these remote regions the hand of unlimited and unconstitutional power hath pursued us, to strip us of that liberty and property with which *God*, nature, and the rights of humanity have vested us. We are ready and willing to contribute all in our power for the support of his Majesty's Government, if applied to constitutionally, and when the grants are made by our own Representatives, but cannot think of submitting our liberty or property to the power of a venal *British* Parliament, or to the will of a corrupt Ministry.

We by no means desire to shake off our duty or allegiance to our lawful Sovereign, but on the contrary, shall ever glory in being the loyal subjects of a Protestant Prince, descended from such illustrious progenitors, so long as we can enjoy the free exercise of our Religion as Protestants, and our Liberties and Properties as *British* subjects.

But if no pacifick measures shall be proposed or adopted by *Great Britain*, and our enemies will attempt to dragoon us out of those inestimable privileges, which we are entitled to as subjects, and to reduce us to a state of slavery, we declare that we are deliberately and resolutely determined never to surrender them to any power upon earth, but at the expense of our lives.

These are our real, though unpolished sentiments, of liberty and loyalty, and in them we are resolved to live and die.

We are, gentlemen, with the most perfect esteem and regard, your most obedient servants.

TYPICAL FRONTIER BLOCK HOUSE USED FOR PROTECTION AGAINST INDIANS

PART VIII

THE EASTERN SHORE

THE country lying in Virginia and Maryland, between the Chesapeake Bay and the ocean, is known as the Eastern Shore.

The counties of Northampton and Accomac, which occupy the Virginia end of this peninsula, had settlers within a few years after the foundation of Jamestown. Their many advantages caused a rapid increase of population, and by the middle of the seventeenth century they were, for that time, well peopled.

Perhaps nowhere in the world, except in remote parts of England itself, can the people boast of so pure an English strain, and nowhere have the same families so long continued. Of course many names have disappeared, but from the lower end of Northampton County to the Maryland line and from the ocean to the bay, one finds families living upon land on which their forefathers settled in the seventeenth century. These people prove the utter falsehood of any theories of lack of energy on the part of Virginians of the older stock. The two counties are among the very richest and most prosperous agricultural sections in America.

Scattered through both Accomac and Northampton are quaint and interesting houses so numerous that only a few examples can be given here.

MT. CUSTIS

The farm situated on Metompkin Bay, known as Mt. Custis, was first owned by John Michael, who came to Virginia from Holland about 1640. He married the daughter of John Custis the first, who also came to this country from Holland.

John Michael left Mt. Custis to his son Adam, who, dying without heirs, left it to his nephew, Lieutenant-

Colonel Henry Custis, who with Colonel Southey Littleton at one time commanded the militia of Accomac and Northampton Counties.

Colonel Custis is buried in front of the house. He, like his Uncle Adam Michael, died leaving no children. He sold Mt. Custis for the nominal sum of $600.00 to his niece, the wife of General John Cropper, with the proviso that he, Henry Custis, and his wife Mathilda, were to occupy it and enjoy its revenues for life and at his death his widow was to receive an annuity of $100.00 for her life.

Colonel Henry Custis is believed to have built the west

MT. CUSTIS, ACCOMAC COUNTY

end of the Mt. Custis house about 1710, while the older part, built by the Michaels, was found in such a bad state of decay that it was pulled down by the present owner. It had been removed from the house about 1840, by Thomas H. Bayly, when he built the present east side of the house, and was used as an outbuilding.

On the death of the first wife of General John Cropper, who was the niece of Colonel Henry Custis, the farm, by will or gift, became the property of Margaret, the eldest daughter of General Cropper and wife of Colonel Thomas M. Bayly, who represented the First District of Virginia for twenty-seven years in the Congress of the United

States. He died at Mt. Custis about 1834 and his eldest son, Thomas H. Bayly, became owner of the estate.

Judge Thomas H. Bayly, at the time of his death, June, 1856, was chairman of the Ways and Means Committee and also of the Committee of Foreign Affairs. He died just before the completion of his seventh term in Congress, as representative of the same district his father so long represented. Mt. Custis is now held by his only child, Evelyn, wife of Doctor Louis McLane Tiffany, of Baltimore. The Tiffanys occupy the place for five months each year.

During the life of Colonel and Judge Bayly Mt. Custis was the scene of much hospitality and on its walls now hang the letters of several presidents of the United States entertained there. Much old furniture, china and a few portraits still remain to show the style in which the Custises and Baylys lived, but many of these heirlooms have been scattered. As each daughter of the house married, some articles were given her to take to her new home. The portrait of Colonel Henry Custis is still in perfect condition and hangs in one of the rooms, and there is also a fine portrait of Tabitha, wife of John Custis, painted by Sir Peter Lely.

WELBOURNE, HORNTOWN, ACCOMAC COUNTY

WELBOURNE

Welbourne, at Horntown, Accomac County, was built by Drummond Welbourne about 1780. It is a substantial two and a half story house, of brick. A unique feature is an arcade entrance at one corner.

ST. GEORGE'S CHURCH, ACCOMAC COUNTY

This old church was probably built about 1656. It is a brick building originally in the form of a cross and had a brick floor, high-back pews and a pulpit of antique fashion.

In 1861 St. George's was used as a stable by Federal

ST. GEORGE'S CHURCH PUNGOTEAGUE, ACCOMAC COUNTY

troops and at the end of the war the venerable building was a complete wreck. It remained untenanted for years until the church people of the neighborhood determined to restore it for use as a place of worship. As the transepts were unsafe they were taken down, the main building rebuilt with the old bricks, and, after an interval of twenty-five years, services were once more held within the ancient walls.

The first rector of the parish was Reverend Thomas Teackle, who ministered there for over forty years and died in 1696. The records of the parish, with the exception of those of modern date, have, unfortunately, all been lost.

BROWNSVILLE

The Brownsville plantation was granted before 1655 to John Brown, who in his will gave 1262 acres to his son John Brown. The latter disappeared and the property came into the possession of his brother, Thomas Brown.

BROWNSVILLE, NORTHAMPTON COUNTY

He divided the 1262-acre tract, giving 631 acres (the Brownsville tract) to his daughter Sarah, wife of Arthur Upshur, and the other half to his daughter Anne, wife of Joseph Preeson, and, later, wife of Andrew Hamilton, of Philadelphia.

The property descended from Sarah Brown Upshur through several generations to its late owner, Thomas T. Upshur, whose family now resides there.

We have no tradition of any residence having been built on the land prior to the " Old Hall " mentioned below. John Brown lived in the territory now included in Accomac, and Thomas Brown also, for years after his father's death. Thomas Brown, however, did not die on this land, for by his will in 1705 he gave his home place (600 acres) to his daughter, Elizabeth Preeson, the wife of Thomas Preeson, and this tract was probably the land now known as " T. B." because its boundaries were marked by carving " TB " on pine shingles and nailing them on a line of trees. If there was a building prior to " Old Hall," it was probably a cheap log house.

The " Old Hall," which stood a few feet eastward of the present house, had a brick at the shoulder of the south end chimney marked 1691, and it is believed this was intended to indicate the date of building. The south end of the structure was of brick, with a large Dutch bake oven included in it. The joists and timbers were of best heart pine, dressed and beaded. It was 20 feet wide, 35 feet long, with four rooms, a small hall and an attic and some curious little closets in the upstairs rooms. It probably had shed rooms also, while occupied by the white family, but after 1806 it was used for negro quarters, and about 1898 was moved out on the farm and is now a good tenant house.

The present brick house was built in 1806, by John Upshur, at a cost of over $10,000.00. The bricks were made on the farm. The brick part is 42 by 40 feet, two and a half stories high and is handsomely finished. The parlor, which is considered the handsomest old style room on the Eastern Shore, is embellished with hand carving, rope molding, mosaic work and other designs. The frame part of the house, 52 by 20 feet, with a cook room 16 by 20 feet added, was built some time after the brick part of the house by John Upshur, who also purchased the 631 acres of the original tract belonging to Anne Preeson, and bequeathed it, with other farms, to his children in 1842. In 1884 the land was again divided by the will of William Brown Upshur, and the home place now containing 300 acres became the property of Thomas T. Upshur.

The first of the Upshur family in Virginia was Arthur

Upshur, who emigrated from Essex, England, and settled in Northampton County in 1664. He patented " Upshur Neck "—2300 acres in Accomac County—and in 1674 removed to that place, where he died, in 1709, in the eighty-fifth year of his age. His son, Arthur Upshur II, married Sarah Brown, who in 1734 gave Brownsville—then containing 631 acres—to their youngest son, Thomas Upshur. This Thomas Upshur was the father of Thomas Upshur II, who married Anne Stockley and was the father of John Upshur, the builder of the present Brownsville house.

Thomas Upshur II was an officer in a company of minute men during the Revolution.

Thomas T. Upshur IV entered the Confederate States Army June 8, 1861, and remained in service until early in May, 1865, when he was paroled by General Ord in Richmond. He was a scout for Generals R. E. Lee, R. S. Ewell, Jubal A. Early and Stonewall Jackson as a member of Company B, Thirty-ninth Virginia Battalion of Cavalry.

Mr. Upshur, who died in 1910, was long an earnest student of the history and genealogy of the Eastern Shore.

VAUCLUSE, NORTHAMPTON COUNTY

VAUCLUSE

Vaucluse, in Church Neck, near the mouth of Hungar's Creek, was once the residence of the distinguished statesman, Abel P. Upshur. Here many noted guests, including President Tyler and his cabinet, were entertained. Vaucluse is now owned by the Wilkins family, who bear another ancient Eastern Shore name.

WEST HOUSE

The West House, on Deep Creek, is shown by its ~~hip~~ gambr roof and great chimneys to be one of the oldest houses on

WEST HOUSE, DEEP CREEK

the Eastern Shore. It was once the home of Revil West, son of Anthony West and Eleanor Revil, and a member of one of the oldest families of this part of Virginia.

DUCKINGTON

Duckington is picturesquely situated on Mattawaman Creek, about three miles from Eastville. This long two-storied frame house was an old residence of the Eastern Shore family of Corbin.

DUCKINGTON, NORTHAMPTON COUNTY

CESSFORD, EASTVILLE, NORTHAMPTON COUNTY

CESSFORD

Cessford, at Eastville, Northampton County, was long the home of the Kerr family. Its name is derived from a seat of the famous Scotch border clan of Kerr. The Virginia house is an attractive residence surrounded by many fine trees.

SHEPHERD'S PLAIN

Shepherd's Plain, in Accomac County, is of unknown age, though evidently an ancient house. As is the case with

SHEPHERD'S PLAIN, ACCOMAC COUNTY

many Eastern Shore houses, the waters of the creek come up to the yard. The name Accomac, originally Accowmake or Accawmacke, is derived from the Indian chief who ruled there, and was formerly the designation of the whole of the Eastern Shore of Virginia.

About 1902 Shepherd's Plain came into the possession of Dr. A. T. L. Quesian, who restored it to its pristine beauty.

THE MELVIN HOUSE

The Melvin House, near Horntown, was built in 1775. It is a type of the smaller story and a half, dormer-windowed house. The long " sweep " of the well nearby adds to its air of antiquity.

MELVIN HOUSE, ACCOMAC COUNTY

CUSTIS HOUSE DEEP CREEK

THE CUSTIS HOUSE

The Custis House, Deep Creek, is not very large but bears every mark of antiquity. Here formerly lived many generations of the Custis family descended from a brother of John Custis, of Arlington.

CALLAHAN HOUSE

One of the quaintest old houses on the Eastern Shore was that at Locust Mount, Accomac County, which was the residence of Reverend Griffin Callahan (1759–1833), who was a pioneer Methodist minister in the West, and was long one of the leading men in his church.

CALLAHAN HOUSE, LOCUST MOUNT, ACCOMAC COUNTY

MARGARET ACADEMY

Margaret Academy was chartered in 1787. The original minute book of the trustees is still in existence. The spacious and substantial brick house will be a surprise to those who are under the impression that there was hardly any equipment for secondary education in Virginia at that day.

MARGARET ACADEMY, ACCOMAC COUNTY

WALLOP HOUSE, ACCOMAC COUNTY

WALLOP HOUSE

On Mosquito Creek, near Chincoteague Bay, is an ancient structure, long the residence of an old family from which it takes its name.

MOUNT WHARTON

This old home of the Parramore family is situated on Watts's Bay, opposite Assateague Island. It is evidently an exceedingly old house.

MOUNT WHARTON, ACCOMAC COUNTY

HUNGARS CHURCH, NORTHAMPTON COUNTY

BY T. B. ROBERTSON

Surrounded and concealed by a body of pine woods in the midst of an ancient grove of sycamores some seven miles north of Eastville is old Hungars Episcopal Church. It is beautifully located on the north side of Hungars creek at the head of navigation for small craft, and near by is the old village of Bridgetown, at which in the early years of the settlement the courts were held.

Hungars Church is one of the oldest church edifices in the State, and has been in use for over two hundred years, for the tradition is that it was built about 1690 to '95, and there are evidences that this is the actual fact, though the exact record is unfortunately lost.

Hungars parish was made soon after the county was established and the first minister was Rev. Wm. Cotton, and the first vestry was appointed in 1635. The following is the order made at that time:

"At a court holden in Accawmacke the 14th day of Sept. 1635;" (Northampton being then called Accomack.)

"At this court Mr. Wm. Cotton, minister, presented an order of the court from James City, for the building of a Parsonage house upon the Glebe land which is by

HUNGARS CHURCH, NORTHAMPTON COUNTY

this board referred to be ordered by the vestry and because there have heretofore been no formal vestry nor vestrymen appointed, we have from this present day appointed to be vestrymen those whose names are underwritten:

"Wm. Cotton, minister, Capt. Thos. Graves, Mr. Obedience Robins, Mr. John Howe, Mr. Wm. Stone, Mr. Burdett, Mr. Wm. Andrews, Mr. John Wilkins, Mr. Alex. Mountjoy, Mr. Edw. Drew, Mr. Wm. Beniman, Mr. Stephen Charlton.

"And further we do order that the first meeting of the

syd, vestrymen shall be upon the feast day of St. Michael the Arch-Angel, being the 29th day of September."

In accordance with that order of the court the vestry meeting was held and record entered of the same as follows:

" A vestry heald, 29th day of Sept. 1635.

" PRESENT

" Capt. Thomas Graves, Mr. John Howe, Mr. Edward Drew, Mr. Obedience Robins, Mr. Alex. Mountjoy, Mr. Wm. Burdett, Mr. Wm. Andrews, Mr. Wm. Stone, Mr. Wm. Beniman."

At this meeting an order was made providing for building the parsonage house.

At one time there were two parishes, the upper or Hungars, and the lower. In 1691 the parishes were united, as will be noted in the order following, entered in the old records in the clerk's office:

" Att a council held att James City, Apr. the 21st, 1691.

" PRESENT

" The Rt. Hono'ble Francis Nicholson Esq. Lt. Gov. &. council.

" Major John Robins and Mr. Thos. Harmonson, Burgesses of the County of Northampton, on behalf of the County, by their petition setting forth that the said county is one of the smallest in the colony, doth consist of a small number of tithables, and is divided in two parishes, by reason whereof the Inhabitants of both parishes are soe burdened that they are not able decently to maintain a minister in each parish and therefore prayed the said parishes might be joyned in one and goe by the name of Hungars parish, not being desirous to infringe any gift given to Hungars parish, and more especially one by the last will of Stephen Charlton, which parishes soe joyned will not only be satisfactory to the inhabitants but make them capable to build a decent church and maintain an able divine. On consideration whereof itt is the opinion of this board and accordingly ordered that the whole county of Northampton be from henceforth one parish and goe by the name of Hungars Parish, and that the same shall be noe prejudice to the gift of the aforesaid Charlton to the said parish of Hungars and it is further ordered that the Inhabitants of the sd. parish shall meet at such time and place as the court of the said county shall appoint and make choice of a vestry according to law. Cop. vera, test, W. Edwards, cl. cou."

Then, in accordance with the appointment of the court, at a meeting of the inhabitants of the said county of Northampton, at the court house thereof the 22nd day of June, 1691, the following vestrymen were elected:

Major John Robins, Capt. Custis, Capt. Foxcroft, John Shepheard, Benj. Stratton, Priece Davis, Benjamin Nottingham, John Powell, Jacob Johnson, Thomas Eyre, John Stoakley, Michael Dickson. It was evidently soon after this step was taken that the Hungars church building was erected.

The church in lower Northampton was perhaps older than Hungars. It was situated in what is locally known as the Magothy Bay section and on the old Arlington estate. Unfortunately it was allowed to go to decay and in 1824 the walls and some of the material was sold. Nothing but the foundation is now left to mark the spot. The communion set, now used in Christ Church, Eastville, was " a gift of John Custis of W^{m}burgh to the lower church of Hungars Parish, 1741," according to the inscription. The plate now used in Christ Church is inscribed " Ex dono Francis Nicholson," who was Lieutenant Governor 1690–2, and again later.

Christ Church, Eastville, was erected as near as can be stated in 1826 or 7.

Old Hungars Church became untenable in 1850 so as to be unfit for holding services.

It was repaired in 1851 and reduced somewhat in size, but practically unchanged in general appearances from its original style. It is an interesting landmark that has stood like a beacon light to many generations.

BOWMAN'S FOLLY *

Edmund Bowman, who was a justice of Accomac in 1663, a sheriff, burgess, and successively held the military titles of Captain and Major, built the old mansion house known as Bowman's Folly on Folly Creek. His daughter Gertrude married John Cropper, a young Englishman, and several generations of the descendants of the Cropper family inherited and lived at Bowman's Folly. The most distinguished was John Cropper (1755-1821), a distinguished officer of the Virginia Continental Line, serving with the rank of Colonel, afterwards a General of State Militia.

BOWMAN'S FOLLY, ACCOMAC COUNTY

The original house built by Edmund Bowman was pulled down and the present one built by General Cropper in 1815. Before the dwelling was built the General's slaves were taken from their usual labors and for several

* Barton H. Wise in *Virginia Historical Collection*, vol. xi, pp. 275–315.

months made to haul earth to make a mound upon which to build.

After General Cropper's death, Bowman's Folly became the property of Thomas R. Joynes, a son of Colonel Levin Joynes. Mr. Joynes was clerk of Accomac County for seventeen years, an able lawyer, and a member of the Virginia Convention of 1829–30. He was the father of Judge W. T. Joynes, of the Court of Appeals, and Dr. Levin S. Joynes, of Richmond. In 1822 he moved to Bowman's Folly, which he called Montpelior, and resided there until his death in 1858. In 1870 the property had passed into the hands of the Browne and later the Gibb family, and in about 1889 became the property of Mr. John Cropper, a grandson of the General.

ROSELAND, AT ACCOMAC

ROSELAND

"Roseland," the home of Mr. and Mrs. William Parramore Bell, is situated at Accomac Court House. The house was built in the early part of the nineteenth century by a Mr. Walker, who married Anne Parramore, and is one of the best examples of the style which obtained in the early days of the Eastern Shore of Virginia. It is long and rambling and there are three stairways leading to three upper floors entirely separated from each other. In the front yard is a beautiful grove of trees, some of them very rare, and were brought from South America. The grove and much of the shrubbery was planted by Dr. S. S. Satchell when he owned it and made his home there.

OLD WARREN HOUSE
See page 57

INDEX

CPSIA information can be obtained at www.ICGtesting.com
Printed in the USA
BVOW041953121212

308079BV00003B/124/P

9 781147 210606